From Stephen

Thanks for all the
help with the Car - Nov 82

Down the 19th Fairway

Augusta National

Down the 19th Fairway

A *Golfing Anthology*

Peter Dobereiner

Illustrated by Tim Havers

 ANDRE DEUTSCH

Contents

List of illustrations   viii
Acknowledgements   ix
Introduction   xi

'Ony pastymes or gammis upoun the Sabboth day, sic as Gof'

The Links of Leith	*Tobias Smollett*	3
The 13th Century	*Steven van Hengel*	3
The Coming of Gowf	*P.G.Wodehouse*	5
Golf as a Cross-Country Game	*Robert Browning*	20
The Game of Goff or Golf	*Hoyle's Games*	22
American Origins	*Charles Price*	24
Professionals and Caddies	*Horace Hutchinson*	26

An Applied Science and a Black Art

The Bogey Man	*George Plimpton*	29
The Feel of a Golf Club	*Bobby Jones*	31
Golfers and Other Strangers	*Alistair Cooke*	32
What it Takes to Win the Open	*Jack Reddy*	38
The Art of Driving	*Harry Vardon*	40
Golf as an Art	*Peter Black*	45
When Bobby Putts	*Keith B.Marshall*	49
Mathematics for Golfers	*Stephen B.Leacock*	50
The Character of Golf	*Arnold Haultain*	54
An Effeminate Game?	*B.J.T.Bosanquet*	55

Love thy Baffie and thy Stotter

The Care of Clubs	*Major Guy Campbell*	59
My First Driver	*Sam Snead*	60
How to Go about Buying a Putter	*John L.Low*	64
The Choice and Care of Clubs	*Harry Vardon*	65
Good Stotters	*Willie Park Jr*	67
The Ideal Golfer	*Paul Gallico*	68

Deed of Derring-Do and the Derring-Doers

Dr Johnson on the Links	*Andrew Lang*	73
Ben Hogan – Greatest Ever	*P.A.Ward-Thomas*	73
Southern Hospitality	*Mark Wilson*	78
George Low	*Dan Jenkins*	83
King Lear at Pebble Beach	*Alistair Cooke*	87
Harry Vardon	*Herbert Warren Wind*	89
The Ryder Cup	*Hugh McIlvanney*	93
Bernard Darwin	*Peter Ryde*	95
Joe Kirkwood	*Nick Seitz*	102
Old Tom Morris	*H.S.C.Everard*	106
Severiano Ballesteros	*Hugh McIlvanney*	107
Slow-Play Flo	*Dan Jenkins*	110

Over the Spinney and into the Pond

The Links of Eiderdown	*Bernard Darwin*	125
Mullion	*A.P.Herbert*	127
St Andrews	*Horace Hutchinson*	129
18 of the Best	*Peter Dobereiner*	132
St Andrews, Old Course		132
Augusta National		134
Gleneagles		135
Oakmont		137
Muirfield		139
Pebble Beach		141
Turnberry		142
Pine Valley		144
Sunningdale		146
Cypress Point		147
Royal County Down		149
Pinehurst No. 2		150
Royal Birkdale		152
National Golf Links		154
Ballybunion		156
Merion		157
Walton Heath		159
Seminole		161

Take a Fertile Imagination and a Golfing Theme

The Strange Case of the Ambitious Caddy	Ogden Nash	165
Naval Occasion	Ben Travers	166
How to Become a Scratch Golfer	Patrick Campbell	169

Oddments Retrieved from behind the Locker

Swearing	Lord Balfour	181
The Charm of Golf	A.A. Milne	182
Once You've Had 'em, You've Got 'em	Henry Longhurst	184
Gamesmanship	Stephen Potter	188
Golftopia	Henry Longhurst	192
The People in Front	Bernard Darwin	194
Swing Time	A.A. Milne	196
Par for POW at the Stalag	P.A. Ward-Thomas	198
Match Days	Patric Dickinson	203

List of Illustrations

Augusta National *Frontispiece*

Old Masters *2*

Worplesdon *28*

Royal and Ancient *58*

Pebble Beach *72*

Turnberry, 6th Tee *124*

Sotogrande, Spain *164*

Sunningdale Old Course *180*

Acknowledgements

The publishers would like to acknowledge the kind permission to reprint the following copyright material in this book: Steven van Hengel for *The 13th Century*; Hutchinson Publishing Group Ltd and Scott Meredith Literary Agency Inc. for *The Coming of Gowf* by P. G. Wodehouse; J. M. Dent & Sons Ltd for *Golf as a Cross-Country Game* from *A History of Golf* by Robert Browning; John Farquharson Ltd for *American Origins* from *The World of Golf* by Charles Price; Longman Group Ltd for *Professionals and Caddies* and *St Andrews* by Horace Hutchinson from The Badminton Library; André Deutsch Ltd for *The Bogey Man* by George Plimpton; Doubleday & Company Inc. and Chatto and Windus Ltd for *The Feel of a Golf Club* from *Bobby Jones on Golf* by Robert Tyre Jones; Alastair Cooke for *Golfers and Other Strangers* and *King Lear at Pebble Beach*; United States Golf Association for *What it Takes to Win the Open* by Jack Reddy, copyright United States Golf Association *Golf Journal*, November 1966; *Golf World Magazine* for *Golf as an Art* by Peter Black and *Ben Hogan – Greatest Ever* by P. A. Ward-Thomas; Dodd, Mead & Company, The Bodley Head Ltd and McClelland and Stewart Ltd for *Mathematics for Golfers* from *Short Circuits* by Stephen B. Leacock; Reginald Bosanquet for *An Effeminate Game?* by B. J. T. Bosanquet; Joan Daves for *My First Driver* from *The Education of a Golfer* by Sam Snead with Al Stump; Methuen London for *The Choice and Care of Clubs* from *The Complete Golfer* by Harry Vardon; Frederick Muller Ltd and Esquire Inc. for *The Ideal Golfer* by Paul Gallico from *Esquire's World of Golf* by Hubert Graffis; B. T. Batsford Ltd for *Southern Hospitality* by Mark Wilson from *The Golfer's Bedside Book* edited by Donald Steel; *Golf Digest Magazine* for *George Low* by Dan Jenkins, *Joe Kirkwood* by Nick Seitz, and *Once You've Had 'em, You've Got 'em* by Henry Longhurst, copyright Golf Digest/Tennis Inc.; The Sterling Lord Agency Inc. for *Harry Vardon* from *Herbert Warren Wind's Golf Book* by Herbert Warren Wind; *The Observer* for *The Ryder Cup* and *Severiano Ballesteros* by Hugh McIlvanney; A. & C. Black Ltd for *Bernard Darwin* from *Mostly Golf* by Peter Ryde; *Sports Illustrated* for *Slow-Play Flo* by Dan Jenkins, copyright Time Inc.; The Estate of the late Bernard Darwin for *The Links of Eiderdown* and *The People in Front* from *Playing the Like* by Bernard Darwin; Lady Herbert for *Mullion* from *Mild and Bitter* by A. P. Herbert; Curtis Brown Ltd and Little, Brown and Company for *The Strange Case of the Ambitious Caddy* by Ogden Nash; Curtis Brown Ltd for *The Charm of Golf* from *Not that it Matters* and *Swing Time* from *A Holiday Round* by A. A. Milne; William Heinemann Ltd and International Management Ltd for *Gamesmanship* from *The Complete Golf Gamesmanship* by Stephen Potter; Victor Gollancz Ltd for *Match Days* from *The Good Minute* by Patric Dickinson; P. A. Ward-Thomas for *Par for POW at the Stalag*; Andrew Morgan for *Naval Occasion* from *The Temptation of Admiral Juddy* by Ben Travers; Macmillan Publishers Company for Cassell Ltd for *Golftopia* from *Only On Sundays* by Henry Longhurst; Holt-Saunders Inc. for *How to Become a Scratch Golfer* by Patrick Campbell. The publishers have made every effort to trace the holders of all copyright material included in this book, but if any necessary acknowledgements have been omitted, or any articles included without permission, we hope that the copyright holders will accept our apology.

Introduction

When I embarked on the task of gathering material for a new golf anthology I had visions of myself in the reading room of the British Museum poring over rare volumes and selecting gems of literature. The work could not be hurried, of course, for this was to be a treatise of genuine scholarship. It would explore the remote origins of golf, assembling every known reference to the progenitors of golf, plus a few original discoveries. Here would be found fully documented accounts of paganica, episkyros (that would have been rendered in the original Cyrillic text, natch), jeu de mail, kolf, het kolven, chole and the Celtic cross-country game played with ball and hurley. I even picked up the scent of a Pharaoh who amused himself by hitting balls with a club on what sounded remarkably like Croydon driving range without the Coca-Cola machine.

The text would be peppered with little symbols, stars and daggers and suchlike – so much more interesting than figures – referring the spellbound reader to half a page of footnotes on each folio. For illustration I would persuade the enthusiastic publisher to furnish me with one of those cameras which focus themselves and adjust the aperture automatically (I know my technical limitations) and despatch me to travel the world, capturing pictorial evidence such as the Roman golfing fresco in Florence and possibly some funereal relics from the Valley of the Kings.

Ten years should do the trick.

Then the book would explode in the academic world. Historians in senior common rooms at Oxford and Cambridge would reel in admiration at the glittering scholarship. *Dobereiner on Golf (Vol. 1)* would be acclaimed as THE standard work, a model of research and a bright beacon of literary merit to illuminate the soul even as it nourished the mind.

Philistine forces entirely beyond my control caused a revision of my plan. There was a bank manager who wore half-moon glasses and drummed his fingertips on his desk in a most disconcerting manner. There was an unaccountable reluctance on the part of the publisher to cough up an advance of £200,000 which I had calculated would see me through if I limited my diet to water and dried apricots. There were sundry pests such as sports editors and wives who brandished bits of paper – tournament schedules, gas bills, etc. – and figuratively threw themselves down on the path of progress, impeding my journey in search of the Holy Grail of Golfing Truth. None of this could deter a determined Lancelot of the Links. I would do it, although I had to modify my research programme and fit it in with a working regime which involves spending 200 days a year overseas reporting golf tournaments and about 100 days a year away from home reporting golf in Britain. Normally I devote the remaining 65 days a year to knocking out a couple of books and the odd film script. What finally deflected me from my original high purpose was the quality of the material. The Latin was quite promising, e.g. the description by Procopius of the Roman provinces of Britain: 'That part of the island nearest Gaul is still inhabited and fertile, but it is divided from the rest of the island by a wall* beyond which lies a region infested by wild beasts, with an atmosphere fatal to human life, wherefore it is tenanted only by the spirits of the departed.'†

I know a hotel in Carnoustie which to this day testifies to the essential truth of Procopius's judgment. What switched me off my scholastic kick was the English writing about the game of golf. After all, my proposed classic was to be, in part, a compendium of fine writing. But where was this fine writing? The first book devoted to the game was 'The Goff' a self-styled herio-comic poem, published in Edinburgh in 1743. What do you make of this:

> 'Yea here great F------s, patron of the juft,
> The dread of villains, and the good man's truft,
> When fpent with toils in ferving human kind,
> His body recreates, and unbends his mind.'

On first reading I thought that great F------s was plural, for even in the eighteenth century the Scots were notorious f------s, but the subsequent singular case reveals him to be an individual, some kind of judge, presumably. We are given no clue as to his identity, not even in a footnote, so although the poem may have been a hoot in 1743 when we may suppose the reader could readily recognise great F------s and knew all about him, a quarter of a millennium later the thing is pretty well meaningless. It is the same with all the early golf writing. On my one visit to the reading room of the British Museum I had to be woken up by a kindly attendant at closing time. To twentieth-century man the stuff is sheer codfwallop.

Clearly I had to change tactics. My next approach was to seek out pieces of golf writing which I judged would appeal to different categories of reader. Reading, say, Eleanor Helme's *Family Golf* I

* Believed to be the rampart erected by Lollius Urbicus for the Emperor Antonius Pius XX *c*. A.D. 140 between the Firths of Forth and Clyde. Cf. *Celtic Scotland* by W. F. Skene.

† Definitely and positively the last footnote to appear in this book.

would come across a passage which produced the reaction: 'Hm, not quite my cup of tea but somebody's ageing aunt, possibly a veteran of the Worplesdon Foursomes, might enjoy it.' In this way I accumulated a mass of material in which I had absolutely no faith.

Finally I gave in to a distressing tendency to arrogance. To hell with the customers; I would collect my favourite pieces and lump them all together in one book in an orgy of self-indulgence. I would cock a snook at anticipated criticism, such as 'Darwin's *People in Front* has already appeared in six different anthologies'. 'So what?,' I snarl. 'Now it is in a seventh anthology. Read it again; it's well worth reading seven times, or ten, or a hundred.'

Apart from the fact that your taste is unlikely to coincide entirely with mine in every case, you may find items which puzzle you. Why did he include *that*? Well, some of them are reproduced for personal, not to say private, reasons. Many of the authors are my friends, or were in certain lamented instances, and I have been privy to the background of their writing. Stephen Potter's *Golf Gamesmanship* is worthy of another airing in its own distinguished right, of course, but it will serve as an illustration because of what prompted me to make it my first selection. When the book was first published, I reviewed it for my newspaper and concluded my remarks by saying that the author's object was to make us laugh. Potter wrote to me and said, in part: 'This was not the original purpose of Lifemanship and Gamesmanship. As a diffident young man I had often been the victim of both. It struck me that deficiency in the powers of quick riposte could be made good by working something out beforehand – one could learn to 'counter' as I call it. Years later, in a humble imitation of Swift's *Ironia*, I decided to deliver a diatribe against the psychological warfare side of games in the form of a lecture on How To (Instead of How Not To) Behave. Next month [October, 1968] Gamesmanship comes of age. Now that I have written my final volume I hope, if I can find the right vehicle, to describe the secrets of its birth and publication.'

So far as I know, Potter never had the opportunity to make public the details of how gamesmanship and lifemanship started as a serious defensive exercise to protect a shy youngster from being put down, and I therefore welcome this opportunity to disclose the fact if not, alas, the delightful detail with which Potter would have embellished the revelation.

The background of certain other contributions in the book must remain locked within my bosom. Myself excepted, golf writers tend to be a raffish lot with imaginative ideas of how to unwind after the stern labours of the day. In my role as a neutral observer of the human scene I have occasionally tagged along, greatly against my puritanical instincts, you understand, purely in order to obtain a well-rounded picture of life. Obviously, one does not want to appear conspicuous on such hell-raising occasions by sitting quietly in the corner sipping lemonade, and some of these distasteful forays have given me some small experience of waking up with a drug-crazed steel band blasting away inside my head. That is all right; it gives one an insight into the problems of other people. On such occasions, as I lay slumped in a chair and emitting faint groans, I have often been disturbed by the sound of a chorus of pneumatic drills. This, as I subsequently observe, is caused by a colleague tapping at the keys of his typewriter. Knowing him to be even further *in extremis* than myself, I have marvelled at the sight and, when the vital life support forces began to tick over again, I have begged to read what I know to be the result of a miracle of dedication and professionalism. Out of sheer admiration for anyone who could write so much as 'The cat sat on the mat' in such circumstances, I have included a few of these miracles. I present all the offerings with the hope that they will give you a modicum of the pleasure that they have given to me.

P.D.

xiv

'Ony pastymes or gammis upoun the Sabboth day, sic as Gof'

Raising wistful speculation about what kind of world it would be if the Scottish churchmen had banned golf for seven days a week – and if they had made the law stick.

.... Old Masters

The Links of Leith

Hard by, in the fields called the Links, the citizens of Edinburgh divert themselves at a game called Golf, in which they use a curious kind of bats tipped with horn, and small elastic balls of leather, stuffed with feathers, rather less than tennis balls, but of a much harder consistence. These they strike with such force and dexterity from one hole to another, that they will fly to an incredible distance. Of this diversion the Scots are so fond, that, when the weather will permit, you may see a multitude of all ranks, from the senator of justice to the lowest tradesman, mingled together, in their shirts, and following the balls with the utmost eagerness. Among others, I was shown one particular set of golfers, the youngest of whom was turned of four-score. They were all gentlemen of independent fortunes, who had amused themselves with this pastime for the best part of a century without having ever felt the least alarm from sickness or disgust; and they never went to bed without having each the best part of a gallon of claret in his belly. Such uninterrupted exercise, co-operating with the keen air from the sea, must, without all doubt, keep the appetite always on edge, and steel the constitution against all the common attacks of distemper.

TOBIAS SMOLLETT, *The Expedition of Humphrey Clinker, 1771*

All books on golf are useless. JAMES AGATE

The 13th Century

In the fateful year of 1296 Count Florence V of Holland was murdered near Muyden castle, on the 27th June. We need not go into the background of this event. The noble murderers, the leaders of which were Gerard van Velsen and Herman van Woerden, were pursued by the countryfolk of the area and reached castle Kronenburg in nearby Loenen on the Vecht. They barricaded themselves in this fortress and were besieged by their pursuers. On Boxing Day of that year the castle was surrendered. Gerard van Velsen was killed by the besiegers at the castle's gate.

To commemorate the surrender of Kronenburg Castle and the revenge for the murder of the count (Florence V had been very popular with countryfolk), the villagers of Loenen thereafter each year played a game of golf on Boxing Day.

The two sides were made up of four players each, an 8-ball in modern words. The game was played with wooden clubs and balls. The first hole ran from the courthouse in Loenen along well defined roads to Kronenburg Castle. The 'hole' there was the kitchen door. The winning side was treated to beer by the lord of the castle. The losers and spectators were showered with apples from the upper floors. The lord of Kronenburg incidentally also met the cost of the damage done to private property in the course of the game. The second hole ran from the castle's courtyard to the windmill near Loenen where again the door served as hole. The third hole ran from there to the front door of 'te Velde' Castle where there were beer and apples again and the last hole ran thence to the door of the courthouse of Loenen.

It is worth noting that Gerard van Velsen had taken refuge in one of the castles of his brother-in-law Gijsbrecht van Amstel (lord of Amsterdam) who, although he was not involved in the actual murder, was involved in the plot. The four 'holes' were played on the four properties of Gijsbrecht in Loenen-village of which he was also lord. The game went around the whole village.

The game was played until 1830, thereafter Kronenburg was no longer inhabited, in 1837 the castle was pulled down.

The length of the course was:

1st hole (courthouse to Kronenburg Castle)	660 yds
2nd hole (Kronenburg Castle to mill)	1870 yds
3rd hole (mill to 'te Velde' castle)	1980 yds
4th hole ('te Velde' castle to courthouse)	440 yds
	4950 yds

No other game of golf in history can yet look back on its 430th anniversary.

The Coming of Gowf

After we had sent in our card and waited for a few hours in the marbled ante-room, a bell rang and the major-domo, parting the priceless curtains, ushered us in to where the editor sat writing at his desk. We advanced on all fours, knocking our head reverently on the Aubusson carpet.

'Well?' he said at length, laying down his jewelled pen.

'We just looked in,' we said humbly, 'to ask if it would be all right if we sent you an historical story.'

'The public does not want historical stories,' he said, frowning coldly.

'Ah, but the public hasn't seen one of ours!' we replied.

The editor placed a cigarette in a holder presented to him by a reigning monarch, and lit it with a match from a golden box, the gift of the millionaire president of the Amalgamated League of Working Plumbers.

'What this magazine requires,' he said, 'is red-blooded, one-hundred-per-cent dynamic stuff, palpitating with warm human interest and containing a strong, poignant love-motive.'

'That,' we replied, 'is us all over, Mabel.'

'What I need at the moment, however, is a golf story.'

'By a singular coincidence, ours is a golf story.'

'Ha! say you so?' said the editor, a flicker of interest passing over his finely-chiselled features. 'Then you may let me see it.'

He kicked us in the face, and we withdrew.

On the broad terrace outside his palace, overlooking the fair expanse of the Royal gardens, King Merolchazzar of Oom stood leaning on the low parapet, his chin in his hand and a frown on his noble face. The day was fine, and a light breeze bore up to him from the garden below a fragrant scent of flowers. But, for all the pleasure it seemed to give him, it might have been bone-fertilizer.

The fact is, King Merolchazzar was in love, and his suit was not prospering. Enough to upset any man.

Royal love affairs in those days were conducted on the correspondence system. A monarch, hearing good reports of a neighbouring princess, would despatch messengers with gifts to her Court, beseeching an interview. The Princess would name a date, and a formal meeting would take place; after which everything usually buzzed along pretty smoothly. But in the case of King Merolchaz-zar's courtship of the Princess of the Outer Isles there had been a regrettable hitch. She had acknowledged the gifts, saying that they were just what she had wanted and how had he guessed, and had added that, as regarded a meeting, she would let him know later. Since that day no word had come from her, and a gloomy spirit prevailed in the capital. At the Courtiers' Club, the meeting-place of the aristocracy of Oom, five to one in *pazazas* was freely offered against Merolchazzar's chances, but found no takers; while in the taverns of the common people, where less conservative odds were always to be had, you could get a snappy hundred to eight. 'For in good sooth,' writes a chronicler of the time on a half-brick and a couple of paving-stones which have survived to this day, 'it did indeed begin to appear as though our beloved monarch, the son of the sun and the nephew of the moon, had been handed the bitter fruit of the citron.'

The quaint old idiom is almost untranslatable, but one sees what he means.

As the King stood sombrely surveying the garden, his attention was attracted by a small bearded man with bushy eyebrows and a face like a walnut, who stood not far away on a gravelled path flanked by rose bushes. For some minutes he eyed this man in silence, then he called to the Grand Vizier, who was standing in the little group of courtiers and officials at the other end of the terrace. The bearded man, apparently unconscious of the Royal scrutiny, had placed a rounded stone on the gravel, and was standing beside it making curious passes over it with his hoe. It was this singular behaviour that had attracted the King's attention. Superficially it seemed silly, and yet Merolchazzar had a curious feeling that there was a deep, even a holy, meaning behind the action.

'Who,' he inquired, 'is that?'

'He is one of your Majesty's gardeners,' replied the Vizier.

'I don't remember seeing him before. Who is he?'

The Vizier was a kind-hearted man, and he hesitated for a moment.

'It seems a hard thing to say of anyone, your Majesty,' he replied, 'but he is a Scotsman. One of your Majesty's invincible admirals recently made a raid on the inhospitable coast of that country at a spot known to the natives as S'nandrews and brought away this man.'

'What does he think he's doing?' asked the King, as the bearded one slowly raised the hoe above his right shoulder, slightly bending the left knee as he did so.

'It is some species of savage religious ceremony, your Majesty. According to the admiral, the dunes by the seashore where he landed were covered with a multitude of men behaving just as this man is doing. They had sticks in their hands and they struck with these at small round objects. And every now and again——'

'Fo-o-ore!' called a gruff voice from below.

'And every now and again,' went on the Vizier, 'they would utter the strange melancholy cry which you have just heard. It is a species of chant.'

The Vizier broke off. The hoe had descended on the stone, and the stone, rising in a graceful arc, had sailed through the air and fallen within a foot of where the King stood.

'Hi!' exclaimed the Vizier.

The man looked up.

'You mustn't do that! You nearly hit his serene graciousness the King!'

'Mphm!' said the bearded man nonchalantly, and began to wave his hoe mystically over another stone.

Into the King's careworn face there had crept a look of interest, almost of excitement.

'What god does he hope to propitiate by these rites?' he asked.

'The deity, I learn from your Majesty's admiral is called Gowf.'

'Gowf? Gowf?' King Merolchazzar ran over in his mind the muster-roll of the gods of Oom. There were sixty-seven of them, but Gowf was not of their number. 'It is a strange religion,' he murmured. 'A strange religion, indeed. But, by Belus, distinctly attractive. I have an idea that Oom could do with a religion like that. It has a zip to it. A sort of fascination, if you know what I mean. It looks to me extraordinarily like what the Court physician ordered. I will talk to this fellow and learn more of these holy ceremonies.'

And, followed by the Vizier, the King made his way into the garden. The Vizier was now in a state of some apprehension. He was exercised in his mind as to the effect which the embracing of a new religion by the King might have on the formidable Church party. It would be certain to cause displeasure among the priesthood; and in

7

those days it was a ticklish business to offend the priesthood, even for a monarch. And, if Merolchazzar had a fault, it was a tendency to be a little tactless in his dealings with that powerful body. Only a few mornings back the High Priest of Hec had taken the Vizier aside to complain about the quality of the meat which the King had been using lately for his sacrifices. He might be a child in worldly matters, said the High Priest, but if the King supposed that he did not know the difference between home-grown domestic and frozen imported foreign, it was time his Majesty was disabused of the idea. If, on top of this little unpleasantness, King Merolchazzar were to become an adherent of this new Gowf, the Vizier did not know what might not happen.

The King stood beside the bearded foreigner, watching him closely. The second stone soared neatly on to the terrace. Merolchazzar uttered an excited cry. His eyes were glowing, and he breathed quickly.

'It doesn't look difficult,' he muttered.

'Hoo's!' said the bearded man.

'I believe I could do it,' went on the King, feverishly. 'By the eight green gods of the mountain, I believe I could! By the holy fire that burns night and day before the altar of Belus, I'm *sure* I could! By Hec, I'm going to do it now! Gimme that hoe!'

'Toots!' said the bearded man.

It seemed to the King that the fellow spoke derisively, and his blood boiled angrily. He seized the hoe and raised it above his shoulder, bracing himself solidly on widely-parted feet. His pose was an exact reproduction of the one in which the Court sculptor had depicted him when working on the life-size statue ('Our Athletic King') which stood in the principal square of the city; but it did not impress the stranger. He uttered a discordant laugh.

'Ye puir gonuph!' he cried, 'whitkin' o' a staunce is that?'

The King was hurt. Hitherto the attitude had been generally admired.

'It's the way I always stand when killing lions,' he said. 'In killing lions,' he added, quoting from the well-known treatise of Nimrod, the recognized text-book on the sport, 'the weight at the top of the swing should be evenly balanced on both feet.'

'Ah, weel, ye're no killing lions the noo. Ye're gowfing.'

A sudden humility descended upon the King. He felt, as so many men were to feel in similar circumstances in ages to come, as though he were a child looking eagerly for guidance to an all-wise master – a child, moreover, handicapped by water on the brain, feet three sizes too large for him, and hands consisting mainly of thumbs.

'O thou of noble ancestors and agreeable disposition!' he said, humbly. 'Teach me the true way.'

'Use the interlocking grup and keep the staunce a wee bit open and slow back, and dinna press or sway the heid and keep yer e'e on the ba.'

'My which on the what?' said the King, bewildered.

'I fancy, your Majesty,' hazarded the Vizier, 'that he is respectfully suggesting that your serene graciousness should deign to keep your eye on the ball.'

'Oh, ah!' said the King.

The first golf lesson ever seen in the kingdom of Oom had begun.

Up on the terrace, meanwhile, in the little group of courtiers and officials, a whispered consultation was in progress. Officially, the King's unfortunate love affair was supposed to be a strict secret. But you know how it is. These things get about. The Grand Vizier tells the Lord High Chamberlain; the Lord High Chamberlain whispers it in confidence to the Supreme Hereditary Custodian of the Royal Pet Dog; the Supreme Hereditary Custodian hands it on to the Exalted Overseer of the King's Wardrobe on the understanding that it is to go no farther; and, before you know where you are, the varlets and scurvy knaves are gossiping about it in the kitchens and the Society journalists have started to carve it out on bricks for the next issue of *Palace Prattlings*.

'The long and short of it is,' said the Exalted Overseer of the King's Wardrobe, 'we must cheer him up.'

There was a murmur of approval. In those days of easy executions it was no light matter that a monarch should be a prey to gloom.

'But how?' queried the Lord High Chamberlain.

'I know,' said the Supreme Hereditary Custodian of the Royal Pet Dog. 'Try him with the minstrels.'

'Here! Why us?' protested the leader of the minstrels.

'Don't be silly!' said the Lord High Chamberlain. 'It's for your good just as much as ours. He was asking only last night why he never got any music nowadays. He told me to find out whether you supposed he paid you simply to eat and sleep, because if so he knew what to do about it.'

'Oh, in that case!' The leader of the minstrels started nervously. Collecting his assistants and tip-toeing down the garden, he took up his stand a few feet in Merolchazzar's rear, just as that much-enduring monarch, after twenty-five futile attempts, was once more addressing his stone.

Lyric writers in those days had not reached the supreme pitch of excellence which has been produced by modern musical comedy. The art was in its infancy then, and the best the minstrels could do was this – and they did it just as Merolchazzar, raising the hoe with painful care, reached the top of his swing and started down:

> *'Oh, tune the string and let us sing*
> *Our godlike, great, and glorious King!*
> *He's a bear! He's a bear! He's a bear!'*

There were sixteen more verses, touching on their ruler's prowess in the realms of sport and war, but they were not destined to be sung on that circuit. King Merolchazzar jumped like a stung bullock, lifted his head, and missed the globe for the twenty-sixth time. He spun round on the minstrels, who were working pluckily through their song of praise:

> *'Oh, may his triumphs never cease!*
> *He has the strength of ten!*
> *First in war, first in peace,*
> *First in the hearts of his countrymen.'*

'Get out!' roared the King.

'Your Majesty?' quavered the leader of the minstrels.

'Make a noise like an egg and beat it!' (Again one finds the chronicler's idiom impossible to reproduce in modern speech, and must be content with a literal translation.) 'By the bones of my ancestors, it's a little hard! By the beard of the sacred goat it's tough! What in the name of Belus and Hec do you mean, you yowling misfits, by starting that sort of stuff when a man's swinging? I was just shaping to hit it right that time when you butted in, you——'

The minstrels melted away. The bearded man patted the fermenting monarch paternally on the shoulder.

'Ma mannie,' he said, 'ye may no' be a gowfer yet, but hoots! ye're learning the language fine!'

King Merolchazzar's fury died away. He simpered modestly at these words of commendation, the first his bearded preceptor had uttered. With exemplary patience he turned to address the stone for the twenty-seventh time.

10

That night it was all over the city that the King had gone crazy over a new religion, and the orthodox shook their heads.

We of the present day, living in the midst of a million marvels of a complex civilization, have learned to adjust ourselves to conditions and to take for granted phenomena which in an earlier and less advanced age would have caused the profoundest excitement and even alarm. We accept without comment the telephone, the automobile, and the wireless telegraph, and we are unmoved by the spectacle of our fellow human beings in the grip of the first stages of golf fever. Far otherwise was it with the courtiers and officials about the Palace of Oom. The obsession of the King was the sole topic of conversation.

Every day now, starting forth at dawn and returning only with the falling of darkness, Merolchazzar was out on the Linx, as the outdoor temple of the new god was called. In a luxurious house adjoining this expanse the bearded Scotsman had been installed, and there he could be found at almost any hour of the day fashioning out of holy wood the weird implements indispensable to the new religion. As a recognition of his services, the King had bestowed upon him a large pension, innumerable *kaddiz* or slaves, and the title of Promoter of the King's Happiness, which for the sake of convenience was generally shortened to The Pro.

At present, Oom being a conservative country, the worship of the new god had not attracted the public in great numbers. In fact, except for the Grand Vizier, who, always a faithful follower of his sovereign's fortunes, had taken to Gowf from the start, the courtiers held aloof to a man. But the Vizier had thrown himself into the new worship with such vigour and earnestness that it was not long before he won from the King the title of Supreme Splendiferous Maintainer of the Twenty-Four Handicap Except on Windy Days when It Goes Up to Thirty – a title which in ordinary conversation was usually abbreviated to The Dub.

All these new titles, it should be said, were, so far as the courtiers were concerned, a fruitful source of discontent. There were black looks and mutinous whispers. The laws of precedence were being disturbed, and the courtiers did not like it. It jars a man who for years has had his social position all cut and dried – a man, to take an instance at random, who, as Second Deputy Shiner of the Royal Hunting Boots, knows that his place is just below the Keeper of the Eel-Hounds and just above the Second Tenor of the Corps of

11

Minstrels – it jars him, we say, to find suddenly that he has got to go down a step in favour of the Hereditary Bearer of the King's Baffy.

But it was from the priesthood that the real, serious opposition was to be expected. And the priests of the sixty-seven gods of Oom were up in arm. As the white-bearded High Priest of Hec, who by virtue of his office was generally regarded as leader of the guild, remarked in a glowing speech at an extraordinary meeting of the Priest's Equity Association, he had always set his face against the principle of the Closed Shop hitherto, but there were moments when every thinking man had to admit that enough was sufficient, and it was his opinion that such a moment had now arrived. The cheers which greeted the words showed how correctly he had voiced popular sentiment.

Of all those who had listened to the High Priest's speech, none had listened more intently than the King's half-brother, Ascobaruch. A sinister, disappointed man, this Ascobaruch, with mean eyes and a crafty smile. All his life he had been consumed with ambition, and until now it had looked as though he must go to his grave with this ambition unfulfilled. All his life he had wanted to be King of Oom, and now he began to see daylight. He was sufficiently versed in Court intrigues to be aware that the priests were the party that really counted, the source from which all successful revolutions sprang. And of all the priests the one that mattered most was the venerable High Priest of Hec.

It was to this prelate, therefore, that Ascobaruch made his way at the close of the proceedings. The meeting had dispersed after passing a unanimous vote of censure on King Merolchazzar, and the High Priest was refreshing himself in the vestry – for the meeting had taken place in the Temple of Hec – with a small milk and honey.

'Some speech!' began Ascobaruch in his unpleasant, crafty way. None knew better than he the art of appealing to human vanity.

The High Priest was plainly gratified.

'Oh, I don't know,' he said, modestly.

'Yessir!' said Ascobaruch. 'Considerable oration! What I can never understand is how you think up all these things to say. I couldn't do it if you paid me. The other night I had to propose the Visitors at the Old Alumni dinner of Oom University, and my mind seemed to go all blank. But you just stand up and the words come fluttering out of you like bees out of a barn. I simply cannot understand it. The thing gets past me.'

'Oh, it's just a knack.'

'A divine gift, I should call it.'

'Perhaps you're right,' said the High Priest, finishing his milk and

12

honey. He was wondering why he had never realized before what a capital fellow Ascobaruch was.

'Of course,' went on Ascobaruch, 'you had an excellent subject. I mean to say, inspiring and all that. Why, by Hec, even I – though, of course, I couldn't have approached your level – even I could have done something with a subject like that. I mean, going off and worshipping a new god no one has ever heard of. I tell you, my blood fairly boiled. Nobody has a greater respect and esteem for Merolchazzar than I have, but I mean to say, what! Not right, I mean, going off worshipping gods no one has ever heard of! I'm a peaceable man, and I've made it a rule never to mix in politics, but if you happened to say to me as we were sitting here, just as one reasonable man to another – if you happened to say, 'Ascobaruch, I think it's time that definite steps were taken,' I should reply frankly, 'My dear old High Priest, I absolutely agree with you, and I'm with you all the way.' You might even go so far as to suggest that the only way out of the muddle was to assassinate Merolchazzar and start with a clean slate.'

The High Priest stroked his beard thoughtfully.

'I am bound to say I never thought of going quite so far as that.'

'Merely a suggestion, of course,' said Ascobaruch. 'Take it or leave it. I shan't be offended. If you know a superior excavation, go to it. But as a sensible man – and I've always maintained that you are the most sensible man in the country – you must see that it would be a solution. Merolchazzar has been a pretty good king, of course. No one denies that. A fair general, no doubt, and a plus-man at lion-hunting. But, after all – look at it fairly – is life all battles and lion-hunting? Isn't there a deeper side? Wouldn't it be better for the country to have some good orthodox fellow who has worshipped Hec all his life, and could be relied on to maintain the old beliefs – wouldn't the fact that a man like that was on the throne be likely to lead to more general prosperity? There are dozens of men of that kind simply waiting to be asked. Let us say, purely for purposes of argument, that you approached *me*. I should reply, "Unworthy though I know myself to be of such an honour, I can tell you this. If you put me on the throne, you can bet your bottom *pazaza* that there's one thing that won't suffer, and that is the worship of Hec!" That's the way I feel about it.'

The High Priest pondered.

'O thou of unshuffled features but amiable disposition!' he said, 'thy discourse soundeth good to me. Could it be done?'

'Could it!' Ascobaruch uttered a hideous laugh. 'Could it! Arouse

13

me in the night-watches and ask me! Question me on the matter, having stopped me for that purpose on the public highway! What I would suggest – I'm not dictating, mind you; merely trying to help you out – what I would suggest is that you took that long, sharp knife of yours, the one you use for the sacrifices, and toddled out to the Linx – you're sure to find the King there; and just when he's raising that sacrilegious stick of his over his shoulder –'

'O man of infinite wisdom,' cried the High Priest, warmly, 'verily hast thou spoken a fullness of the mouth!'

'Is it a wager?' said Ascobaruch.

'It is a wager!' said the High Priest.

'That's that, then,' said Ascobaruch. 'Now, I don't want to be mixed up in any unpleasantness, so what I think I'll do while what you might call the preliminaries are being arranged is to go and take a little trip abroad somewhere. The Middle Lakes are pleasant at this time of year. When I come back, it's possible that all the formalities have been completed, yes?'

'Rely on me, by Hec!' said the High Priest grimly, as he fingered his weapon.

The High Priest was as good as his word. Early on the morrow he made his way to the Linx, and found the King holing-out on the second green. Merolchazzar was in high good humour.

'Greetings, O venerable one!' he cried jovially. 'Hadst thou come a moment sooner, thou wouldst have seen me lay my ball dead – aye, dead as mutton, with the sweetest little half-mashie-niblick chip shot ever seen outside the sacred domain of S'nandrew, on whom' – he bared his head reverently – 'be peace! In one under bogey did I do the hole – yea, and that despite the fact that, slicing my drive, I became ensnared in yonder undergrowth.'

The High Priest had not the advantage of understanding one word of what the King was talking about, but he gathered with satisfaction that Merolchazzar was pleased and wholly without suspicion. He clasped an unseen hand more firmly abut the handle of his knife, and accompanied the monarch to the next altar. Merolchazzar stooped, and placed a small round white object on a little mound of sand. In spite of his austere views, the High Priest, always a keen student of ritual, became interested.

'Why does your Majesty do that?'

'I tee it up that it may fly the fairer. If I did not, then would it be apt to run along the ground like a beetle instead of soaring like a

14

bird, and mayhap, for thou seest how rough and tangled is the grass before us, I should have to use a niblick for my second.'

The High Priest groped for his meaning.

'It is a ceremony to propitiate the god and bring good luck?'

'You might call it that.'

The High Priest shook his head.

'I may be old-fashioned,' he said, 'but I should have thought that, to propitiate a god, it would have been better to have sacrificed one of these *kaddiz* on his altar.'

'I confess,' replied the King, thoughtfully, 'that I have often felt that it would be a relief to one's feelings to sacrifice one or two *kaddiz*, but The Pro for some reason or other has set his face against it.' He swung at the ball, and sent it forcefully down the fairway. 'By Abe, the son of Mitchell,' he cried, shading his eyes, 'a bird of a drive! How truly is it written in the book of the prophet Vadun, 'The left hand applieth the force, the right doth but guide. Grip not, therefore, too closely with the right hand!' Yesterday I was pulling all the time.'

The High Priest frowned.

'It is written in the sacred book of Hec, your Majesty, "Thou shalt not follow after strange gods".'

'Take thou this stick, O venerable one,' said the King, paying no attention to the remark, 'and have a shot thyself. True, thou are well stricken in years, but many a man has so wrought that he was able to give his grandchildren a stroke a hole. It is never too late to begin.'

The High Priest shrank back, horrified. The King frowned.

'It is our Royal wish,' he said, coldly.

The High Priest was forced to comply. Had they been alone, it is possible that he might have risked all on one swift stroke with his knife, but by this time a group of *kaddiz* had drifted up, and were watching the proceedings with that supercilious detachment so characteristic of them. He took the stick and arranged his limbs as the King directed.

'Now,' said Merolchazzar, 'slow back and keep your e'e on the ba'!'

A month later, Ascobaruch returned from his trip. He had received no word from the High Priest announcing the success of the revolution, but there might be many reasons for that. It was with unruffled contentment that he bade his charioteer drive him to the

15

palace. He was glad to get back, for after all a holiday is hardly a holiday if you have left your business affairs unsettled.

As he drove, the chariot passed a fair open space, on the outskirts of the city. A sudden chill froze the serenity of Ascobaruch's mood. He prodded the charioteer sharply in the small of the back.

'What is that?' he demanded, catching his breath.

All over the green expanse could be seen men in strange robes, moving to and fro in couples and bearing in their hands mystic wands. Some searched restlessly in the bushes, others were walking briskly in the direction of small red flags. A sickening foreboding of disaster fell upon Ascobaruch.

The charioteer seemed surprised at the question.

'Yon's the muneecipal linx,' he replied.

'The what?'

'The muneecipal linx.'

'Tell me, fellow, why do you talk that way?'

'Whitway?'

'Why, like that. The way you're talking.'

'Hoots, mon!' said the charioteer. 'His Majesty King Merolchazzar – may his handicap decrease! – hae passit a law that a' his soobjects shall do it. Aiblins, 'tis the language spoken by The Pro, on whom be peace! Mphm!'

Ascobaruch sat back limply, his head swimming. The chariot drove on, till now it took the road adjoining the royal Linx. A wall lined a portion of this road, and suddenly, from behind this wall, there rent the air a great shout of laughter.

'Pull up!' cried Ascobaruch to the charioteer.

He had recognized that laugh. It was the laugh of Merolchazzar.

Ascobaruch crept to the wall and cautiously poked his head over it. The sight he saw drove the blood from his face and left him white and haggard.

The King and the Grand Vizier were playing a foursome against the Pro and the High Priest of Hec, and the Vizier had just laid the High Priest a dead stymie.

Ascobaruch tottered to the chariot.

'Take me back,' he muttered, pallidly. 'I've forgotten something!'

And so golf came to Oom, and with it prosperity unequalled in the whole history of the land. Everybody was happy. There was no more unemployment. Crime ceased. The chronicler repeatedly refers to it in his memoirs as the Golden Age. And yet there remained one man on whom complete felicity had not descended. It was all right while he was actually on the Linx, but there were blank, dreary stretches of the night when King Merolchazzar lay sleepless on his couch and mourned that he had nobody to love him.

Of course, his subjects loved him in a way. A new statue had been erected in the palace square, showing him in the act of getting out of casual water. The minstrels had composed a whole cycle of up-to-date songs, commemorating his prowess with the mashie. His handicap was down to twelve. But these things are not all. A golfer needs a loving wife, to whom he can describe the day's play through the long evenings. And this was just where Merolchazzar's life was empty. No word had come from the Princess of the Outer Isles, and, as he refused to be put off with just-as-good substitutes, he remained a lonely man.

But one morning, in the early hours of a summer day, as he lay sleeping after a disturbed night, Merolchazzar was awakened by the eager hand of the Lord High Chamberlain, shaking his shoulder.

'Now what?' said the King.

'Hoots, your Majesty! Glorious news! The Princess of the Outer Isles waits without – I mean wi'oot!'

The King sprang from his couch.

'A messenger from the Princess at last!'

'Nay, sire, the Princess herself – that is to say,' said the Lord Chamberlain, who was an old man and had found it hard to accustom himself to the new tongue at his age, 'her ain sel'! And believe me, or rather, mind ah'm telling ye,' went on the honest man, joyfully, for he had been deeply exercised by his monarch's troubles, 'her Highness is the easiest thing to look at these eyes hae ever seen. And you can say I said it!'

'She is beautiful?'

'Your Majesty, she is, in the best and deepest sense of the word, a pippin!'

King Merolchazzar was groping wildly for his robes.

'Tell her to wait!' he cried. 'Go and amuse her. Ask her riddles! Tell her anecdotes! Don't let her go. Say I'll be down in a moment. Where in the name of Zoroaster is our imperial mesh-knit underwear?'

A fair and pleasing sight was the Princess of the Outer Isles as she stood on the terrace in the clear sunshine of the summer morning, looking over the King's gardens. With her delicate little nose she sniffed the fragrance of the flowers. Her blue eyes roamed over the rose bushes, and the breeze ruffled the golden curls about her temples. Presently a sound behind her caused her to turn, and she

17

perceived a godlike man hurrying across the terrace pulling up a sock. And at the sight of him the Princess's heart sang within her like the birds in the garden.

'Hope I haven't kept you waiting,' said Merolchazzar, apologetically. He, too, was consious of a strange, wild exhilaration. Truly was this maiden, as his Chamberlain had said, noticeably easy on the eyes. Her beauty was as water in the desert, as fire on a frosty night, as diamonds, rubies, pearls, sapphires, and amethysts.

'Oh, no! said the Princess, 'I've been enjoying myself. How passing beautiful are thy gardens, O King!'

'My gardens may be passing beautiful,' said Merolchazzar, earnestly, 'but they aren't half so passing beautiful as thy eyes. I have dreamed of thee by night and by day, and I will tell the world I was nowhere near it! My sluggish fancy came not within a hundred and fifty-seven miles of the reality. Now let the sun dim his face and the moon hide herself abashed. Now let the flowers bend their heads and the gazelle of the mountain confess itself a cripple. Princess, your slave!'

And King Merolchazzar, with that easy grace so characteristic of Royalty, took her hand in his and kissed it.

As he did so, he gave a start of surprise.

'By Hec!' he exclaimed. 'What hast thou been doing to thyself? Thy hand is all over little rough places inside. Has some malignant wizard laid a spell upon thee, or what is it?'

The Princess blushed.

'If I make that clear to thee,' she said, 'I shall also make clear why it was that I sent thee no message all this long while. My time was so occupied, verily I did not seem to have a moment. The fact is, these sorenesses are due to a strange, new religion to which I and my subjects have but recently become converted. And O that I might make thee also of the true faith! 'Tis a wondrous tale, my lord. Some two moons back there was brought to my Court by wandering pirates a captive of an uncouth race who dwell in the north. And this man has taught us——'

King Merolchazzar uttered a loud cry.

'By Tom, the son of Morris! Can this truly be so? What is thy handicap?'

The Princess stared at him wide-eyed.

'Truly this is a miracle! Art thou also a worshipper of the great Gowf?'

'Am I!' cried the King. 'Am I!' He broke off. 'Listen!'

18

From the minstrels' room high up in the palace there came the sound of singing. The minstrels were practising a new pæan of praise –words by the Grand Vizier, music by the High Priest of Hec – which they were to render at the next full moon at the banquet of the worshippers of Gowf. The words came clear and distinct through the still air:

> 'Oh, praises let us utter
> To our most glorious King!
> It fairly makes you stutter
> To see him start his swing!
> Success attend his putter!
> And luck be with his drive!
> And may he do each hole in two,
> Although the bogey's five!'

The voices died away. There was a silence.

'If I hadn't missed a two-foot putt, I'd have done the long fifteenth in four yesterday,' said the King.

'I won the Ladies' Open Championship of the Outer Isles last week,' said the Princess.

They looked into each other's eyes for a long moment. And then, hand in hand, they walked slowly into the palace.

EPILOGUE

'Well?' we said, anxiously.

'I like it,' said the editor.

'Good egg!' we murmured.

The editor pressed a bell, a single ruby set in a fold of the tapestry upon the wall. The major-domo appeared.

'Give this man a purse of gold,' said the editor, 'and throw him out.'

P. G. WODEHOUSE, *The Golf Omnibus*

The wit of man has never invented a pastime equal to golf for its healthful recreation, its pleasurable excitement and its never ending source of amusement. LORD BALFOUR

Golf as a Cross-country Game

Of the history of golf prior to the famous Act of Parliament of 1457 in which we find it coupled with football as one of the two great national sports of Scotland, nothing certain is known. As a similar Act of the previous reign, passed in 1424, refers to football but not to golf, it has been conjectured that the rise of golf to popular favour must have taken place during the intervening quarter of a century, but its origin is lost in the mists of antiquity.

Sir Walter Simpson in his *Art of Golf* draws a fanciful picture of a shepherd idly striking a round pebble with his crook and accidentally knocking it into a rabbit scrape, essaying to repeat the stroke, and calling a companion to join in the new game. But this guess at the origin of golf has nothing to support it beyond a pleasing plausibility – hardly even that, for I cannot imagine that the game began from the wrong end, with the holing out. That, I fancy, would be devised as an extra touch, when two players in a cross-country game had reached their goal in an equal number of strokes and were looking for some amusing method of deciding the tie.

On the other hand there actually is some vague evidence in favour of the idea that golf may have been an offshoot of the older game of hurley or shinty, the equivalent of the English hockey, and may have originated in a form of 'practice' indulged in by hurley players journeying across country. When the Aonach Tailteann, the Irish Olympic Games, were revived some years ago, golf was included on the score of this supposed Celtic origin. An epic account of Cuchullain, one of the heroes of Ulster legend, is quoted to show him amusing himself with golf on his journey. 'The boy set out then, and he took his instruments of pleasure with him; he took his hurly of creduma and his silver ball, and he took his massive Clettini . . . and he began to shorten his way with them. He would give the ball a stroke of his hurly and drive it a great distance before him; and would cast [?swing] his hurly at it, and would give it a second stroke that would drive it not a shorter distance than the first blow;' – using the same club or hockey-stick as both driver and brassie, so to speak.

The Hon. Ruaraidh Erskine of Marr, in an article in *Golfing*, drew attention to a passage to somewhat similar effect in the Gaelic tale of Gaisgeach na Sgeithe Deirge, in which the 'Hero of the Red Shield' meets three of his foster-brothers, and they 'go out in the morning to drive the ball.' The hero pitted himself against the three, and 'he would put a half-shot down and a half-shot in on them.' Apparently what is meant is that without putting out his whole strength he could defeat the three, but precisely how is not quite so clear. It is possible that the reference is only to some sort of scrambling game of shinty with one player against three. But it is at least equally possible that what is meant is that he played the best ball of the three at some primitive form of golf, and giving them half a stroke could still beat them – probably only in point of distance covered, for we have no reason to suppose that at this stage there was any 'holing out.'

A half-way stage between hockey and golf is represented by the game of *chole*, which still survives in Belgium and, under the name of *soule*, in various departments of Northern France. The game, however, is very old. The earliest references to golf and to the Dutch *kolven* both date back to the middle of the fifteenth century, but Mr Andrew Lang, in the first chapter of the Badminton *Golf*, mentions that Ducange, in his *Lexicon of Low Latin* quotes various references to *chole* from legal documents of 1353, 1357, etc. – dates earlier by a century than any of the references to the other two games. A missal of 1504, also referred to in the Badminton *Golf*, shows peasants engaged in playing *chole* with clubs with heads of a steely blue that would seem to indicate that they were of iron. This is consistent with the modern practice, for in the game as now played in Belgium the ball is of beechwood and the club a quaintly shaped lofting iron.

Zola, in *Germinal*, has a somewhat flamboyant description of the game as played by the French miners, but a better idea of it can be gleaned from M. Charles Deulin's tale of 'Le Grand Choleur,' in his *Contes du Roi Gambrinus*, a translation of which, by Mrs Anstruther Thomson, was published in *Longmans' Magazine* (June 1889) under the title of 'The Devil's Round.' The tale, which describes how St Peter and St Anthony came to the wheelwright of the hamlet of Coq, near Condé-sur-l'Escaut, to have a club reshafted for a match they were to play on Shrove Tuesday, and rewarded his good nature and skill in repairing it by granting his wish to become the greatest golfer (*choleur*) in the world, is quite fantastic, but there is no reason to question the references to the technique of the play.

The general idea of the game is not in doubt. The two opponents (or the two opposing sides into which the players have divided themselves, if there are more than two players) begin by agreeing upon a goal to which they are to play, a cemetery gate, a church door, or the like. This mark may be as much as two, three, or even four leagues distant from the starting point. Then the opponents 'bid' the number of 'turns' (of three strokes each) in which they will undertake to reach the goal, always remembering that after each 'turn' of three strokes the other side is entitled to a stroke in which to *dechole*, i.e., to strike the ball backward away from the goal, or into a difficult place. The side which bids the smallest number of turns is 'in' and strikes off, and after each three strokes the 'out' side, the *decholeurs*, have their chance to hit the ball back or into any 'hazard' they can find. (It is difficult to avoid translating the technical terms into those of golf, but, of course, each game has its own glossary.) Inasmuch as we have here the idea of attack and defence, with both sides playing the same ball, *chole* retains some of the elements of hockey, but in its general conception it is a sort of cross-country golf.

ROBERT BROWNING, *A History of Golf*

In golf it is not the how which counts but the how many? LLOYD MANGRUM

The Game of Goff, or Golf

The favourite Summer Amufement in Scotland, is played with Clubs and Balls. The Club is taper, terminating in the Part that ftrikes the Ball, which is faced with Horn, and loaded with Lead. But of this there are fix Sorts ufed by good Players; namely, the *Common Club*, ufed when the Ball lies on good Ground; the *Scraper* and *Half Scraper*, when in long Grafs; the *Spoon*, when in a Hollow; the *Heavy Iron Club*, when it lies deep amongft Stones or Mud; and the *Light Iron ditto*, when on the Surface of chingle of fandy Ground.

The Balls are confiderably fmaller than thofe ufed at Cricket, but much harder; they are made of Horfe Leather, ftuffed with Feathers in a peculiar Manner, and boiled.

The Ground may be circular, triangular, or a femicircle. The Number of Holes are not limited; that always depends on what the Length of the Ground will admit. The general diftance between one Hole and another is about a Quarter of a Mile, which commences and terminates every Game; and the Party who gets their Ball in by the feweft Number of Strokes are the Victors.

Two, four, fix, eight, or as many as choofe, may play together; but what is called the good Game never exceeds four; that Number being allowed to afford beft Diverfion, and not fo liable to Confufion as fix, eight, ten or twelve might be.

The more rifing or uneven the Ground, requires the greater Nicety or Skill in the Players: on which Account it is always given the Preference to by Proficients.

Light Balls are ufed when playing with the wind, and heavy ones againft it.

At the Beginning of each Game the Ball is allowed to be elevated to whatever Height the Player choofes, for the Convenience of Striking; but not afterwards. This is done by Means of Sand or Clay, called a *Teeing*.

The Balls which are played off at the Beginning of the Game muft not be changed until the next Hole is won, even if they fhould happen to burft.

When a Ball happens to be loft, that Hole is loft to the Party.

If a Ball fhould be accidentally ftopped, the Player is allowed to take his Stroke again.

Suppofe four are to play the Game, A and B againft C and D, each Party having a Ball, they proceed thus:

A ftrikes off firft – C next; but perhaps does not drive his Ball above half the Diftance A did, on which Account D, his Partner, next ftrikes it, which is called *one more*, to get it as forward as that of their Antagonifts, or as much beyond it as poffible; if this is done, then B ftrikes A's Ball, which is called playing *the Like*, or equal, of their Opponents. But if C and D, by their Ball being in an awkward Situation, fhould not be able, by playing *any more*, to get it as forward as A's, they are to play, in turn, *two*, *three*, or as many more until that is accomplifhed, before B ftrikes his Partner's Ball; which he calls *one to two*, or *one to three*, or as many Strokes as they required to get to the fame Diftance as A did by his once playing. The Ball is ftruck alternately if the Parties are equal, or nearly fo.

Hoyle's Games, 1790

American Origins

The first authentic reference to the game in the United States is preserved in an advertisement dated April 21, 1779, from *The Royal Gazette*, which was published in New York City by an Englishman, named James Rivington, who was in the combined businesses of printing and importing. Rivington had recently received a shipment of play clubs and featheries from Scotland, and advertised their sale in his publication. Whether or not he sold them is anybody's guess.

There is also evidence, from old pamphlets, of a golf club of sorts having been formed in Charleston, South Carolina, in 1786, the members of which apparently played a form of miniature golf on a local public green that was not more than a few acres in area. Not long afterward there was also, apparently, a club in Savannah, for we have evidence dated 1796 that its members celebrated an anniversary (although we don't know which one) on the first of October of that year. To substantiate Savannah's claim as the cradle of American golf, there is also in existence an invitation sent out by the members of the club to a ball in honor of a Miss Eliza Johnston for New Year's Eve, 1811. It is one of the tantalizing curiosities of history that there is no positive evidence, beyond the implication of this invitation and the announcement of the club's anniversary, of golf actually having been played at the Savannah Golf Club – no old clubs or balls, not even a remnant of what might have been a course. So there is a strong suggestion that the club might have served only a social purpose.

Whatever its purpose, the club does not seem to have survived the War of 1812, and no doubt the Civil War excluded any possibility of the game's taking another toe hold elsewhere in the country until the early eighties. In those years, we know, golf was tried out as a curiosity in Sarasota and a course was built and a club called Oakhurst was formed in 1884 by some New Englanders at a private estate in the Alleghenies of West Virginia, only a few miles from the graybeard resort at White Sulphur Springs. Both the club and the course died out in a matter of a few years, however.

American golf may be said to have really begun, by one of the many happy coincidences with which his life was marked, in the golf shop of Old Tom Morris in 1887. There one day that year two dozen gutties and a set of six clubs were purchased by a traveling American businessman named Robert Lockhart on commission by another American named John Reid, a transplanted Scotsman who, like Lockhart, had got an inkling of what the game was all about as a boy growing up near the links of Musselburgh. Lockhart requested Old Tom to ship the clubs and balls to him. When they arrived at his home in New York City that winter, Lockhart tested them out on a vacant lot near Seventy-second Street and what would now be Riverside Drive. Satisfied that they had arrived in sound condition, he sent them to his friend Reid at the latter's home in suburban Yonkers.

February 22, 1888 – Washington's Birthday – was an uncommonly balmy day that came less than three weeks before the greatest blizzard in that city's history. Itching to try out his new clubs, Reid took advantage of the weather to invite a group of his sports-loving cronies to watch him and a friend play an improvised three holes which Reid had laid out in a nearby cow pasture. Thus, on the birthday of the man who is alleged never to have told a lie in his life, was played the round which presaged a pastime that has since created more lying Americans than any other save fishing.

After the blizzard, Reid and his friends returned in earnest to the game. So appealing did they find it that in April they decided to construct a six-hole course on a larger tract off Broadway that was owned by their local butcher. This they used as their course for the remainder of the summer and the fall. On November 14, Reid invited the group to a dinner at his home, and after it he and his friends drew up a membership list and elected officers to a club, to which they gave the not altogether original name of St Andrews.

CHARLES PRICE, *The World of Golf, 1962*

Golf is a game whose aim is to hit a very small ball into an even smaller hole, with weapons singularly ill-designed for the purpose.
WINSTON CHURCHILL

Professionals and Caddies

The profession offers prizes, as we have said, in the shape of engagements as keepers of golf greens, but otherwise its solid inducements are few and its temptations very many. Especially to be reprobated is the practice at some clubs of offering a 'drink' to a professional at the close of a round. If you leave him to himself there is no danger of his damaging his health by drinking too little. No golf professional is recorded to have died of thirst. On the other hand, the lives of many have been shortened and degraded by thirst too often satiated. Some of the clubs of the North would be greatly more pleasant places if a fixed price were authoritatively named for the recompense of professional caddies and players. There is a delightful uncertainty upon this point which more than the actual cost deters many from taking out a professional. The 'dour' silence in which he accepts your fee when you give him enough, and the sense of self-contempt for the moral weakness which prompts you to give him too much, are equally annoying with his open dissatisfaction and probable profanity if you give him too little.

On the whole, the professional is not a bad fellow. He has little morality; but he has good, reckless spirits, a ready wit and humour which is only denied to the Scotch by those who do not know them, and he will show a zeal and loyalty in defending your performances behind your back – provided you overpay him sufficiently – very much at variance with the opinion which he expresses to your face. He is apt to be insolent in order to show you that he imagines himself to have some self-respect – which is a self-delusion – but if you can endure a certain measure of this, he is a good companion. Never, however, bet with him; for so will it be best for him and best for you, as he is unlikely to pay you if he loses. This he is apt to do, for he is a bad judge of the merits of a golf match, a point which requires a delicacy of estimate usually beyond his powers.

HORACE HUTCHINSON, *The Badminton Library, 1980*

An Applied Science and a Black Art

Being an attempt to prise the back off the genus Golfer, and to examine his works through various optical glasses in an attempt to determine what, if anything, makes him tick.

Worplesdon

The Bogey Man

My woes in golf, I have felt, have been largely psychological. When I am playing well, in the low 90's (my handicap is 18), I am still plagued with small quirks – a suspicion that, for example, just as I begin my downswing, my eyes straining with concentration, a bug or a beetle is going to suddenly materialize on the golf ball.

When I am playing badly, far more massive speculation occurs: I often sense as I commit myself to a golf swing that my body changes its corporeal status completely and becomes a *mechanical* entity, built of tubes and conduits, and boiler rooms here and there, with big dials and gauges to check, a Brobdingnagian structure put together by a team of brilliant engineers but manned largely by a dispirited, eccentric group of dissolutes – men with drinking problems, who do not see very well, and who are plagued by liver complaints.

The structure they work in is enormous. I see myself as a monstrous, manned colossus poised high over the golf ball, a spheroid that is barely discernible 14 stories down on its tee. From above, staring through the windows of the eyes, which bulge like great bay porches, is an unsteady group (as I see them) of Japanese navymen – admirals, most of them. In their hands they hold ancient and useless voice tubes into which they yell the familiar orders: 'Eye on the ball! Chin steady! Left arm stiff! Flex the knees! Swing from the inside out! Follow through! Keep head down!' Since the voice tubes are useless, the cries drift down the long corridors and shaftways between the iron tendons and muscles, and echo into vacant chambers and out, until finally, as a burble of sound, they reach the control centers. These posts are situated at the joints, and in charge are the dissolutes I mentioned – typical of them a cantankerous elder perched on a metal stool, half a bottle of rye on the floor beside him, his ear cocked for the orders that he acknowledges with ancient epithets, yelling back up the corridors, 'Ah, your father's mustache!' and such things, and if he's of a mind, he'll reach for the controls (like the banks of tall levers one remembers from a railroad-yard switch house) and perhaps he'll pull the proper lever and perhaps not. So that, in sum, the whole apparatus, bent on hitting a golf ball smartly, tips and convolutes and lunges, the Japanese admirals clutching each other for support in the main control center up in the head as the structure rocks and creaks. And when the golf shot is on its way the navymen get to their feet and peer out through the eyes and report: 'A shank! A shank! My

God, we've hit another shank!' They stir about in the control center drinking paper-thin cups of rice wine, consoling themselves, and every once in a while one of them will reach for a voice tube and shout:

'Smarten up down there!'

Down below, in the dark reaches of the structure, the dissolutes reach for their rye, tittering, and they've got their feet up on the levers and perhaps soon it will be time to read the evening newspaper.

It was a discouraging image to carry around in one's mind; but I had an interesting notion: a month on the professional golf tour (I had been invited to three tournaments), competing steadily and under tournament conditions before crowds and under the scrutiny of the pros with whom I would be playing, might result in 5, perhaps even 6, strokes being pruned from my 18 handicap. An overhaul would result. My Japanese admirals would be politely asked to leave, and they would, bowing and smiling. The dissolutes would be removed from the control centers, grumbling, clutching their bottles of rye, many of them evicted bodily, being carried out in their chairs.

The replacements would appear – a squad of scientific blokes dressed in white smocks. Not too many of them. But a great tonnage of equipment would arrive with them – automatic equipment in gray-green boxes and computer devices that would be placed about and plugged in and set to clicking and whirring. The great structure would become almost entirely automatized. Life in the control center would change – boring, really, with the scientists looking out on the golf course at the ball and then twiddling with dials and working out estimations, wind resistance, and such things, and finally locking everything into the big computers; and with yawns working at the corners of their mouths because it was all so simple, they would push the 'activate' buttons to generate the smooth motion in the great structure that would whip the golf ball out toward the distant green far and true. Very dull and predictable. The scientists would scarcely find very much to say to each other after a shot. Perhaps 'Y-e-s,' very drawn out. 'Y-e-s. Very nice.' Occasionally someone down in the innards of the structure would appear down the long glistening corridors with an oil can, or perhaps with some brass polish to sparkle up the pipes.

GEORGE PLIMPTON, *The Bogey Man*, 1969

The Feel of a Golf Club

There is nothing occult about hitting a golf ball. In fact, although the application may be a bit more complicated, we use no more than the ordinary principles of motion we encounter numberless times every day. Once started upon a correct path, the club will tend to hold to its course until outside forces cause a change.

The great fault in the average golfer's conception of his stroke is that he considers the shaft of the club a means of transmitting actual physical force to the ball, whereas it is in reality merely the means of imparting velocity to the club head. We would all do better could we only realize that the length of a drive depends not upon the brute force applied but upon the speed of the club head. It is a matter of velocity rather than of physical effort of the kind that bends crowbars and lifts heavy weights.

I like to think of a golf club as a weight attached to my hands by an imponderable medium, to which a string is a close approximation, and I like to feel that I am throwing it at the ball with much the same motion I should use in cracking a whip. By the simile, I mean to convey the idea of a supple and lighting-quick action of the wrists in striking – a sort of flailing action.

BOBBY JONES, *Bobby Jones on Golf*, 1966

Golf can become a drug to which the victims,
powerless to escape, are addicted twice a day.
JOYCE WETHERED

Golfers and Other Strangers

Just after dawn on a brisk but brilliant December day a couple of years ago, I was about to ask Raquel Welch if she was all set for a droll caper I had in mind, when the telephone went off like a fire alarm, and an eager voice shouted, 'All set?' It was, alas, not Raquel but my golf partner, a merry banker of indestructible cheerfulness who calls all stock-market recessions 'healthy shake-outs'. I climbed out of my promising dream and out of bed, and in no time I was washing the irons, downing the Bufferin, rubbing resin on the last three fingers of the left hand, inserting the plastic heel cup, searching for my Hogan cap – performing the whole early morning routine of the senior golfer. This was the great day we had promised ourselves ever since I had suffered the shock of hearing Herbert Warren Wind confess he had never played Century, the tough and beautiful rolling course in Purchase, New York, where Ben Hogan had his first job as a teaching pro. It seemed ridiculous that the man who had helped Hogan lay down 'The Modern Fundamentals of Golf' should never have played the course on which Ben laid them down. Another telephone call alerted Wind to get the hell out of his own variation on the Welch fantasy. An hour later we were on our way, up the West Side Highway and the Saw Mill River Parkway, and on to Purchase.

Century is the private domain of some very well-heeled gents from Wall Street, but they are so busy watching those healthy shake-outs that none of them has much time for weekday golf. Furthermore, in December, the caviar and hamburgers are stacked in the deep freeze. But, since it is very difficult to close a golf course, the course is open. The caddie master had been briefed about the signal honor that Wind was going to confer on one of the fifty toughest courses in America and he had obligingly mobilized two of his veteran caddies.

As we swung around White Plains and began to thread up through the country lanes of Purchase, we were puzzled to see strips of white cement smearing the grassy banks of the highway. They got thicker as we turned into the club driveway, and as we came out on the hill that overlooks the undulating terrain, we saw that the whole course was overlaid not with cement but with snow. The caddies were already there and looking pretty glum. They greeted us by stomping their feet and slapping their ears and otherwise conveying that, though our original idea was a brave one, it had obviously been aborted by the weather. 'You serious about this thing, Mr Manheim?' one of the caddies asked the banker, 'Sure,' said Manheim, who would play golf in a hammock if that's what the rules called for.

We started off with three reasonable drives, which scudded into the snow the way Hawaiian surfers skim under a tidal wave. The caddies went after them like ferrets and, after a lot of burrowing and signaling, retrieved them and stood there holding the balls and looking at us, as the song says, square down in the eye, as if to say, 'What are you going to do with these damn things?' We had to find little slivers of exposed ground (no nearer the hole) and drop them and swipe off once more. The greens were either iced over or had sheets of ice floating in little lakes. After several five-putts on the first two greens, we decided that anybody who could hold a green deserved the concession of two putts.

This went on for eight holes, at the end of which, however, Wind allowed that Hogan sure loved to set himself problems. Plodding up the long ninth fairway, with Cooke beginning to turn blue and the banker humming happily to himself (it was the two-putt rule that did it), Wind turned and said, 'Tell me, Manheim, do you do this because you're nuts or because your p.r. man says its good for your image?' We three-putted the ninth green, which 'held' with the consistency of rice pudding, and that was it.

As I recall this Arctic expedition, there is a blustery wind bending the trees in Central Park and a steady rain, a combination of circumstances that fires many a Scotsman to rush out and play a round of golf in what one of them once told me are 'the only propair condeetions.' But, because this is America, they are conditions that immediately empty the golf courses from Maine to San Diego, forcing the sons of the pioneers to clean their clubs, putt on the bedroom carpet or sink into the torpor of watching a football game. We have it from the Mexican ambassador himself, His Excellency Lee Trevino, that there are Texans who will not play at all whenever the temperature toboggans below 80° Fahrenheit. And there are by now many generations of Dutchmen who gave up the game once it moved off ice onto grass.

It is a wonderful tribute to the game or to the dottiness of the people who play it that for some people somewhere there is no such thing as an insurmountable obstacle, an unplayable course, the wrong time of the day or the year. Last year I took Manheim – whose idea of a beautiful golf course was a beautiful park – to play his first links course. It is the home course of the English golf writer Pat Ward-Thomas (Ward-Thomas's idea of the most beautiful golf course in the world is his home course). It is up in the bleak stretch of southeastern England known as Norfolk, a sort of miniature prairie exposed to the winds whistling out of Siberia. The course is called Brancaster, and you can drive up to the rude clubhouse, a kind of Charles Addams gabled shack, and start asking people where is the golf course. For ahead of you is nothing but flat marshland – which floods at the high tide – and beyond that the gray North Sea and a chorus of squawking gulls. The flags are about two feet high, so as to encourage the notion that a man has not been known to tamper with a masterpiece of nature.

When we went into lunch it was spitting rain and when we came out it was raining stairrods. The wind gauge at the clubhouse entrance registered forty-three knots. There was Ward-Thomas; a handsome and imperturbable Englishman named Tom Harvey; Manheim and I. There was also two caddies, aged about ten, already half-drowned and cowering in the whirling sand like two fugitives from Dotheboys Hall.

Nobody raised a question or lifted an eyebrow, so Manheim and I – remembering the good old White House slogan – soldiered on. By about the seventh, Manheim, who wears glasses, had to be guided to the proper tees. We were all so swollen with sweaters and raingear we looked like the man in the Michelin ads. Well, sir, they talked throughout in well-modulated tones about 'sharp doglegs' and 'a rather long carry' and 'it's normally an easy five-iron, but maybe with this touch of wind you'd be safer with a four-iron, even a four-wood, I shouldn't wonder.' We were now all water-logged, from the toenails to the scalp, and Manheim came squelching over to me and said, 'Are these guys nuts?' I told him that on the contrary this was for them a regular outing: 'You know what the Scotsman said – "If there's nae wind, it isn't gawf."' Manheim shook his head like a drenched terrier and plodded on. The awful thing was that Harvey, a pretty formidable golfer, was drawing and fading the damn thing at will, thus proving the sad truth that if you hit it right, even a tornado is not much of a factor.

Outward bound, we'd been carried downwind. But as we were bouncing like tumbleweed down to the ninth green, Ward-Thomas came staggering over. I should tell you that he is a gaunt and a very engaging gent who looks like an impoverished Mexican landowner (a hundred acres in beans and not doing very well), and he has a vocabulary that would have qualified him for an absolutely top advisory post in the last Republican administration. He came at me with his spiky hair plastered against his forehead and water blobbing off his nose and chin. He screamed confidentially into the gale: 'If you think this (expletive deleted) nine is a (expletive deleted) picnic, wait till we come to the (expletive deleted) turn!'

He was right. We could just about stand in the teeth of the gale, but the balls kept toppling off the tees. It was a time to make you yearn for the old sandbox. Manheim's glasses now looked like the flooded windshield of a gangster escaping through a hurricane in an old Warner Brothers movie. Moreover, his tweed hat kept swiveling around, making him stand to the ball like a guy who'd been taught about his master eye by a one-eyed pirate. At this point, Ward-Thomas offered up the supreme sacrifice. He is a longtime idolater of Arnold Palmer and he cried, 'Hold it!' and plunged into his bag. He came up with a faded sunhat and tendered it to Manheim with the reverent remark: 'It was given to me by Palmer. Try it.' As everybody knows, Palmer's head is on the same scale as his forearms, and this one blotted out Mannheim's forehead, nose, glasses, master eye and all. What we did from then on was to slop our way down the last nine, pity the trembling caddies and throw murderous glances at Harvey, who was firing beautiful woods into the hurricane.

Very little was said as we retired to Harvey's home, fed every strip of clothing into a basement stove and stewed in baths that would have scalded a Turk. At dinner it came out. All through the first nine, Harvey and Ward-Thomas had been muttering to each other just as Manheim and I had been doing: 'They must be out of their minds, but if this is what they're used to. . . .' Harvey said, 'We decided that since you were our guests, the only thing to do was to stick it out.'

If these are fair samples of maniacal golfers, how about crazy golf courses?

You would not think, looking at the stony rampart of the mountain face back of Monte Carlo, that anyone could plant a one-hole putting green between those slabs of granite. But when you get to the top, there the indomitable British have somehow contrived a course that lurches all around the Maritime Alps. There is rarely a straightaway drive. On the very first tee, you jump up in the air and see the flag fluttering in a depression way to the left. You ask the caddie for the line. He points with a Napoleonic gesture to a mountain far to the right. 'La ligne!' he commands. And if you believe him and bank away at the mountain top, you then see the ball come toppling about a hundred yards to the left and going out of sight. Which is the proper trajectory to the green.

The golf 'clubu' at Istanbul is, if anything, more improbable still. The banks of the Bosporus are studded with more boulders than Vermont. But when the Scots took Constantinople at the end of World War I and laid in an adequate supply of their *vin du pays*, what else was there to do but build a golf course? The original rude layout is still there in the 'clubu' house, and on paper it looks like a golf course. In fact, it is simply a collection of flags stuck at random on a mountainside of boulders. Every ball comes to rest against a rock. The local rule is a free drop on every stroke. You drop it and drop it till it stops, and never mind the fussy business of 'no nearer the hole.'

In Bangkok, before the natives took to cement and the automobile, the canals looked like irrigation ditches slicing every fairway. Forecaddies, as nimble as grasshoppers, spent the day diving into the canals and surfacing with an ear-to-ear grin while they held aloft a ball drenched with cholera. Once they'd wiped it and dropped it, you were on your way again, and free to enjoy the great game in a dripping temperature of 110°.

A lion, you might guess, is not a normal item of wildlife on your course or mine. But in Nairobi once, a tawny monster strolled out of the woods, sniffed at my ball and padded off again, while my partner, a British native of the place, tweaked his mustache and drawled: 'You're away, I think.' At about the third hole I pushed my drive into the woods, and when I started after it, the host screamed at me to cease and desist. 'Snakes, man, snakes!' he hissed; 'leave it to the forecaddies.' They plunged into shoulder-high underbrush, and I meekly muttered, 'How about *them*?' 'Them?' the man said, 'Good God, they're marvelous. Splendid chaps; lost only two this year.' That round, I recall, was something of a nightmare, what with my pushed drives and the caddies (the ones who survived) chattering away in Swahili. The whole place was so exotic that I began to wonder if any of the normal rules of golf applied. One time, we came on a sign which read, 'GUR.' I gave it the full Swahili treatment. 'What,' I said, 'does GHOOOR mean?' He gave a slight start, as if some hippo were pounding in from the shade. Then he saw the sign. 'That,' he said firmly, 'means Ground Under Repair.' And he sighed and started to hum a Sousa march. After all, you must expect anything in golf. A stranger comes through; he's keen for a game; he seems affable enough, and on the eighth fairway he turns out to be an idiot. It's the rub of the green, isn't it?

Well, it takes more sorts than you and I have dreamed of to make up the world of golf. In Japan, they take a ski lift up to the tee of a famous par three. In Cannes, the club members never bat an eyelid as they board a ferry from one green to the next tee.

But for sheer systematic nuttiness, nothing can compare with an annual ceremony put on by the Oxford and Cambridge Golfing Society, a collection of leather-elbowed oldsters and shaggy-haired youngsters who play for the President's Putter, no less, every year in the first week of January at Rye, on the coast of Sussex, another treeless links course fronting on a marsh which gives out into the English Channel. This tournament is intended to prove the English boast that 'we can play golf every day of the year.' If they can do it at Rye in January, they can do it at the South Pole, which in some sharp ways Rye resembles. At any rate, under the supervision of Gerald Micklem, a peppery stockbroker in his 60s who is the Genghis Khan of British amateur golf, these maniacs go through with this tournament on the scheduled date no matter what. Snow, hail, wind, torrents – nothing can keep them from the swift completion of their Micklem-appointed rounds.

I was there four years ago. On the first morning, the small town and the course were completely obliterated in a fog denser than anything in Dickens. It seeped into the hotels so you needed a links boy to light your way to your plate of bacon, baps and bangers. I assumed the whole thing was off, till a telephone call warned a few dallying competitors that their tee-off time was about to strike. We crawled out to the course, and the first person I ran into, marching around the clubhouse, was Micklem. I asked him if anyone was out there, and if so, why. 'Nonsense,' he barked, 'they're all out there. Haven't lost a ball yet.' He motioned toward the great gray nothingness outside, not fog, not landscape, but what John Milton (thirteen handicap) once called 'not light but darkness visible.' I hopped off into what might very well have been the edge of the world, as it was conceived by those Portuguese mariners who would have liked very much to discover America but who were afraid to sail out into the Atlantic, beyond sight of land, for fear of falling off. The word, God knows how it got through, was that Donald Steel was doing nicely toward repeating his win of the previous year. He had just teed off on the second nine. I ran into a swirl of nothingness and, sure enough, there emerged, like a zombie on the heath in a horror film, a plumpish, confident figure recognizable at three yards as Steel. He took out an iron for his approach shot, though what he thought he was approaching I have no idea – San Salvador, no doubt.

He hit it low and clean, and a sizable divot sailed away from him and vanished. He went off after it and vanished too. I kept following in the gloom, and from time to time a wraith swinging a golf club would loom up, take two steps and be gone.

It was true! They all finished, and nobody lost a ball. I felt my way back to the clubhouse, and at the end the last ghost was in. Within five minutes they were up against the bar, chests out, faces like lobsters, beer mugs high, slapping thighs, yokking it up. Queer fish, the Oxford and Cambridge Golfing Society. They behave just as if they'd been out for a round of golf. What they play every year on that barren fork of Sussex that reaches out to the Channel, and Holland, and eventually to the Bering Strait, is a wholly new game: Invisible Golf.

ALISTAIR COOKE, *Golf*, 1957

Some golfers, we are told, enjoy the landscape; but properly the landscape shrivels and compresses into the grim, surrealistically vivid patch of grass directly under the golfer's eyes as he morosely walks towards where he thinks his ball might be. JOHN UPDIKE

What it Takes to Win the Open

During each of the last four Open Championships the USGA has conducted a research project to determine how well the players drive, hit fairway woods and irons, execute recovery shots, and putt. Patterns have evolved which may be said to describe the games of the very best golfers. Let's examine these patterns for they are likely to be repeated at Baltusrol.

First, let's look at the actual scores. The winner has gone as low as 278 at Olympic in 1966 and at Congressional in 1964, and as high as 293 at The Country Club in 1963 when strong, gusty winds sent scores to their highest level since 1935.

The score needed to survive the 36-hole cut (60 and ties beginning in 1966 and 50 and ties earlier) has been remarkably constant. It has varied only between 150 and 152.

Another constant factor has been the average score per round of those who play through 72 holes. With the exception of 1963, which has been discarded because of extraordinary weather conditions, the average score for those who make the cut has varied only between 73.8 strokes at Bellerive in 1965 to 74.1 strokes at Congressional in 1964. This indicates clearly that, despite the architectural differences of the courses, the USGA's method of preparing the course establishes a comparable test year in and year out.

The difference between the average scores of those who finish in the top 10 and those who finish well down the list is relatively slight. To determine what does separate the wheat from the chaff, so to speak, we have to consider what the very best players have been doing in recent Opens. After doing so, we can say with relative certainty that the man who wins at Baltusrol will meet the following standards:

Driving distance: He will consistently drive between 240 and 270 yards. His average drive is likely to be close to 250 yards. Casper averaged 253 yards last year; Gary Player 250 yards in 1965; Ken Venturi 248 yards in 1964. The average distance for the entire Open field has been 249 yards. A chart on page 206 shows the distances achieved by some of the players on a long par-4 hole at Olympic last year. Incidentally, our research shows that there is a tendency for the public and for the news media to exaggerate the lengths of drives. We have observed only one drive of more than 300 yards in four years, that a 301-yard wallop by Jack Nicklaus in 1964.

Driving accuracy: The Open Champion will drive in a fairway about 35 yards wide about 80% of the time. He will not have to be terribly long off the tee, but it is essential that he be accurate because of the rough that borders the Open fairways. On the 18th hole at Olympic last year the average score for players who drove into the rough was 4.57, compared to 4.04 for those who drove in the fairway.

Fairway woods: When a wood is called for on the second shot, as it will be on Baltusrol's 17th and 18th holes, the winner's second shot will usually come to rest 460 yards to 510 yards from the tee.

Long irons: The Champion will hit his No. 2- and No. 3-irons a little more than 200 yards and he will come within 40 feet of the hole generally.

39

Medium irons: He will get to within 30 feet of the pin when he is 150 to 175 yards from the hole. In general, a well-struck iron should come to rest less than 7% of the original distance from the hole.

Long putts: On putts of 75 feet, the winner will come to within 4½ feet of the cup, and proportionately closer as the distance of the putt diminishes. Thus, his 40-foot putt will stop about 2.4 feet from the hole and a 30-footer only 1.8 feet away.

Short putts: The winner will hole *everything* up to 2½ feet; will make 50% of his 7-footers; and about one out of seven from 20 feet. He is likely to have one hot round when he will markedly better this standard.

Chip shots: He will chip from grass cut at fairway height just about as well as he would putt from the same distance, so that he will encounter only a slight penalty for missing the green *if* the ball doesn't stop in the rough.

Recovery shots: He will miss many greens, but he will recover from rough near the greens and from bunkers to within 12 feet of the pin when he is playing from 75 feet away. Even the Champion will miss more putts than he will make from 12 feet.

JACK REDDY, *US Open Programme, 1967*

The first rule usually is no woman-chasing after Wednesday. TONY LEMA

The Art of Driving

It has been said that the successful driving of a golf ball is a knack. The statement may be true, but I am certain that the only way to acquire the knack is to study the art, and that mental capacity cannot afford greater assistance to physical strength than by allotting to the latter its proper and rather modest place in the scheme of the tee-shot.

A long drive is not usually made purely by virtue of hard hitting.

There are a few men – veritable golfing goliaths, and good luck to them! – who depend mainly upon what we may term 'brute strength' for the admirable length of their drives. They slog for all they are worth; they time the shots well; and, as a consequence, they make the ball travel great distances. They are gifted souls. What the average moderate player does not realise (so, at least, it seems to me after many years of experience) is that Nature never intended him to be a slogger. He is not endowed for the part. And yet he persists in trying to play it. He seems to make up his mind during the preliminary waggle that the most important matter of all is to give the ball a terrific thump. He tightens all his muscles in his determination to accomplish a mighty shot. That is just where he fails. I can assure him that this constricted condition of the muscles, which is easily cultivated in the case of the man who thinks that physical power and hefty hitting are of supreme importance, is the worst thing imaginable for the purpose of long driving.

As a rule, it produces a foozle. What happens is easily explained. The player induces such a state of rigidity in his resolve to hit with desperate force that he simply cannot swing the club freely. The muscles of his arms are so contracted in the vehement desire to triumph by means of strength that the victim cannot go through with the shot. What he usually does – unwittingly, but none the less surely – is to begin to stop the club before it reaches the ball. His arms are not sufficiently free to allow the driver to do the work for him. And as he starts involuntarily to check the club, he endeavours to use all his bodily strength; in a way, he hurls himself at the ball. It is a curious fact that, in spite of the employment of so much energy, one is not likely to send the ball 150 yards when adopting these methods. It may be struck fairly, cleanly, but there is no real power behind it. One of the most common mistakes of the indifferent golfer is that he makes downright hard work of driving. The practice is not merely useless; it renders a long shot a rarity except in the case of an exceptionally constituted individual.

In saying this, I do not mean to suggest that there is no necessity to invest the stroke with any strength at all. The power must be there, but it must be inveigled into exercising its influence at the right instant. What I wish to indicate is that it is not likely to be brought into profitable operation by mere violence on the part of the player; that is to say, by a desperate tightening of the muscles and a mere lunging of the body at the ball. A first-class golfer who executes a long tee shot uses in the process most, if not all, of the strength that Nature has given him, but he uses it in such a way that he scarcely realises that he is hitting hard, and, indeed, the strain for him is not so great as for the man who is fiercely workmanlike. This, then, is the knack of successful driving, and the only way to master it is to study the swing, which is the art of golf. And I venture to say that there is no reason why anybody should be incapable of learning sufficient about that art as would enable him to drive tolerably well. People vary in their aptitude for games, but the main principles of the golf swing are so clear that their assimilation is largely a matter of perseverance.

For the man who is endeavouring to acquire a knowledge of how to drive I always recommend the use of the brassie. Its stiffer shaft renders it easier to control than the driver and the slight loft on its face imparts confidence. The simpler the task can be made at the outset, or when one is off one's driving and practising in the hope of remedying the defect, the more rapid is likely to be the progress. Having secured satisfactory results with the brassie, there ought to be no difficulty in doing equally well with the driver, since the two clubs are (or, at any rate, most certainly should be) of the same length and the same 'lie'.

As to the stance, let it be as natural and unconstrained as possible. The toes should point outwards, and it is best, I think, to have the right foot a few inches in front of the left. Certainly it is bad to have the left foot in front of the right, although I have seen people stand in that manner. It almost precludes the possibility of a proper finish. There are golfers, too, who stand exceedingly straddle legged, and others who have their feet too close together. All these points are worthy of consideration; there is a kind of 'happy medium' about the character of the correct stance, the idea of which can be conveyed better by illustration than by the written word. So I would refer my reader to the picture showing the stance.

I daresay that every student of the game has heard that the main secret of the successful up-swing is to screw the body from the hips and keep the head still instead of allowing the body to sway. All the same, I feel that this point cannot be emphasised too frequently or too strongly, for it is certain that there are thousands of golfers who, even though they have been told that it is the principle of ninety-nine good players in every hundred, do not give to it the attention it deserves. Probably the explanation is that they think they are performing the correct thing when, all the while, they are swaying in a way which completely upsets their balance and renders a good shot practically impossible unless they chance to be so fortunate as to recover the proper position at the proper moment – a pleasant dispensation which comes to few people. As a means of detecting head-movement, which means swaying of the body, I have seen nothing so good as the little device of Colonel Quill which, of late, has attracted considerable attention. It shows a golfer at once whether he is committing the most disastrous of all the faults to which the golfing flesh is heir, and it is valuable to be able to settle that matter when one is out for a little quiet practice and reflection in splendid isolation.

It is an important matter always to let the club-head lead. I have pointed out the danger of allowing the body to lead by the act of lurching away from the ball at the beginning of the upswing; similarly would I lay stress on the mistake of snatching the club-head away by a hasty movement with rigid wrists. As the club starts to go back, allow the left wrist to turn slightly inwards towards the body. That small operation will help very considerably to secure the correct position of the wrist and club-head at the top of the swing. Then, if you determine to wind up the body at the hips and keep your head steady, so that the screwing operation ceases, so to speak, at the neck, you ought to be able to learn the knack of driving. As the club goes up the right leg will stiffen, the left leg will bend inwards at the knee, and the left heel will rise from the ground. All these happenings are the natural outcome of the winding up of the body; they do not occur – at any rate, in the same degree – when the player sways. Resolve that the left heel shall not turn outwards more than an inch or so (less if possible) and, at the top of the swing, you will be correctly poised. The pivoting will have been done on the inside of the left foot (on that portion of the member in question which extends from the big toe to the big joint) and the right foot will be resting firmly on the ground.

When you are practising it is instructive to inspect your left wrist at the top of the swing in order to ascertain whether it is in the proper position. That it should be so is important, and inasmuch as you are in no great hurry during these purely personal proceedings, it is as well to turn your head and examine the left wrist. If it is bent outwards, the club-head is necessarily in the wrong position. This highly important left wrist should be bent inwards so that it constitutes the base of a curve of which the hand and the arm are the continuations. That being so, the club-head will be pointing to the ground, as it should be.

In coming down, it is highly important to let the club-head lead. Do not throw your arms forward as though you were trying to mow grass. Just give the club a start, and in the first stage of the downward swing – a stage which lasts for only a brief instant, but which is of vast importance to the ultimate issue – let the left hip go forward a trifle. Then bring the club round with rhythmic vim, its pace increasing until it is travelling at its fastest when it reaches the ball, and go right through with the shot so that the hands finish high and the chest faces the line of play at the end of the stroke. Beware, above all things, of hurling the arms forward at the beginning of the downward swing. It is one of the most frequent of errors, and it nearly always produces a shot which flies in any but the straight path.

There is much to be said for the aphorism 'slow back'; but it is not desirable to perform the upward movement at funereal pace. It is necessary to remember that you are going to play a free and full shot; you are not attempting merely to flick a fly five yards. Consequently, excessive slowness during the backward swing is apt to do more harm than good. The slight inward turn of the left wrist; the winding-up of the body from the hips to the neck; and the resolve to let the club-head lead instead of allowing the arms to throw it forward at the beginning of the downward swing – these are golden principles. And keep your own head down until you have struck the ball; keep smelling at the ball, as it were, until you have despatched it on its journey.

The grip is a matter of fancy. I should be something less (or, perhaps more) than human if I advocated any but the overlapping grip. Its details are shown in the illustration. It may not suit all golfers, but I have no hesitation in saying that it is the ideal manner of holding the club. It is agreed by all students of the game that the two hands should work as a whole. That was one of the first floods of light that came to us in the old days in Jersey. When I became a professional, about the earliest thing that I did was to consider the question of the grip. For a full year I tried various ways of holding the club, until at length I decided in favour of the method which I now employ. It seems to me to weld the two hands into one; the beauty of it is that neither hand works against the other. That, I am sure, is just what is wanted. For the man who has practised the old-fashioned palm grip for a long while the system which I advocate may be difficult at the outset, but familiarity breeds friendliness with it. It is a matter of placing the little finger of the right hand over the forefinger of the left, with the thumbs and forefingers forming V's down the hand of the club. It produces a confederacy of the kind which is not easily secured in any other way.

As regards general details, I would suggest a low tee for the drive, because, if you have a high one, you are likely to see difficulties (which do not actually exist) in the brassie shot, and, indeed, every other shot through the green. You start with the ball poised high above the ground, and you are not altogether prepared for the shock of having to play it when it is sitting down on the turf. Another useful hint is to be sure of securing a comfortable stance on the teeing ground. It is the only place at which you have the right to choose a stance, and you may as well make the most of it. So hunt for a favourable spot on which to tee the ball. And, when there is an out-of-bounds area to be taken into consideration, tee the ball as far from it as the limits of the teeing ground will allow. These are matters which at times count heavily.

HARRY VARDON, *Fry's Magazine*

No man should attempt to play golf who has not good legs to run with and good arms to throw with, as well as a modicum of brain power to direct his play. PHILADELPHIA TIMES

Golf as an Art

It must be forty years since I picked up an old cleek belonging to my father and swung at a golf ball with it; and, Lord, the changes I have seen. Why, there must be quite a few readers who were stumped just by the word cleek. It was a fairly straight-bladed iron with a fairly shallow face, and you used it when you wanted to hit a low, boring shot into the wind. Now the cleek, so far as it exists at all, is called the number one iron. The numbering of clubs came in with the steel shaft and the possibility of manufacturing matched sets, and I often meet young sparks who wonder what the old fool is rambling on about with his talk of brassies, spoons, mashies and niblicks. The only club to have kept its name is the putter.

Golf was never as snobbish as outsiders thought. I remember a scene at St George's Hill before the war when a dentist was elected captain against the wishes of a determined bloc who saw in this event the shadow of the tumbrils. It was always hard to get into the kind of golf club James Bond belonged to, and still is. Swinley Forest, near Ascot, limits its membership to two hundred and has, I believe, a ten-year waiting list. But there were always middle and lower class clubs, where the members played in cycle clips with their trousers tucked into their socks, and called each other Mister.

On the whole, though, golf has moved with the times. The snobbery has altered in stance. The questions now are Who do you know? and Can you afford it? not, What do you do? and What was your school? Alongside this, as you would expect, there's been a sharp decline in observance of golf etiquette. The bastards won't let you through.

It is a much harder game than it used to be. Until 1950 the par of a course was based on the score a reasonably average golfer would achieve if he made no mistakes. Now the par is based on the absurd prognosis that on top of making no mistakes he can hit a ball two hundred and fifty yards. The result of this has been the disappearance of all those better than scratch handicaps, the Plus Two, Three, even Four men that used to figure on the trophy boards.

It's cleaner, too, thanks to the influence of televised golf. When I was a boy only a handful of golfers ever saw Bobby Jones, Henry Cotton, Gene Sarazen, Walter Hagen, and half a hundred more that I could name without needing a reference book. Today everyone knows Jack, Gary, Arnie and Jacko; and their presence on the box has transformed the look and odour of golf. Golfers look prettier and smell nicer. The fragrance of old shoes and sweaters that used to give men's locker-rooms their peculiar atmosphere has given way to the whiff of Brut and Old Spice and talcum powder.

The central truth of golf, though, remains the same. It isn't really a game; it's an art.

If it were a game, played at an unreflective speed, such as hockey, you would use one club only. Most golfers carry fourteen for the same reason that a painter's easel can accommodate fourteen or more brushes; they are not too many for the delicate, varied and agonisedly solitary and introspective making of strokes.

It is the introspection that makes the art. The actual swing of a golf club at a ball is no more complicated physically than the act of swinging an axe at a selected spot on a tree. There's nothing to it. Max Faulkner told me once that by the time a good golfer had passed his twentieth birthday he should have trained his muscles to deliver the perfect swing every time. (We all show this perfect command of muscle memory every time we drop a finger unerringly on the light switch in the middle of the night.) In theory, said Max, all you needed to do was to switch your mind off, first telling your muscles to get on with it. It is because you cannot switch off your mind, because under pressure it transmits the possibility of failure to the muscles, that competitive golf, even on the level of the monthly medal, tests will and determination more than beef and co-ordination. The art is in willing the muscles to stop fooling.

Bobby Jones's swing was the perfection of drowsy elegance, as Bernard Darwin called it. But when he won the British Open in 1930 he fought round the seventy-two holes without ever, as Darwin wrote, playing really well. Most of the time he was retrieving errors. He said in his book, *Bobby Jones on Golf*, that of all the rounds of golf he'd played only five had been easy – five times when, as he put it, 'I have to make no special effort to do anything.'

Now, the unique appeal of golf, the thing that keeps you at it, is that it is impossible to play eighteen holes without playing one shot as well as Bobby Jones could have done it, even though it may only be the holing of an eight-foot putt and of no more significance than leaving a good set of footprints in a sand trap. Everyone can do it right sometimes. It seems intolerable not to do it always. No; not just intolerable: shameful; humiliating; undeserved.

I used to mind playing badly so much that a miasma of gloom appeared to play about my head, rather like the unholy nimbus with which early painters surrounded the head of the foul fiend. I no longer burn, but I have compassion for those who do. I was playing one day last summer with an Australian, normally a strong, steady golfer, whose game had become so unhinged that he was incapable of doing more than disturb the ball a few yards. After one such blow that must almost have dislocated his shoulderblades he took off his Gary Player-type cap, lifted his eyes skywards and said: 'You work hard all the week. You look forward to your golf. All you want is to enjoy your one afternoon out. And what happens? You get *punished!*' I thought he expressed himself delicately and truthfully.

You have noticed that without actually saying so, I have sug-gested to you that I am very good at golf. Well, it's quite true. I am extremely good; and it's a constant puzzle to me why I don't play better. With this admission we approach the inner truth of golf. *Golfers mind playing badly because it seems an unjust reflection of their normal game.*

Henry Longhurst rouses much bitterness in his golf commentar-ies on TV by constantly drawing attention to what his audience does not in its bones accept – that there is a difference between the way they can play and the way Gary, Jack and Arnie can. 'This is just the kind of shot the club golfer dreads,' Henry will say as

47

Palmer shapes up to a pitch over a bunker. 'He knows he'll pop it into the sand.'

Not true. The club golfer looks forward keenly to such a shot. He sees it clearly with his inner eye. Perfectly struck, the ball thumps down by the flag and squirms to a stop. The only thing is, just that once he didn't hit it right. But to say that he can't is ridiculous.

The multi-million pound golf industry refutes the learned Longhurst. The accessory and clothing industry could not have flourished (it is of course based on one of the oldest myths, that one can acquire strength by eating the strong) if golfers did not know in their hearts that they were good players having an off day. There would be no point in buying a set of Lee Trevino woods if they couldn't use them; they might just as well stick to their old Jack Nicklaus's. A more striking example is the success of the books. Every instructional book ever written about golf assumes that the reader can do what it says. 'For the fade shot,' wrote Bill Cox in his Penguin, *Improve Your Golf*, 'the ball should be played from just inside the left heel with the stance very slightly open.' Tommy Armour's *How To Play Your Best Golf All The Time* was based on the principle of placing each shot to set oneself up well for the next. The ingenious Tommy knew he could rely for sales on every golfer's belief that he can hit the ball where he's aiming.

And there's a kind of logic – perhaps the truth within the inner truth – that says Armour is right. Sometimes you can split every fairway with a stroke that looks, feels and sounds triumphantly right. Next week it will have gone. But it is still there, somewhere; and it's no more absurd to believe that the good swing was the normal one, and the other is some demoniac intervention, than to put it the other way round.

PETER BLACK, *Piccadilly World of Golf*

When Bobby Putts

You immediately relapse into silence. Bobby Locke has just strolled on to the green. The solemn business of putting a little white ball into a four-and-a-quarter-inch-diameter hole is about to begin.

No easy matter this. No time for merry-making. No smile anywhere. No noise at all.

Among the gathering round the green, there are those who stand sedately; and those who sit uncomfortably, on shooting-sticks, on haunches, on honest-to-goodness bottoms; but, no matter what the preference, all are engrossed with the line of Bobby's putt and the secret undulations of the green.

Bobby sides with the squatters. For that is precisely what he does when everyone has settled down quietly to watch. Down on his haunches, carefully weighing distance, undulations, line and pace.

Perhaps, if you weren't a golfing man, you might think of him as an Indian squatting before a fire. But, of course, an Indian in a white Palm Beach cap is extraordinarily difficult to imagine.

Meanwhile Bobby ponders, and spies impressively along the line of putt. He keeps at it too. Little short of a severe attack of cramp would move this guy from his line of putt.

Then, just as you begin to think he's dozed off, he surprises you. He gets up and walks slowly away from the ball, out in the direction of square-leg.

But not directly there. No. He chooses a somewhat circuitous route through the out-field, looking intently the while at ball, hole and green.

Arriving at square-leg, he squats again and, for an interval, plays the same old Indian before the same old fire.

Next comes the hole. Not the ball. The hole. He's not interested in the ball until he's had a good look at the hole.

It's deathly cold and the north wind blows disagreeably, yet no one seems to mind, each apparently saying to the other: 'Bobby's gone to look at the hole,' and the other replying sagely: 'That's the

49

way to do it . . . boy . . . that's the way.' Still, no matter what they say, it's a damned cold wind to stand there looking at a hole!

Albeit ruefully, we let him go, but I feel that the grey haired little lady at my side thinks him awfully vague and forgetful. I'm sure she's quite bewildered, saying to herself: 'Why does he walk about the green and sit so often? Has he forgotten his ball?'

Bobby stands at the holeside and, stooping above, looks suspiciously at and in it, jerking his head, this way, that way, up, down and sideways. After watching him on many occasions, I think he observes how the hole has been cut and notes any peculiarities it may have. I may be wrong. Everyone is entitled to his own opinion, and the chap who thinks he's looking to see if the previous players have left a ball in there, may be more accurate.

Next the anti-litter campaign. Every inch of the putt comes under a microscopic eye. Infinitesimal bits of grass and grit are carefully removed until, at long last, the ball is reached.

Bobby then takes up his stance for putting – but not immediately to putt. Positioning himself rather wide of the ball, he takes two little 'fresh-air' practice swings before he's ready to strike.

Now, however, the big moment nears. Bobby's white shoes creep forward an inch or two to the final position, and the ball, beautifully and precisely struck, rolls holewards along the right line, at the right pace, curves obediently down the almost imperceptible slope of the green, and dives into the hole like a cat-chased mouse.

So there you are. That's the way to putt. All you have to do when you've holed a cruel twenty-five footer is charmingly touch your white Palm Beach cap and smile at the applause which greets you.

KEITH B. MARSHALL, *Golf Galore, 1960*

The man who can putt is a match for anyone.
WILLIE PARK

Mathematics for Golfers

It is only quite recently that I have taken up golf. In fact, I have played for only three or four years, and seldom more than ten games in a week, or at most four in a day. I have had a proper golf vest for only two years. I bought a 'spoon' only this year and I am not going to get Scotch socks till next year.

In short, I am still a beginner. I have once, it is true, had the distinction 'of making a hole in one,' in other words, of hitting the ball into the pot, or can, or receptacle, in one shot. That is to say, after I had hit, a ball was found in the can, and my ball was not found. It is what we call circumstantial evidence – the same thing that people are hanged for.

Under such circumstances I should have little to teach anybody about golf. But it has occurred to me that from a certain angle my opinions may be of value. I at least bring to bear on the game all the resources of a trained mind and all the equipment of a complete education.

In particular I may be able to help the ordinary golfer, or 'goofer' – others prefer 'gopher' – by showing him something of the application of mathematics to golf.

Many a player is perhaps needlessly discouraged by not being able to calculate properly the chances and probabilities of progress in the game. Take for example the simple problem of 'going round in bogey'. The ordinary average player, such as I am now becoming – something between a beginner and an expert – necessarily wonders to himself, 'Shall I ever be able to go around in bogey; will the time ever come when I shall make not one hole in bogey, but all the holes?'

To this, according to my calculations, the answer is overwhelmingly 'yes'. The thing is a mere matter of time and patience.

Let me explain for the few people who never play golf (such as night watchmen, nightclerks in hotels, night operators and astronomers) that 'bogey' is an imaginary player who does each hole at golf in the fewest strokes that a first-class player with ordinary luck ought to need for that hole.

Now an ordinary player finds it quite usual to do one hole out of the nine 'in bogey' – as we golfers, call it; but he wonders whether it will ever be his fate to do all the nine holes of the course in bogey. To which, we answer again with absolute assurance, he will.

The thing is a simple instance of what is called the mathematical theory of probability. If a player usually and generally makes one hole in bogey, or comes close to it, his chance of making any one particular hole in bogey is one in nine. Let us say, for easier calculation, that it is one in ten. When he makes it, his chance of doing the same with the next hole is also one in ten; therefore, taken

51

from the start, his chance of making the two holes successively in bogey is one-tenth of a tenth chance. In other words, it is one in a hundred.

The reader sees already how encouraging the calculation is. Here is at last something definite about his progress. Let us carry it farther. His chance of making three holes in bogey one after the other will be one in 1000, his chance of four, one in 10,000, and his chance of making the whole round in bogey will be exactly one in 1,000,000,000 – that is, one in a billion games.

In other words, all he has to do is to keep right on. But for how long? he asks. How long will it take, playing the ordinary number of games in a month, to play a billion? Will it take several years? Yes.

An ordinary player plays about 100 games in a year, and will, therefore, play a billion games in exactly 10,000,000 years. That gives us precisely the time it will take for persons like the reader and myself to go round in bogey.

Even this calculation needs a little revision. We have to allow for the fact that in 10,000,000 years the shrinking of the earth's crust, the diminishing heat of the sun, and the general slackening down of the whole solar system, together with the passing of eclipses, comets and showers of meteors, may put us off our game.

In fact, I doubt if we shall ever get around in bogey. Let us try something else. Here is a very interesting calculation in regard to 'allowing for the wind'.

I have noticed that a great many golfers of my own particular class are always preoccupied with the question of 'allowing for the wind'. My friend Amphibius Jones, for example, just before driving always murmurs something, as if in prayer, about 'allowing for the wind'. After driving he says with a sigh, 'I didn't allow for the wind'. In fact, all through my class there is a general feeling that our game is practically ruined by the wind. We ought really to play in the middle of the Desert of Sahara where there isn't any.

It occurred to me that it might be interesting to reduce to a formula the effect exercised by the resistance of the wind on a moving golf ball. For example, in our game of last Wednesday, Jones in his drive struck the ball with what, he assures me, was his full force, hitting it with absolute accuracy, as he himself admits, fair in the center, and he himself feeling, on his own assertion, absolutely fit, his eye being (a very necessary thing with Jones) absolutely 'in', and he also having on his proper sweater – a further necessary condition of first-class play. Under all the favorable circumstances the ball advanced only 50 yards! It was evident at once that it was a simple matter of the wind: the wind, which was of treacherous character. It had impinged full upon the ball, pressed it backward, and forced it to the earth.

Here, then, is a neat subject of calculation. Granted that Jones – as measured on a hitting machine the week the circus was here – can hit 2 tons, and that this whole force was pressed against a golf ball only one inch and a quarter in diameter. What happens? My reader will remember that the superficial area of a golf ball is r^3, that is $3 \cdot 141567 \times (5/8 \text{ inches})^3$. And all of this driven forward with the power of 4000 pounds to the inch!

In short, taking Jones's statements at their face value, the ball would have travelled, had it not been for the wind, no less than 6½ miles.

I give next a calculation of even more acute current interest. It is in regard to 'moving the head'. How often is an admirable stroke at golf spoiled by moving the head! I have seen members of our golf club sit silently and glum all evening, murmuring from time to time, 'I moved my head'. When Jones and I play together I often hit the ball sideways into the vegetable garden from which no ball returns (they have one of these on every links; it is a Scottish invention). And whenever I do so Jones always says, 'You moved your head.' In return when he drives his ball away up into the air and down again ten yards in front of him, I always retaliate by saying, 'You moved your head, old man.'

In short, if absolute immobility of the head could be achieved, the major problem of golf would be solved.

Let us put the theory mathematically. The head, poised on the neck, has a circumferential sweep or orbit of about 2 inches, not counting the rolling of the eyes. The circumferential sweep of a golf ball is based on a radius of 250 yards, or a circumference of about 1600 yards, which is very nearly equal to a mile. Inside this circumference is an area of 27,878,400 square feet, the whole of which is controlled by a tiny movement of the human neck. In other words, if a player were to wiggle his neck even 1/190 of an inch the amount of ground on which the ball might falsely alight would be half a million square feet. If, at the same time, he multiplies the effect by rolling his eyes, the ball might alight anywhere.

I feel certain that after reading this, any sensible player will keep his head still.

A further calculation remains – and one perhaps of even greater practical interest than the ones above.

Everybody who plays golf is well aware that on some days he plays better than on others. Question – How often does a man really play his game?

I take the case of Amphibius Jones. There are certain days, when he is, as he admits himself, 'put off his game' by not having on his proper golf vest. On other days the light puts him off his game; at other times the dark; so, too, the heat: or again the cold. He is often put off his game because he has been up late the night before; or similarly because he has been to bed too early the night before; the barking of a dog always puts him off his game: so do children: or adults; or women. Bad news disturbs his game; so does good; so also does the absence of news.

All of this may be expressed mathematically by a very simple application of the theory of permutations and probability; let us say that there are, altogether, 50 forms of disturbance any one of which puts Jones off his game. Each one of these disturbances happens, say, once in ten days. What chance is there that a day will come when not a single one of them occurs? The formula is a little complicated, but mathematicians will recognize the answer at once as $x/1 + x^2/1 + \ldots \ldots x^n/1$. In fact, that is exactly how often Jones plays at his best. Worked out in time and reckoning four games to the week and allowing for leap years and solar eclipses, it comes to about once in 2,930,000 years.

And from watching Jones play, I think that this is about right.

STEPHEN B. LEACOCK, *The World of Mathematics, Vol. 4,* edited by James R. Newman, 1956

A man who can approach does not require to putt. J. H. TAYLOR

The Character of Golf

There is no other game in which the three fundamental factors of life – the physiological, the psychological, and the social or moral – are so extraordinarily combined or so constantly called into play. Some sports, such as football, polo, rowing, call chiefly for muscular activity, judgment, and nerve; others, such as chess, draughts, backgammon, call upon the intellect only. In no other game that I know of is, first, the whole anatomical frame brought into such strenuous yet delicate action at every stroke; or, second, does the mind play so important a part in governing the actions of the muscles; or, third, do the character and temperament of your opponent so powerfully affect you as they do in Golf. To play well, these three factors in the game must be most accurately adjusted, and their accurate adjustment is as difficult as it is fascinating. . . .

An eminent Scots philosopher once told me that the eminence of Scottish philosophy was due to the fact that Scots philosophers were brought up on the Shorter Catechism. I venture to think that he might have extended his axiom to the St. Andrew's game. At any rate, this much is certain: Golf is a game in which attitude of mind counts for incomparably more than mightiness of muscle. Given an equality of strength and skill, the victory in Golf will be to him who is captain of his soul. Give me a clear eye, a healthy liver, a strong will, a collected mind, and a conscience void of offense both toward God and toward man, and I will back the pigmy against the giant. Golf is a test, not so much of the muscle, or even of the brain and nerves of a man, as it is a test of his inmost veriest self; of his soul and spirit; of his whole character and disposition; of his temperament; of his habit of mind; of the entire content of his mental and moral nature as handed down to him by unnumbered multitides of ancestors.

ARNOLD HAULTAIN, *Atlantic Monthly, 1908*

Excessive golfing dwarfs the intellect.
SIR W. G. SIMPSON

An Effeminate Game?

Sir,

The sooner it is realized that golf is merely a pleasant recreation and inducement to indolent people to take exercise the better. Golf has none of the essentials of a great game. It destroys rather than builds up character, and tends to selfishness and ill-temper. It calls for none of the essential qualities of a great game, such as pluck, endurance, physical fitness and agility, unselfishness and *esprit de corps* or quickness of eye and judgement. Games which develop these qualities are of assistance for the more serious pursuits of life.

Golf is of the greatest value to thousands, and brings health and relief from the cares of business to many but to contend that a game is great which is readily mastered by every youth who goes into a professional's shop as assistant (generally a scratch player within a year!) and by the majority of caddies is childish. No one is more grateful to golf for many a pleasant day's exercise than the writer, or more fully recognizes the difficulties and charm of the game, but there is charm and there are difficulties in (for instance) lawn tennis and croquet. It certainly seems to the writer that no game which does not demand a certain amount of pluck and physical courage from its exponents can be called great, or can be really beneficial to boys or men.

The present tendency is undoubtedly towards the more effeminate and less exacting pastimes, but the day that sees the youth of England given up to lawn tennis and golf in preference to the old manly games (cricket, football, polo, &c.) will be of sad omen for the future of the race.

I am, yours, &c.

B. J. T. BOSANQUET

The Times, June 4th, 1914

Love thy Baffie and thy Stotter

An examination of the spiritual bond between the golfer and what soul-less pragmatists would mistakenly describe as inanimate objects, his clubs.

Royal and Ancient

The Care of Clubs

And now let us approach the actual care of clubs. Years ago, when I was of an age for hero-worship, I went back with a good golfer and famous player to his rooms after a match, and I have never forgotten the impression he made upon me by the care he showed for his clubs. It had been raining, and in consequence his bag was wet, the heads and shafts of his clubs were damp, and the heads of the wooden clubs were rubbed. He said to me, 'Now, young man, I'll show you how to look after your clubs.' He started by sending his bag to be dried in the kitchen – not too near the fire. Then he went into his study with his clubs, and carefully dried them with a towel. When they were quite dry he wiped them over with a rag on which there was a little furniture polish. He then took a hare's foot and dipped it very lightly into a saucer which contained a mixture of varnish and oil. With this he brushed the shafts and heads of his wooden clubs and the shafts of his iron clubs, and stood them up to dry.

How, When, and Why

While they were drying he gave me the following advice: 'If you look after your clubs they will look after you. Never let your bag of clubs drop on to the ground, but always put it down carefully. This will prevent the wooden heads getting scratched, the iron heads from being nicked, and the shafts from being dented and strained. For the same reason, never pull your clubs out from the bag quickly or put them back in a hurry, and in pulling them out and putting them back, do so with a twisting motion. Now I'll tell you the reason for what I have done so far. I sent my bag to be dried at once because otherwise the sail-cloth would rot. I dried the heads and shafts of my wooden clubs to prevent the wet getting into any scratches, and the heads of the irons to prevent rust starting. I touched up the heads of the wooden clubs and all the shafts with the oil and varnish to give them a waterproof cover. The clubs ought to be dry now – they are right!' He took the iron clubs and cleaned the heads with a rather worn piece of emery cloth. 'Always clean your iron heads from toe to heel,' he went on. 'This preserves a true face, for if you put on a cross marking you will find in time that the heads get a hollow at the toe and heel and a lump in the centre. Now we'll put the clubs away for the night.'

MAJOR GUY CAMPBELL, *Golf for Beginners*, 1922

My First Driver

The first drive I have any recollection of making was hit outside the Ashwood, Virginia, Methodist Church one Sunday morning when I was around seven years old. My folks, Harry and Laura Snead, had a little cow-and-chicken farm in Ashwood, a few miles from Hot Springs. Ashwood wasn't much: some said the 400 people in the town didn't match the number of moonshiners up in the timber.

When the chores was finished, all of us Snead kids scattered for the hills. We were rounded up on Sunday the way they call hogs. My mother, who had a good, strong voice, would let out a war whoop that could be heard over the next mountain, and when we straggled in they scraped off the mud and wood ticks and put us into clean clothes for churchgoing.

My older brothers – Homer, Jesse, Lyle, and Pete – weren't quite as wild as me. One Sunday I sneaked away from Bible class and spent the morning fixing an old wooden clubhead I'd found to a buggy whip.

The organ was finishing off the sermon when I came down the road, swinging at rocks and dried-up horse turds. One of the rocks took off like a bullet, went through a church window, and sprayed the congregation with glass.

The preacher, whose name was Tompkins, was the first one out of the door, but all he found was an empty road. I stayed in the woods until dark, then wouldn't admit a thing when they gave me the third degree. They never did prove it on me.

Years later, in 1949, I presented the Ashwood Methodist Church with a new electric pipe organ – just another sinner who came to repent.

My brother Homer was my hero, but he was twelve years older than me and without much time for us little kids, Homer was a star at every sport – football, swimming, boxing – and could rip a golf ball about as far as anyone I've ever seen. He'd let me shag balls for him in the pasture. Then he'd leave for his job – as an electrician – and his club would go with him. So I'd cut a swamp maple limb with a knot on the end, carve a rough clubface with a penknife, leaving some bark for a grip, and swing by the hour, imitating Homer's roundhouse wallop.

Barefoot, with that swamp stick, I could hit for twenty fence posts, about 125 yards. If the ball sliced, it fell into some mucky bottomland. By trying different grips and stances, I got so it would sail both far and fairly true.

The way I became a caddie was that a Negro kid named Franklin Jefferson Jones came along one day when I was seven and a half and said, 'Sam, let's go swipe us some candy.'

We went down to a crossroads store, waited until the old man who ran the place stepped out, and grabbed all the chocolate bars we could carry. Back in our hideout I tried to eat some but couldn't. I began to bawl. 'That poor old man,' I said. 'We're gonna put this stuff back.' So we had to hide in the brush by the store all that hot day until we got a chance to creep in and replace the candy, which by now had melted into a sticky mess.

Frankie thought I was out of my mind but suggested that we could earn candy money by packing clubs over at The Homestead Hotel links in Hot Springs. A set of clubs weighed nearly as much as my sixty-five pounds. Since my shoulders weren't wide enough to support a bag, I hung it around my neck and staggered along behind the golfers.

Eighteen holes of this was worth fifty cents to a caddie, but the trouble was that the track was too long for me: after eighteen, I fell down and couldn't get up. The hotel doctor came along and saw me stretched out in exhaustion. He said that if any more golfers let an unformed infant carry their clubs, he'd knock them so high that they'd starve to death coming down.

'Why, this baby can ruin his health,' he said.

My folks didn't know about it, since I was always missing from home, anyway – to spear bullfrogs or chase coon – and so my caddying didn't end until winter came and a man hired me to pack for him in the snow. Being barefoot, after nine holes I couldn't feel a thing below my shins. 'Mister,' I said, 'I think I'm froze.' Dropping his bag, I started to run.

When I reached the caddie house and got next to a fire, they found that all ten toes were frostbit and in a few more minutes might have been permanently damaged. So then they took away my caddie badge for good.

That hurt, because I was a hurrying kid with ambition. Horse-hair Brinkley and Piggie McGuffin, two pals of mine, had to run to keep up with me. I tried every which way to learn to play golf on a real course, but when I was ten and twelve years old there wasn't a chance. The Homestead and Cascades Hotel courses were for wealthy tourists only. Any time we peckerwoods sneaked onto the local 'Goat Course,' which was a nine-holer for hotel employees, a cop would holler, 'Hey, you little bastards!' – and we'd have to scatter for the woods without even time to putt out.

Since that door was closed, I went back to pasture practice, got so I could knock a ball out 200 yards or more in my bare dogs using a swamp maple, and then made myself a little five-hole course by sinking tomato cans around the farmyard. The hazards were loose chickens, the pump, a hayrake, and the outhouse.

In order to judge where a long drive should go, you need some depth perception. Likewise on chips, pitches, and putts. I think mine came from playing horseshoes with an uncle of mine. Back of the barn we tossed ringers by the day and week. A long time later, while winning the Brazilian Open at São Paulo, I stunned a gallery by shooting three straight holes without taking a putt – chipping in from off the green each time from distances of 40, 25, and 100 feet. It all went back to those horseshoe matches.

Me and Horsehair and Piggie and my brother Pete couldn't wait until the frost was gone so we could stop wearing shoes. By the next winter my toenails were practically all torn off and my feet were tougher than boot leather. I could stomp a chestnut burr and not feel a thing.

Matter of fact, when I got older and wore shoes they didn't feel normal. Right then golf began to get complicated for me. Instead of just swinging from the heels, I began thinking about what I was doing. Thinking instead of acting is the No. 1 golf disease.

If I could have played barefoot all these years, I believe my scores would have been lower. Footwork, which I'll discuss later, is the most overlooked factor in golf: when you're really dug into Mother Earth, you have a true feeling of balance – and I proved it to myself in 1942 at the Augusta Masters Championship. Taking off my shoes, I played two of the toughest holes barefoot and birdied both. Then (and I'll tell about this, too) Gene Sarazen and others raised hell because they claimed it wasn't dignified, and back on went the shoes.

Not to claim that this is any sort of secret, but any time I've had balance trouble I've kicked off my shoes and found myself hitting straight again.

If you lead a horse away from water, he'll find it somewhere else. Not having the opportunity to play much golf as a kid, when I got to high school other sports became my main interest and pasture pool faded out so far that I almost never came back to it.

At Valley High School, which had only 150 students, I turned out for everything – baseball, football, basketball, swimming, track, and tennis. As a halfback for the Hornets, my running was slippery enough to cause college scouts to take a look and make offers. Virginia Poly, Davis-Elkins College, and Virginia U. wanted to sign me, but several things happened that got in the way.

For one, I damned near got killed in football.

While we were a puny country school, the schedule often sent us against Class A high schools of 1,000 or more kids, and the slaughter was terrible to watch. We had three substitutes as our whole bench; the other schools had two dozen or more. Against Covington, I was the ballcarrier on a sweep around end, where a gang of tacklers piled in at once and buried me in a water puddle. By the time I was lifted out, I was half choked to death on mud and had to be carried away and pounded on the back until I was breathing again.

After making a diving catch of a pass for a touchdown against Victoria, the opposition laid for me and on the next play separated my rib muscles and knocked loose some teeth. In the huddle I spit blood and told my teammates, 'Now, look, I've had enough. Let somebody else carry the ball.'

Nobody else would. We'd either send Snead in to be butchered or else do the only thing left – throw a long, incomplete pass.

Finally, after cracking a bone in my hand, I turned to baseball and track, where I ran the 100-yard dash in ten seconds flat. For a while there, I had my mind set on becoming a professional pitcher – especially after a game with Eagle Rock when I struck out eighteen batters and had a no-hitter going in the ninth innings, when the hitter lefted a high fly to center field. Our outfielder crossed his legs, fell down, and the ball rolled into a cornfield behind him. While he was hunting for it amongst the corn stubble, the run scored that beat me 2–1.

Things like that helped me make up my mind to stick to a sport where you didn't depend on other people's efforts – but only on your own.

SAM SNEAD, *The Education of a Golfer, 1962*

How to Go About Buying a Putter

If you wish a good putter, you will hardly expect to find one in a clubmaker's ready-made stock, far less in a toyshop or a tobacconist's window. The putter must be sought for with care and not hastily, for she is to be the friend, be it hoped, of many years. First, then, find out a workman of repute as a maker of putters – and in these days of 'reach-me-down' clubs there are few such artists – and, having found him, proceed warily. It will never do to go and order him to make you a first-class club for your match next morning; you would probably receive only the work of an apprentice. Wait your time and you will find the great man about his shop, or on his doorstep at the dinner hour, and may remark to him that the day is fine; this will be a safe opening, even though rain be falling in torrents, for it will give him the idea that you are a simple fellow and so throw him off his guard.

If a half-empty pipe lies beside him, offer a cigar, and mention that you are afraid that it is not as good as you would have wished, being the last of the box, at the same time giving him to understand that another box is expected that evening. The cigar having been accepted and lighted, you may, in course of conversation, allude to a very fine putter made by a rival clubmaker which, you will tell your friend, is being much talked about and copied. This will be almost certainly a winning card to play, for there is much jealousy among the profession, and as likely as not the remark will be made that So-and-so – naming the rival maker – has about as much idea of fashioning a putter as he has of successfully solving the problem of aerial navigation. Do not press the matter to a conclusion, but meet your man again in similar manner, this time carelessly holding in your hand the club which you have long felt was the cause of the success of some distinguished player. Almost seem to hide it from the clubmaker, and he will be sure to ask to see it, and probably volunteer to make you one on the same lines with slight improvements of his own. In time you will get your putter, and it will

64

probably be a good one; in any case it will be good enough to resell if it does not suit you, which is always a point to be considered.

JOHN L. LOW, *Concerning Golf, 1903*

A few golfers remain, although I believe their numbers are diminishing, who like to make you believe that their nerves never trouble them. But one never quite knows if they are speaking the truth. If they are, one is tempted to exclaim, 'What a pity!' JOYCE WETHERED

The Choice and Care of Clubs

My own clubs seem to most golfers who examine them to be on the short side, and this is a convenient opportunity for giving a few details concerning my favourites, which may prove of interest to the readers of these notes. I should prefix the statement with the observation that I am 5 feet 9¼ inches in height, and that normally I weigh 11½ stones. Young players who might be inclined to adapt their clubs to my measurements should bear these factors in mind, though I seem to be of something like average height and build. Here, then, are the statistics of the chief and most regular occupants of my bag:

Club	Length	Weight
Driver	42 inches	12¾ oz.
Brassy	42 ,,	12½ ,,
,, (more lofted)	42 ,,	12½ ,,
Cleek	37 ,,	13½ ,,
Iron (mongrel)	37 ,,	15 ,,
Mid-iron	36½ ,,	15¼ ,,
Mashie (running)	36½ ,,	15¼ ,,
,, (pitching)	36½ ,,	15¼ ,,
Niblick (Logan's)	37 ,,	19 ,,
Putter	33½ ,,	15 ,,

I could write many things about these clubs of mine, but for the most part the list and the particulars may be left to speak for themselves. It will be seen that I have what I call a 'mongrel' iron in my bag, and by that I mean a club which does not conform exclusively to the idea of any other club with a definite name of its own. Some mongrel clubs are often very excellent things, and this one of mine has become a great favourite. It was given to me once by an American gentleman, and it might be described as being a cross between a mid-iron and a driving iron, and is very powerful. At one time I carried a driving mashie in my bag, but this has to a large extent taken the place of it. The driving mashie used to be a favourite form of club for fairly long shots, and was regarded as being easier to use than a cleek. It has, however, lost much of its old popularity. It is a very good club on dry courses, but is often not suitable to general play on inland courses. The mashie-iron is another kind of club which has become a favourite with many players. As its name indicates, it is an established kind of mongrel, generally with a deep face and the loft of an iron club. It is a powerful club, and is useful for many shots, and especially for play from rough and grassy lies and from long grass. However, if one went in for describing all the new kinds of iron clubs that have been brought into the game in recent times one might never stop. There is the 'Sammy', which is a sort of specially lofted cleek, easier to use than an ordinary cleek, and very effective in some people's hands; and there is the 'jigger', which is a narrow-bladed iron, heavily weighted in the sole, which is a good thing for fairly long iron shots when it is desired to reduce the run on the ball as much as possible. Many of these clubs have merit in them, and often they suit some players as no others could do, but it takes time and experience for players to find out their needs in regard to them, and it is practically impossible to give any advice. Certainly the beginner at the game should limit himself to the plainest types.

HARRY VARDON, *from The Complete Golfer, 1905*

Good Stotters

In selecting gutty balls, care should be taken to see that they are at least six months old; but they should not be much older than this, as, if so, the paint is apt to chip off, and they lose some of their elasticity. They should be good 'stotters' – that is to say, when dropped on a flagstone or pavement they should rebound with a clear, hard click, and those that rebound furthest are generally the best. Some balls when placed in water will float, while others will sink. I prefer those that sink, because they are heavier than the others. Floaters are too light; they leave the club quickly, and their carry is soon exhausted. The size of ball most generally used is 27½, but the larger it is the better, as, in putting, a big ball will fall into the hole more readily than a small one, and is less likely, from its weight, to be deflected by a stiff blade of grass or such obstacle on the green. Of course it requires more strength to play with a big heavy ball than with a light one, and I would say to golfers, 'Play with as big a ball as you are able to manage comfortably.' A golfer who is not a hard hitter will probably play best with a ball that floats in water, but a strong player will knock such a ball out of shape in a very few strokes. Experience will teach every one the ball best adapted to his game better than anything that can be written on the subject. Some makers have recently brought out balls made of selected material, which are sold at a correspondingly selected price. I think, however, that they are too light in weight, and for a powerful player ordinary balls are preferable.

After a ball has been played with a few times the life gets knocked out of it, and it loses the elasticity which characterises a new ball. Although not good enough for using in an important match, it is good enough for practice; but by degrees it will become useless, from hacks made with clubs and the chipping off of the paint. Balls arrived at this stage can be remade at moderate cost; but in remaking there

67

is always a slight loss of material, and thus a 27½ when remade will be scarcely larger than a 27. Remade balls are not as a rule so good as new balls; at the same time, a ball remade for the first time is not much inferior, and I could name certain balls that are rather improved by the remaking process. After being remade a couple of times any ball is useless, as it gets too small, and fresh gutta-percha cannot be added satisfactorily.

WILLIE PARK JR, *from The Game of Golf, 1896*

Walk up to the ball and hit it hard.
TOMMY ARMOUR

The Ideal Golfer

Came across a fascinating advertisement – and what a Christmas present – of a new vehicle called the 'Autoette Golfmobile', advising 'the smart way to play golf . . . more fun, too!'

It then goes on to say that this is a 'New approach to golf – the Autoette Electric Golfmobile. Keeps you fresher to play better golf, with more fun as you go. Carries two players and their clubs without damage to turf. You'll love one.'

The illustration shows a handsome young fellow accompanied by a beautiful young girl. He is seated in the little buggy, while she is just about to enter it, I gather to rest from the exertion of having hit a mashie shot into a bunker. The clubs are already aboard and the two are consulting their score cards with evident pleasure.

The point is that this new invention, or rather new adaptation of a rather older invention called the wheel, does away with one of the features of golf that a number of would-be players have found tedious and painful, and that is the walk, from the spot where they have hit the ball to the place where this has come to rest. Sometimes this is a soothingly brief stroll, a matter of seven inches, but at others, if by ill luck one has stroked the ball squarely, it could be a matter of two hundred yards, or two whole city blocks, a distance which otherwise, if you were where you could get one, would be a taxi ride.

68

The golfmobile then does away with the dangers of this harmful exercise which might set the blood to circulating through the system and lead one to acquire a glow in the eyes and a flush to the cheek which envious gossips might ascribe to other causes. One simply climbs aboard after having hit the ball, which should only be a few steps at most, turns on the juice and rides to the next stop.

There is only one fault to find with this boon to humanity; it does not go far enough, in the sense that while it unquestionably eliminates the walk, it has not provided for the strain upon the system caused by swinging the golf club and hitting the ball.

However, I have solved this little detail, for I remembered having seen another advertisement once for a golf ball with a tough cover and it told how at the factory a driving machine had been developed to hit the ball over and over again, and with the same force, to test it for distance as well as toughness.

Well!

I have written to that company, as well as to the Autoette people out in Long Beach, California, for the rights to *combine* these two wonderful machines, thus taking all the effort out of the game.

So this Christmas, give him a Gallico Eezie-Duzzit Three-in-one Automogolf, the only machine that is absolutely guaranteed to take the game out of golf.

Has place for three, two players and a putter, besides two golf bags. On tees, or through the fairways, back the Automogolf up to the ball and get out of the way. The built-in, automatic striker hits the ball with just the right force. Then get aboard and ride in comfort to where your ball has come to rest and repeat the process. Comes equipped with caterpillar tractors for bunker play. No need to keep count of your strokes. The built-in automatic stroke compiler keeps track of you, while the Patent built-in Selenium Eye also keeps track of your opponent's strokes. At the end of the round, the Stroke Compiler delivers you the totalled card, with holes won and lost, along with your weight and your fortune and the time spent at the refreshment stand at the ninth.

Using the Gallico Automogolf, you do not lift a finger from tee to green. For when your ball has come to rest upon the green, stop the Automogolf at the edge. The putter then gets off, putts for you and returns to the vehicle. The Automogolf can even be set to give you a few more strokes a hole, if you're playing with a client whose next order will bring your take-home to the point where you can join a more expensive golf club.

Yes, give him a Gallico Automogolf this Christmas. For he does not even have to go out on the golf course to drive it himself, risking the rigours of fresh air. A friend or an employee can take it around the layout for him, returning to the clubhouse with his card where he can enjoy studying his round in the more healthful conviviality of the locker room.

PAUL GALLICO, *Esquire's World of Golf, 1966*

Deeds of Derring-Do and the Derring-Doers

A chance selection of memorable moments on the golf course and a parade of some of the characters who inhabit the extraordinary world of golf.

Pebble Beach

Dr Johnson on the Links

He was now determined to exercise himself at the game of Golf, which I explained to him as the Scotch form of cricket. Having purchased a ball and club, he threw himself into the correct attitude, as near as he could imitate it, and delivered a blow with prodigious force. Chancing to strike at the same time both the ball and the ground, the head of his club flew off to an immense distance. He was pleased with this instance of his prowess, but declined, on the score of expense, to attempt another experiment.

'Sir,' he said, 'if Goldsmith were here, he would try to persuade us that he could urge a sphere to a greater distance and elevation than yonder gentleman, who has just hit over that remote sand-pit.'

Knowing his desire for information, I told him that, in Scotch, a sand-pit is called a Bunker.

'Sir,' said he, 'I wonder out of what *colluives* of barbarism your people have selected the jargon which you are pleased to call a language. Sir, you have battened on the broken meats of human speech, and have carried away the bones. A sand-pit, sir, is a sand-pit.'

ANDREW LANG, *A Batch of Golfing Papers*, 1892

The mistakes that are made that lose a match are always made in the mind. PETER THOMSON

Ben Hogan – Greatest Ever

In any discussion as to the greatest golfer of the past half-century the names of Bob Jones, Ben Hogan and Jack Nicklaus stand alone. To attempt comparison between them, absorbing though it may be, is a purely academic exercise because far too many variables are involved. No man can do more than achieve indisputable supremacy in his own time, and thereby acquire an aura reserved only for those who do something better than anyone else in the world. However familiar as persons these supreme beings may become they quicken feelings far surpassing normal admiration for great skill, feelings of awe, even wonder, that they are not as other men. Never was this feeling more intense than when one was with Hogan.

73

There was a rare sense of the unforgettable about him, not simply because of his matchless skill but because of the force of his personality, a force more compelling in its fashion than the charm of Arnold Palmer, the ebullience of Lee Trevino or the amiable strength of Jack Nicklaus. There was about Hogan in his competitive years, as of no one else, an almost overwhelming sense of a man apart.

Within seconds of meeting him for the first time anyone would be aware that he was in the presence of a most unusual man, even without knowing of his eminence as a golfer. The outlines of his face, indelibly tanned by thousands of days in the sun, are unmistakably powerful, even cruel when the wide mouth is drawn down in concentration; the piercingly direct gaze could be cold as a winter dawn, and his economy of speech fearsome. In the tradition of the Far West Hogan does not believe in wasting words.

Even in a longish conversation I have never heard Hogan waffle; his replies to questions were invariably direct, sometimes alarmingly so; where a monosyllable would suffice he saw no reason to cloak it in useless verbiage. I recall waiting outside an airport for transport to a course some years ago; Hogan and his wife, Valerie, were there and eventually a bustling official approached and asked Hogan if he would care to ride down with Mr Snead. Hogan looked straight at him and said quietly, 'Not particularly.' Not another syllable did he utter and the little man scarcely knew where to look. The Hogans rode alone.

The American Press as a whole are not famous for their deep insight into golf or for watching it and the players can be asked stupid questions. On one such occasion Hogan is said to have remarked that, 'One day a deaf mute will win a tournament and no one will know what happened.' Another time I was talking with him when a man approached and said, 'I suppose you come to Augusta now to see your friends,' – a lethal misunderstanding. Hogan chilled him with a glance and replied, 'I see my friends in Fort Worth.' On the other hand, if Hogan knew that a writer was genuinely interested, and watched the golf, he would take pains to explain the shot.

Tournament golf was not a social occasion for Hogan. He would enjoy chatting and having a drink with old cronies in the locker room, but even in the later mellower years one would never see him pausing here and there about the clubhouse or its precincts. It was as if he had need of no one, either on the course or off it, except for his wife; he seemed a man alone and I imagine sometimes a lonely man.

This very self-sufficiency indicated the force of character that had enabled him to endure and overcome privation and adversity, the like of which none of his great contemporaries have known. As a child he sold newspapers until he heard that he could make 65 cents a round as a caddie. He had to fight to get a place and said that he would run seven miles to the course. Eventually he had one club, a left-handed mashie, and used to tear up the grass in the back yard until his mother would send him to the grocery store and he would hit shots along the road. When he changed to right-handed he said he had the most awful time, and that the effort used to nauseate him.

Hogan started professional golf when he was 18, and all the world knows of the years of struggle and hardship before he could win. His first major victory, the PGA Championship, was not until 1946 when he was two years older than Nicklaus is now. Then, on the threshold of absolute supremacy, came the accident which nearly destroyed him, leaving its mark forever afterwards and compelling him to husband his resources and not tire himself socialising. The ensuing remoteness helped to compound a figure of legend, as indeed he became to a greater extent than any other golfer of his time. You could feel it whenever he appeared.

If Hogan walks into a room you are aware of a presence, although nothing of his manner or outward appearance attracts attention. Always he dresses impeccably, inconspicuously, in modest shades. Vivid colours and cheap gimmicks are not for Hogan; there is nothing about him of the extrovert effusiveness so common in the American male; always in public his manner is quiet and contained. More often than not in those later years he would be addressed as Mr Hogan; others were Arnie, Billy or Sam on the briefest acquaintance, but Hogan was Mr and the title is more meaningful in America than in Britain. Similarly, on the course Hogan never sought acclaim for its own sake, or in any way played to the gallery. An army of screaming fans, like those on which Palmer thrives, meant nothing to him. He allowed his masterful golf to speak for itself and it usually did. The applause that greeted him as he approached every green had a note of respect reserved for no one else; the people, reverent rather than ecstatic, would clap rather than cheer.

There is no doubt that Hogan came closer than anyone to eliminating the human element from golf. Such was his control of the ball, and completeness of technique, and so true in outline and rhythm was his swing that he seemed immune to the pressures that destroy other golfers. When he was ahead in his great years his command of an event seemed unbreakable; rarely if ever was there any stumbling on the way to victory, such as that which has troubled Nicklaus on occasion and Bob Jones long ago. One of the few regrets that Jones had about his competitive golf was that he sometimes surrendered a commanding position and won far less easily than he should have done. Not so Hogan: as Jones himself said, 'Ben was always so good at finishing the job.'

Probably the greatest instance of this was in 1951 when Oakland Hills had been made savagely penal for the United States Open. Clayton Heafner with a 69 was the only other player to break 70 in the whole Championship. Hogan's scores read 76–73–71–67. The final round conceivably is the greatest he ever played, although when I asked him to confirm this years later he said: 'It is very difficult to get your mind back on to one particular round, analyse it again and say whether it was better than any other one.' This was revealing of the man in that he would estimate greatness by the quality of the shots rather than the winning of a championship. He went on to mention a round he had recently played, some of which I saw. Laurel Valley that day of the PGA Championship was very long and heavy, but he missed no fairways and only one green by three yards, and was round in 70 having taken three putts five times. He thought he had played as well as ever he could; he was then 53.

No modern golfer has ever finished the job more emphatically than Hogan did in 1953. He won the Masters by five strokes with a total of 274 that only Nicklaus has beaten; the United States Open by six and the British by four. His golf at Carnoustie was so masterful that had his putting been fractionally better than moderate the Championship would have been no contest at all. His scores were 73–71–70–68, another ruthless downward progression, and one felt that had a fifth round been necessary it would have been 66. This was the peak of his supremacy.

Hogan won no more championhips, but 10 years later the professionals were still saying that from tee to green he could hit the ball better than any man alive. But even Hogan, tough of spirit as he was, did not have an inexhaustible supply of nerve and gradually putting became an agony and a frustration to him and the worshipping watchers. Leaving the practice ground one morning at Augusta on his way to the putting green he said, 'Now for the bloodbank,' and he meant it.

In the third round of his last appearance in the Masters in 1967 Hogan, rising 55, played the back nine in 30, and the only putts holed of any length were from six, 15 and 25 feet. For thousands a lifetime's memory had been made, but the next day brought tiredness and reaction.

Hogan was the ultimate perfectionist, the more remarkable because he emerged from an age when intensive practice was not the fashion. Once, after a 64 in a tournament he practised for two hours and everyone thought 'I was nuts.' He practised with a ferocity of intent that can never have been surpassed, as if refusing to believe that it was not possible to create a flawless swing. There can never have been a more acute golfing intelligence than Hogan's, and for a great part of his lifetime he concentrated it upon the search for perfection.

I have the impression of him that hitting pure golf shots was the fulfilment of his whole being, as much an expression of his soul as a painting to an artist, a piece of music to a composer, and he was never satisfied. He saw no reason why every hole should not produce a birdie, and I could imagine his feelings when he dreamt one night that he had 17 holes in one, and one in two. Telling this he turned to me almost angrily and said, 'When I woke up I was so goddam mad.'

The pursuit of perfection was not confined to the golf course. When he began to manufacture clubs in 1954 he was so displeased with the output that he insisted on having it all destroyed. Nothing but the finest would appear under his name. The gesture cost the company a great deal of money, but Hogan's pride was satisfied.

The swing he created was not beautiful except in the sense that there is beauty in the smooth working of any machine. The backswing was compact and flatter than the classical concept, but the extension of the arc through the ball was quite remarkable with the right arm remaining straight through to the finish of the swing. The tempo was fastish; it was remote from the lazy effortless grace of Jones or Snead, but there was about it a wonderful sense of precision, like an instrument of flawlessly tempered steel.

For many years his accuracy was phenomenal. He could shape the shots as he willed, and even late in his career he could place drives as precisely as others would medium irons. To watch him fade or draw the ball ever so slightly, usually away from a hazard, was an unforgettable sight. The flight of his long irons had a searing quality, the ball so truly struck that it seemed motionless as if drawn down a plumb-line. If accurate striking be the measure of greatness then Hogan must be classed as the finest of all golfers. Gene Sarazen, who has played with every great player of the half-century since Vardon has often said that no one ever covered the flag like Hogan.

In 14 consecutive United States Opens up to 1960, and the same number of Masters to 1956 he was never outside the first 10, and was in the first four 18 times.

Of all the impressions of Hogan that memory cherishes those of him against the matchless background of Augusta are perhaps the strongest; many of the tees are cool places of green gold shadows, cloistered in the trees. Hogan, swarthy, silent and inscrutable, appears, tees his ball and takes his stance with that impression of massive authority created only by the great ones; the powerful hands, mahogany dark, mould themselves on the club, the swing coils and uncoils, swift and true as a lash of steel; the ball arrows away and Hogan with his stiff rather limping walk moves out of the shade. A moment later he stands in the sunfilled loneliness of the fairway. At such moments there was a rare quality of stillness about him and one could sense the absolute concentration of the cold, shrewd mind as he surveyed the shot.

P. A. WARD-THOMAS, *Piccadilly World of Golf*

---

*Black Care may ride behind the horseman; he
never presumes to walk with the caddie.*
LORD BALFOUR

Southern Hospitality

After four hours of final practice in the Georgia sunshine edging his own game to an acceptable state of sharpness, Arnold Palmer was unceremoniously resting his aching feet on a table, and soothing a parched throat with a liberally iced soft drink amid the many splendours of the East Lake Country Club at Atlanta. Then suddenly he publicly declared the outcome of a Ryder Cup series as tantamount to a foregone conclusion. He did so as if it was the most natural thing to do, and in a manner that suggested it was only right and proper for all to know before paying entrance money.

Alligator shoes, fine alpaca cardigan over a tailored shirt, and lightweight slacks impeccably cut, the American team captain, dollar millionaire and fairway idol, fitted perfectly into the extravagant surrounds of a paradise clubhouse as he faced the 1963 Pressroom inquisition seeking his thoughts on what the October morrow would bring. 'Aw, come on, fellas,' he playfully rebuked for having been asked how strong the British opposition was expected to prove. 'Now you know me better than that. I can't guess how good they are going to be out there. But I'll gladly tell you the message that I've just given my boys in the locker room – and that is there aren't ten golfers from the whole world who could possibly beat us right now.'

To some listening British ears – our own captain John Fallon had contented himself to a 'We are determined to do our very best' pronouncement in contrast – such extreme forthrightness jarred almost the senses of propriety. But experience of the flamboyant American golf scene, so often dedicated to having the best whatever the cost, soon teaches understanding of moments like these. Palmer's expression of unmitigated confidence was sincere and completely justified, as events proved, but in any case nothing less would have been publicly acceptable from him. Modesty can be read as another word for pessimism.

East Lake, a name long familiar as the home course of Bobby Jones, fits snugly into the 'Think Big' pattern. It sets itself the highest standards; obviously enjoys its costly living to them; and unquestionably thrives upon the policy in every sense. When the Ryder Cup was played there the club's well vetted golf membership totalled around 1,000, and that left a waiting list of so many more eager to pay the £300 entrance fee that anyone over forty years of age was credited with scant hope of living long enough to be given the opportunity of parting with his money.

It should not, of course, be thought that East Lake is representative of all American golf, though there are many more country clubs which will claim equal standing. It bestrides a level, however, to which the remainder aspire. The thousand or so who wallowed contentedly in its opulence as members included, by my findings, some of the nicest, most generous and resourceful people ever to have graced the game. Even so, living with them was an arduous business, for common to them all was an insatiable desire to welcome each visitor to the very limit of his endurance and so resolutely is this pursued that only the hardiest of guests is likely to survive more than a couple of days without having to seek a hiding place in which to rest up for a time.

Southern hospitality knew no bounds at East Lake, extending far beyond customary conviviality and the unrestricted use of Thunderbird automobiles driven by women members specially uniformed for the purpose. The assorted problems of the British intake, players and camp followers alike, were seized upon and seen solely as a challenge to the club's ingenuity in solving. Three personal instances, quite unrelated to the normal affairs of a golf centre, may help to illustrate. Immediately upon arrival I discovered my need for a private telephone in the clubhouse with which to make my constant and personal calls to the *Evening Standard* in London. Having just before this faced a considerable installation delay at home in Britain, I posed my problem with trepidation.

Minutes later a club member associated with the Bell company of America was found and brought to me. He listened to the problem and then, almost with embarrassment, declared: 'If only I'd known about this before lunch, Mr Wilson, you would have had that telephone this afternoon. Now we have to wait until tomorrow, but it will be there by breakfast time, I promise you.' It was, too! Having once got my telephone, problem two arose somewhat automatically. On the opening two days of the match the time factor dictated that I would need to be on the line giving the nearest thing to a running golf commentary for the first hour of play. Only that way could I make the last editions of the evening paper in London. But how does one stay with a trans-Atlantic call and at the same time see what is going on about a golf course? Well, that poser cost East Lake no headache, either. The local television station was fully covering that first hour on both days – so a TV set was wheeled in to keep my telephone company.

After all this, problem three was small enough, but the solution was no less big and generous, and certainly more personal. Seeing me without a match for a cigarette, a welcoming member passed his lighter, and then refused to accept it back despite every argument presented. 'No, sir,' he insisted, 'I've got another on me.' I found they enjoyed doing that sort of thing at East Lake. It comes under the heading of Southern hospitality, to which every visitor is entitled.

The East Lake membership pays dearly for its golf, but it gets a full measure of what it demands: the best, the very best. To gloss over the facility range, there is a clubhouse born of the 'If we haven't got it then it's not worth having' way of thinking: two magnificent championship courses; lakes for yachting and fishing; a swimming pool built to precise Olympic standards; and a downtown multi-storey social headquarters which leaves nothing wanting for the pursuit of enjoyment other than a well stacked purse. Four restaurants were operating in the clubhouse by my count at the time of the Ryder Cup, though when another visitor claimed to have seen a fifth through the tinted widows, no one was prepared to argue against him. It was a big place. There were, for instance, rooms for reading, talking, sleeping, games, cards, television and so on.

But oh! the men's locker room. Here was the *pièce de résistance*. Here, 50 yards long, was one huge expanse of wall-to-wall carpeted extravagance. 'Some place for changing your shoes in,' joked a British player taking his first look. The joke was on him. You don't change your golf shoes in the East Lake locker room after play. A coloured club servant takes them at the doorway for instant cleaning – and in exchange you collect a throw-away pair of paper slippers. Needless to say, anything and everything a man could possibly want to revitalise himself after a round of golf is there for the taking.

On one glass shelf in the softly lit washroom I counted fourteen different brands of hair oil, cream, eau de cologne, deodorant, after-shave lotion and talcum powder. If you didn't feel fresh after going through that lot then you certainly smelt it. Yes, they know how to live at East Lake. And I don't blame them, either, for after a day's golf with a group of the members in Georgia heat I felt entitled to any aid science had ever devised for body restoration. We moved a few miles to Druid Hills, another course of superb beauty, of rolling fairways, bordered by pines, and large expanses of water. The clubhouse was less pretentious, not being a country club; more on the Sunningdale lines as I remember.

Georgians, I discovered, take their golf quite seriously. There were rituals to be observed, the purpose of which appeared primarily to be for starting an argument on the first tee and thereby ensuring a needle match with stakes to suit. To Mulligan or not to Mulligan is the first question. The high handicap members of our party stood out for the right to have a second penalty-free drive to start the game if dissatisfied with their first; the better players naturally opposed such levity with the rules, but in this instance they lost. But the greatest argument of all had yet to come.

Despite that fact that all had official club ratings, and played each other every week, my companions quite comfortably spent another ten minutes bargaining for extra strokes. The winner last time out was arbitrarily penalised two shots while someone else was conceded an additional one purely on his word that he had not been to bed the night before. Two others agreed to play level after one of them had put paid to the bantering with a solemn speech in front of the clubhouse. He raised a hand for silence, and then, in a deep Georgian drawl, announced: 'Sir, I'll tell you one last time what you are gonna get off me. You'll gonna get fourteen clubs, five hours of my precious time, and as much conversation as you want. And not a damn thing else.' The Nassau style of wagering, so much for the front nine holes, the back nine and the whole round, plus inducements for eagles, birdies, longest drives, single putts and, it seemed, anything else that could be dreamed up, left me baffled from the start.

Eventually the match began at 9.10 a.m. Five hours and twenty-five minutes later, at a hazy, scorching 2.35 in the afternoon it finished. Every player had holed out on every green, meticulously kept a card and a book of wagers. During the whole of this time the sun had blazed to a point when the temperature topped the 100 mark. I came off the home green utterly dehydrated, and upon returning to the air-conditioned comfort of the East Lake clubhouse by fast car, promptly enjoyed the most exquisite eighty minutes of my whole life – just sitting on the floor of a shower under a constant stream of cool, cool water.

During the match itself I became aware that I was cheating, or rather my young coloured caddie was doing so for me. Whenever one of my shots strayed into the woods which bordered the fairways he would instantly hare off at great speed. On reaching the spot I inevitably found him standing over the ball which offered both a magnificent lie and an easy recovery line through a most convenient gap in the trees. When this had occurred four or five times I decided something must be done about it, though I was anxious to avoid an embarrassing scene with the caddie who would doubtless deny what was obvious. So I approached my East Lake opponents, told them my fears and heartily apologised. Then one confessed in return: 'Don't give it a thought, sir. We had a word with the boy at the start and told him to make sure you enjoyed your game.' 'But that's cheating,' I mildly protested. 'No, sir,' retorted my companion with feeling. 'That's Southern hospitality.'

American caddies include some tremendous characters, as the British team at East Lake discovered. There was one coloured fellow there who was never seen without an expensive-looking cigar in his mouth. And thereby, as they say, hangs a strange tale. Six months before the match a group of fund-raising top US tournament players had staged an exhibition at the club and this young man had carried for one of them.

'What's your name then, son?' he was asked. 'Poe, sah,' he

replied. Joked the youngster's newly found idol, 'Any relation to Edgar-Allan Poe?'

The caddie's surprise was such that he is reported to have dropped his bag on the ground. Then with an innocence matched only by his truthfulness, eyes popping, chest swelling, he blurted out his answer: 'Why, sah, ah is Edgar Allan Poe!' To the everlasting credit of the professional he said no more, and for a young coloured boy life began anew that moment. He must be a famous caddie, even the top players had heard of him, and from that day onwards he never took to the East Lake course without a cigar in his mouth, a status symbol for all to see. Like Palmer, like East Lake itself, like so much of the American golf scene, Edgar Allan Poe had got the message: THINK BIG.

MARK WILSON, *The Golfer's Bedside Book*, 1965

---

*A fluke by an afterthought can with little exercise
of the imagination very soon assume the
proportions of a masterpiece.*
A. H. N. WETHERED

George Low

It just isn't like George Low to turn down a free meal, a free drink or a free anything for that matter.

Thus, it was a jolt to everyone at the Colonial Invitation tournament last May when Low bypassed Jerry Barber's invitation to buy lunch.

Barber, one of the leading money winners on the 1960 PGA tour, was noticeably stunned at Low's refusal. Then the method in George's madness became apparent.

'How much did you win last week at the Tournament of Champions?' Low asked Barber.

'$10,000.'

'Well, I'm saving you for bigger things,' Low explained.

This is a typical demonstration of the free-loading prowess of George Low, the leading character on the men's professional tour and the fellow that the pros will not putt for money on the practice green.

'My yearly income averages about $10,000, but I spend $50,000 more of my friends' money,' George admits with a touch of pride.

Low, a hulking Scot who wears a solemn, jowly, bronzed face behind dark glasses and carries a can of beer, is as much a fixture on the PGA trail as Cary Middlecoff's hay fever or Tommy Bolt's flowered sport coats. No tournament is really complete without him.

It was Paul Grossinger, the New York resort fellow, who tabbed Low 'America's Guest.'

'You gonna use Grossinger's name in this story?' George asked at a recent PGA stop. 'Good. That ought to be worth a freebie.'

Few, except those on the inside of pro golf, realize that Low is probably the game's finest putter – and putting instructor.

Giving putting lessons is Low's primary method of making a buck – 'this way and that,' as he says. He doesn't hustle the business, however. That would be too much like work.

'I was born energetically lazy,' he explains.

Low's reputation as a putter has been growing since about 1946, the year of his last fling at trying to play golf for a living.

He wasn't good enough to match the Byron Nelsons week after week, so he quit playing – except on the putting greens. There was also the matter of an old back injury, traced to a private plane crash in the 1930s. He never fully recovered.

However, Low is in the record books – in a most unusual place.

He was the first pro to break Nelson's fabulous streak of successive victories in 11 official and 12 unofficial events. It was at the 1945 Memphis Open where Freddie Haas, then an amateur, won with 274, Low was second at 275 and Nelson third at 276.

'I seen that Nelson was getting out of hand,' he quips today.

Notoriety is something George doesn't really care about, but it suddenly became unavoidable after Arnold Palmer won his second Masters championship last April.

Within earshot of about 100 golf writers, Palmer credited Low for helping him this season. Talking about the putts that netted him a torrid birdie-birdie finish, Palmer said,

'I kept thinking what my old friend, George Low, always says, "keep your head down and don't move."'

Low refuses to take any credit for helping Palmer, however.

'If I've helped him it was with his confidence. I think he was just giving me a plug because that's the way he is, a great guy who likes to help out his friends.

'It's like the doctor who sits and smiles at the patient and then hands him some sugar pills – and the guy thinks he's got some miracle drugs that will cure him.'

Palmer did not need any technical help, according to George.

'He does everything right,' Low said. 'In putting, he has the quick left wrist that makes you take the clubhead back on the inside. He has most of his weight on the left foot – where it ought to be for balance. And his action is concentrated from the elbows downward.'

Low recommended another thing for good putting: Keeping both thumbs squarely on the shaft for proper feel.

'When you reach in your pocket for a coin,' he explains, 'the last thing that touches the coin is your thumb. You use it to pull out the coin. Right? It's the most sensitive finger. That's why you grip the putter with both thumbs on the top of the shaft.'

Consistency is the key to Low's putting proficiency. That is the reason the pros shy away from engaging him in a putt-for-money session. He can out-putt some of them using a sand wedge.

'The reason I beat them is because that's all I've done for 15 years,' George points out. 'They got other worries, like getting on the green. I'm already there. I hit it the same way every time with the putter. You can putt me for 30 minutes and maybe you'll have a hot streak and win. But if you stay with me for an hour or so, you got no chance because I'm going to keep hitting it the same way and you're not.'

Byron Nelson has been around golf for a while. Is what George says true?

'Don't ever try him,' Nelson warns.

After all these gypsy years, Low is proudest at the moment because a George Low putter is coming on the golf market. Eight different models will bear his name.

Old-timers may remember that George Low Sr., another big Scot, was runner-up for the U.S. Open title in 1899. They may also recall that this George Low was pro at Baltusrol for 27 years where he tutored some early-day White House hackers named William Howard Taft and Warren G. Harding.

That was George Low Jr's father. And George was born at Baltusrol, as a friend suggested, probably in the 19th Hole, the only one he ever parred. He was indeed a child of golf.

Baltusrol acquainted Low with wealth, for an adjacent cottage belonged to the Henry Toppings.

'I thought we was rich, like everybody else,' George says. 'Later on, when I knew I could never afford an overcoat, I had to work it out so's I spent my winters in Florida and Palm Springs.'

Through the years George has become good friends with more wealthy people than any resident of Wall Street. Golf was his entré, along with a sharp humor, a talent for needling people and making them like it, and a basic honesty that makes people like him.

It was Bob Johnson of New York's Roosevelt Raceway who made a classic statement about George that comes close to summing him up.

Low was in a party with Johnson and others one evening and George kept asking the host for another $100 to buy drinks for everyone in the place. Finally Johnson confessed, 'Just to associate with Low is better than having a high Dun and Bradstreet rating.'

There are no official stastistics on it, but Low is sure to have seen more tournaments in his lifetime than practically anyone.

He will average about 30 a year, but he has to get away occasionally to see how things are going with such friends as jockeys Eddie Arcaro and Willie Shoemaker. If golf is his business, then the ponies are his hobby – or vice-versa. Also, he likes to spend some time with Jimmy Demaret in Houston – he Christmases there – and with San Francisco Giant owner Horace Stoneham in Phoenix.

If Low has a home base at present it is Delray Beach, Fla., where he keeps an apartment and a Cadillac. His office?

'I don't have to be back to the office for 30 more years,' he'll tell you.

When last seen by this writer, George was on his way to another tournament, driving Arnold Palmer's car. In the trunk were most of his belongings, including some scrapbooks.

The scrapbooks contain photos of George with almost every big name golfer and celebrity and wealthy sportsman who has ever stepped on a putting green. One of the pictures shows George with his hand in the pocket of Wilbur Clark, the Desert Inn impressario at Las Vegas.

It's the closest George Low has been to big money since he moved out of the Topping's neighborhood at Baltusrol.

DAN JENKINS, *Golf Digest, 1960*

King Lear at Pebble Beach

One of the epic farces in the history of sport is now being endured on the majestic and normally sparkling fairways that overlook Carmel Bay. The annual Bing Crosby Pro-Amateur golf tournament at Pebble Beach, California, is as much of a junket as a tournament, and it always tolerates a high proportion of soaks. Yesterday was, in every sense, the soakiest Crosby in memory.

On the third day of play, after 45 warm and rainless days, a storm came rifling in from the Pacific like a one-iron from Nicklaus on the last hole of a play-off. Sixty-mile-an-hour winds hurled 14 inches of rain on San Francisco to the north, but the main bout was saved for the lovely towering coastline that frames Pebble Beach and Cypress Point, two of the most celebrated courses on earth, and now encloses a third, Spyglass, another nightmare fantasy of Robert Trent Jones, which the pros either praise with a grunt or deplore with a groan.

On these three courses, the best pros and the most audacious amateurs pair off for a four-day assault on a rolling terrain whose hazards include blind holes, over pine forest, scrubby meadows, cliffs and yawning chasms, boisterous winds, tiny greens floating like billiards tables on the bosom of the ocean, perambulating deer and quail, and pelicans with a peculiar appetite for the Haskell ball.

All these normal risks were ludicrously magnified yesterday, as if by a Hollywood director, hot for an Oscar, who had hit on the idea of filming the Goldfinger-James Bond golf game in a typhoon. Not since Clark Gable held on to Lana Turner in 'China Seas' has a television epic swilled more rain into the camera lens, tethered the camera crew to the swaying ground with more rope, amplified to such a drilling pitch the cracking of pine and cypress limbs.

Some 168 players took off in pairs into the raging hurricanes at seven in the morning, and within 30 yards of the tees most of them vanished into the desolate heaths like drama school contestants in a

87

mass audition for Lear and his clown. The flags twanged like catapults, the bunkers vaporised into clouds of sand. The players, transformed by ear muffs, sou'westers and ballooning raincoats into Eskimo midshipmen, prodded and lurched at balls that ran off of their own accord over the fringe of the greens and into the sea.

Three and a half hours of this ordeal were enough for the tournament director of the Professional Golfers' Association. Clawing into the wind at the seventh and eighth fairways, he could see neither course nor players for the whirlwinds of sand from the bunkers and the salt spume from the ocean. When a tree or two bent and expired alongside powerlines, he decided that even the Crosby could pause for a better day. He had the word of the host himself that 'the Navy says the storm will clear by July at the latest.' He called off all play.

By then the storm had registered on the score cards a record as impressive as the weather station's seismograph. Several eminent amateurs had racked up noble scores of 89, 87, and 93. The renowned Billy Farrell took 55 on the first nine holes of Pebble Beach. The New York Metropolitan open champion did even better: a 59 over the same stretch. Once the cancellation was announced, many world-famous pros hastened to tear up their cards.

But there was one indestructible giant, the true King Lear of this delirium, who strode from tee to green 'through ford and whirlpool, o'er bog and quagmire,' challenged the storm to rumble its bellyful, and strove 'in his little world of man to outscorn the to-and-fro conflicting wind and rain.' He was, need it be said, the boy from Columbus, Ohio, that Jack Nicklaus, who regards all natural disasters as annoying distractions from the main business of life: the steady grooving of his swing.. Against the beseechments of the staggering gallery and the advice of his wife, he rooted his colossal legs on the fairways, seized his irons like squalling children, and joined the elements in battering the new Spyglass course, which on any tranquil day is a monster.

After a bogey five and a par five, he holed birdie deuces on the two par three holes. He took another bogey on the sixth and parred the murderous seventh and wound up with another bogey five and a par. In all three bogeys, four pars, and two birdies. As he stalked in through the swaying spectators, a thoughtful frown clouded his pink brow. He had gone out in 39, three over par. But it was his twenty-seventh birthday. And he thought there was 'room for improvement.'

He is, however, the leader after two days with 142, a two-stroke lead for 36 holes. Today he hopes to improve. For those who had seen him at Muirfield and the Masters in 1965 and on other conquering journeys, this first nine in the hurricane at Spyglass will remain the most stupendous round of his career.

The pelicans must have thought so. There was a flock of them pitifully marooned on the eighteenth fairway as incapable of independent flight as the top-heavy California condors. Then there was a blast of wind and a following lull. They were blown into cruising altitude and took off over the foaming seas, flapping their wings for Nicklaus, whom neither snow, nor rain, nor wind, nor heat, nor gloom of night can stay from the swift completion of his appointed round.

ALISTAIR COOKE, *The Guardian, 1967*

How well you play golf depends on how well you control that left hand of yours.
TOMMY ARMOUR

Harry Vardon

The two best-known Vardon anecdotes make him out to be rather a bluff man. In Anecdote One, the year was 1913 and Harry was making his second exhibition tour through America. One afternoon in Chicago his foursome included a left-hander of no particular distinction who enjoyed one of those days when he couldn't miss a shot. After the round, fishing for a compliment, he said to the master, 'If I may be so bold, Mr Vardon, might I enquire who is the best left-handed golfer you've come across in your long career?' Vardon made a little snorting noise. 'Never saw one who was worth a damn,' he said.

In Anecdote Two, the year was 1920, the setting the U.S. Open, at Inverness. In the qualifying round, Vardon was partnered with Bobby Jones, then a boy of eighteen, very much aware of the privilege he was accorded in being paired with the visiting lion. On the seventh, a drive-and-pitch par 4, Vardon made his par in regulation fashion, but Jones looked up on his niblick approach, skulled the ball miles over the green, and ultimately bogeyed the hole. As they walked to the next tee, Jones, trying to dispel his lingering embarrassment, said to Vardon. 'Have you ever seen a worse shot than that, sir?' 'No,' Vardon answered, and nothing more.

The only trouble with these anecdotes is that they tend to be misleading: Vardon comes off as a combination of Ned Sparks, Titus Moody, and Don Rickles. While he preferred not to talk too much on the golf course and could be curt on occasion, fundamentally he was a kind, modest, and unusually gentle man. It is significant that the *Golfer's Year Book*, the familiar British annual that comes bound in red leather, should go out of its way in its short biographical note on Vardon to state that he was of 'placid and serene disposition' and that 'he endeared himself wherever he played'. It is to the point also that he was exceedingly well liked and respected by his fellow professionals and, when he died in March 1937, dozens and dozens of them came from all over Britain to attend his burial in the Totteridge Parish Churchyard, outside of London. As you may know, whenever the Ryder Cup match is played in Britain, the American team makes it a practice to visit Harry Vardon's grave.

He was born on May 9, 1870, just about three months after James Braid and ten months before John Henry Taylor, the two other stalwart men who with him were to form The Triumvirate. In a family of eight, he was the fourth of six sons – George, Phil, Edward, Harry, Tom, and Fred. (It sounds like a roll call in the Turnesa household.) He was born and grew up in the village of Grouville on the island of Jersey in the English Channel. His father was a gardener, and that is what Harry also would have been undoubtedly had golf not entered his life. It did when he was seven. Some golfers over from England gained permission from the constable of Grouville parish to set up some golf holes on the common land. This was to develop, in a matter of years, into the Royal Jersey Golf Club. The local boys acted as the caddie force, and, naturally, they began to play the game. Their course consisted of four holes of their own devising – 50 yards long on the average. For their golf balls they used a big white marble called a taw. They made the shafts for their clubs from either the black thorn or white thorn tree, and whittled their clubheads from a tree called the lady oak. They frequently played at night when the moon was up. As Vardon recollected decades later, 'The moon seemed to shine more clearly at Jersey than in England.'

Harry caddied till he was twelve when he went to work on a dairy farm. (All the cows on Jersey are Jerseys.) After two years of this, he became a page boy for a local doctor and then joined the staff of one Major Spofford of Beauview as an assistant gardener. He played some golf during this period as a member of the workingmen's club in Grouville. He speaks of himself as having been only an ordinary player, about an eight handicap, but some glimmer of his high talent must have been visible since Major Spofford once counseled his young gardener, 'Harry, my boy, take my advice and never give up golf. It may be useful to you some day.'

If that line has a fine Dickensian ring to it, so, too, though in a much harsher register, does a line uttered some years later – 1899, to be precise – by Vardon's father when Harry had just won his third British Open and a friend happened to ask Mr Vardon if he wasn't proud of his famous son. 'Although Harry may win trophies,' came the reply, 'it is Tom who plays the golf.' What underlay this animus between Mr Vardon and his son Harry – or the especial rapport between Mr Vardon and his son Tom – is something we shall never know and really have no need to, but the knowledge that a certain friction existed between Harry Vardon and his father helps to explain some of the mystifying apertures in Harry's makeup and it also helps to explain Tom Vardon's much greater confidence and assertiveness. For example, although Tom was two years younger than Harry, it was he who first made the break from Jersey and got a job for himself in England. He caught on as an assistant with George Lowe at St Anne's and did very well from the outset. It so happened that Lowe was engaged at this time in laying out a nine-hole course at Studley Royal for Lord Ripon, and through Tom's good offices Harry was hired as the professional and greenkeeper. Harry was twenty at the time.

Three years later, in 1893, Vardon entered his first British Open. In the interim he had twice changed his club affiliation, moving from Studley Royal (where there was hardly enough work to keep him busy) to Bury and then on to Ganton. (Tom told him about the opening at Ganton.) He played rather well in his Open debut but he did not really attract attention until he went to Portrush in northern Ireland after the championship with a large group of British pros and there made his way to the final in a big match-play tournament, where Sandy Herd beat him. One of the name stars whom the unknown Vardon knocked out on his way to the final was Andra Kirkaldy, the brawny Scot who had a word – and usually a fairly colourful one – for every occasion. As the story goes, Andra expected to make short work of this young Vardon kid, but he lost one hole and then another and another. At the turn this wonderful exchange took place between Andra and his brother Hugh, a well-known pro in his own right, who happened to be passing down a parallel fairway:

Hugh (cheerily, in the expectation of a happy answer): 'Andra, hoo's the game?'

Andra (with feeling): 'Man alive, I'm five doon.'

Hugh (slapping a palm to his forehead): 'Ma conscience!'

Vardon's first big moment came some three years later in the 1896 British Open. The setting is Muirfield, the comparatively new home of the Honorable Company of Edinburgh Golfers, the oldest golf club in the world. Vardon is playing the seventy-second hole, a long par 4 to a slightly elevated green protected by a fearsome bunker – a deep trough with a sharp front wall capped by a heavy overhanging lip. This is Vardon's fourth Open; he has finished fifth and ninth the two previous years, and now he has a par 4 on this home hole to beat J. H. Taylor, 'the leader in the clubhouse' (as they certainly didn't say in those tasteful days). This is Taylor's fourth Open, too, but there the similarity stops: Taylor has won the last two. . . . All right, Vardon is on the tee. He hits a fine drive, straight and fairly long, but he is still a good two hundred yards from the green. Should he go for the green, gambling for a 4 and outright victory? That means running the risk of burying his second in the face of the bunker and ending up with a possible 6 and no crack at a playoff. Or should he choose the more cautious route – lay up short of the bunker in two, make sure of a 5 and a tie, and take his chances in a playoff? Vardon is still debating the problem with himself when, far down the fairway, just short of the bunker, he recognizes the familiar figure of an old friend, James Kay of Seaton Carew. Kay must be reading Vardon's mind. With the toe of his foot he is tapping the ground in front of him; obviously that is where he thinks Vardon should play his second – short of the bunker. Vardon plays it there. He gets his 5 and ties Taylor at 316.

. . . In the playoff Vardon is leading by two strokes when they come to the thirty-sixth hole. Taylor has no choice in this situation: he must go for the green with his second, a long fairway wood. The ball dives into the wall of the bunker. Vardon wins by four strokes.

HERBERT WARREN WIND, *The Lure of Golf*

The Ryder Cup

Until yesterday the feeling at Lytham was that the Americans, as hosts for the next Ryder Cup match in 1979, should consider holding it at the Little Big Horn Country Club and issuing the British captain with a blond wig.

On Friday night, as he surveyed the rotting corpses of all those optimistic utterances he delivered earlier in the week, Brian Huggett may have decided that in one respect at least, Custer had an easier time of it. Old Yellow Hair did not have to hang around and rationalise the slaughter.

Yesterday's singles, with their heroics from Gallacher, Barnes, Faldo, Oosterhuis and Dawson, hugely eased Huggett's embarrassment and made his noisy defiance on the eve of battle sound less hollow. He is a game, warm and altogether appealing man and we had always known that he would echo the underdog reassurance boomed out in Ecclesiastes Chapter 9, V. 11: 'The race is not to the swift, nor the battle to the strong, neither yet bread to the wise, nor yet riches to men of understanding; nor yet favour to men of skill; but time and chance happeneth to them all.'

But when he started castigating the bookmakers for offering Great Britain and Ireland at 7 to 1 against before the off, we were tempted to remind him of the celebrated Runyon paraphrase: 'The race is not always to the swift, nor the battle to the strong, but that's the way to bet.'

That was, of course, the way the bookmakers did bet and they were never exposed to serious risk. The only genuine question was whether the British lion would be devoured by the American eagle or humiliatingly buried beneath its droppings.

The final score certainly did not represent such a burial but all the exciting achievements of the last day could not weaken the conviction that 50 years of tradition have lumbered British and Irish professional golf with a biennial comparison that is now bereft of any roots in the real status of the nations involved. Brian Barnes may be right when he suggests that the Ryder Cup should be viewed as a friendly get-together combined with a series of exhibition matches but his very willingness to see it that way probably does more than even the discrepancy in the countries' overall golfing manpower to explain the gulf between the teams at Lytham.

It is not carping to remind the British that even their boldest spirits were aided yesterday by the notorious chanciness of the 18 hole matchplay format as a means of judging calibre and, perhaps, still more, by the fact that the Americans went out with the knowledge that their lead from the foursomes and four-balls was almost unassailable.

Individual pride ensured that Nicklaus, Watson and Irwin would not offer themselves as easy victims in the singles but since their side had already won the battle – and this was an occasion when there was very little bread at stake for the wise, or riches for the men of understanding – it was virtually inevitable that their psychological vice should slacken fractionally.

For as long as the match was a contest in one sense, it was no contest in another. It was an exhibition all right but not quite in the way that the admirable Mr Barnes had meant, for what the US players were exhibiting in those earlier stages was the fierce almost puritan zeal for self improvement, that separates them fundamentally from our men. When the issue of winning and losing is being settled, in golf as in other sports, we seem incapable of trying quite as hard, let alone playing quite as well, as they do. They have the working-breakfast approach to the game, and the working-supper too, if necessary.

Reading Jack Nicklaus's great instructional book, 'Golf My Way,' we are quickly made aware that his way is to wrestle with the flaws in his play as earnestly as a medieval theologian wrestling with his conscience.

He did so to such effect after an unbelievably calamitous beginning yesterday that he was able to win back four holes and lost in the finish because he was opposed by quite the biggest heart (and by no means the least considerable talent) in the home team. The Americans have a substantial body of leading professionals with a depth and relentlessness of concentration on the job, a sustained current of energy and will and self-belief, that all but one or two of our fellows find ultimately unnatural.

The discrepancy is most blatant in pitching and putting. Americans attack the short game utterly convinced that if they practise hard enough, concentrate hard enough, read the conditions right and swing and strike right, the ball will have no option but to go down. The British decide much earlier along the way that they have done all they can and the rest is up to the malevolent Gods of the game.

That contrast and its implications were demonstrated perfectly in the match between Barnes and Horton and Green and Watson when, on the seventh green, the Americans were both about 45 feet away with their opponents facing putts of about a quarter of that distance. Horton's caddie said to Barnes's caddie, 'Do you want to ask for a half now?'

The question ceased to be ironic a few seconds later as Green's putt fell into the hole.

'Having two fellows like that on the green or anywhere around it' said Brian Barnes, 'is like having a double-barrelled shotgun pointed at your head.'

The US will surely always carry too many shotguns for us in the Ryder Cup.

HUGH MCILVANNEY, *The Observer*, 1977

There is no such individual as a born golfer.
BEN HOGAN

Bernard Darwin

In 1907 there appeared in *The Times* an article, lugubriously entitled in the manner of the day 'Golf and the Championship'. It was the shallowest of headings, quite inadequate by modern standards to support the two full, unbroken columns that followed. The article is a milestone in sporting journalism. It marked the first step – a giant stride rather – towards a new conception of writing about sport in newspapers. Up to that time 'Sporting Intelligence' as it was still known in *The Times*, was little more than a jumble of figures at the foot of the page. By the time Darwin had finished with it, sports writing had blossomed into a branch of literary journalism.

That introductory article was not the first piece he wrote on golf. *Country Life* also claimed him about that time, and before he took either of these jobs he had been engaged by the *Evening Standard* to write an occasional column. All this happened in 1907, a red-letter year for him because it enabled him to sell his wig and gown and take to the fairways for ever. The championship referred to in the heading is not the Open but the Amateur championship. The amateur game was much the stronger of the two in those days although the presence of the Big Three – Vardon, Braid and Taylor – had already begun to swing the balance. But amateur events had always commanded more space than professional – not that either could get much of a foothold – and Darwin was simply continuing the tradition. It is in the 251st line of an article of 276 lines that the other side of the game gets a mention and then only with the guarded introduction: 'About professional golf there is really very little to say – Braid, Vardon, Taylor and possibly Herd, and there the story seems to end'. This dictum almost serves to pass, along with other memorable aphorisms of his, into the history of the game.

His opening sentence is a reminder of changed times; for while admitting that golf is played all the year round, he says that it has a distinct season which was just beginning. The article is dated 23 May. It is difficult to realise now that apart from the Amateur there was very little else that required covering. The four home championships did not exist, and the only international match of any kind was between England and Scotland, in which Darwin took part with pride. The 'ladies' championship attracted so little attention that it had already taken place when he wrote the article and was not included in his vision of the season. The Amateur championship was everything and he was alarmed at the growing size of the entry. 'The list of entries is swollen by a number of persons with no conceivable claim to be rated as first- or even second-class players. The credit of having approached the position of scratch at small unknown clubs and over meadows bearing the courtesy titles of courses, combined with the wish for three or four days' cheap play over a championship course and with the chance of rubbing shoulders with the giants of the game, inspires an increasing number of players to cumber the gound by entering for a competition in which their legitimate part is as spectators only.' Elegance of style was never an obstacle to his saying what he thought. By modern standards there is more than a trace of snobbishness in the remark, but he was writing of the game nearly three-quarters of a century ago when, except in Scotland, it was the sport of the leisured and the well-breeched. It explains the presence in some of his writing of a touch of condescension in dealing with even the greatest of the earlier professionals, for whom it was still perfectly natural to enter the clubhouse through the back door.

In one respect times have not much changed since that article appeared. 'Scotland', we read, 'literally swarms with players who can come straight to the course from their plastery or plumbing and play a really fine game. Lack of experience is likely to prevent their winning outright, but they may oust some very good players in the earlier rounds.' Among the resounding names of John Ball and Harold Hilton and others who were the highest in the realms of golf, one non-golfer makes his first appearance. It is a precarious entry for he is confined to the last sentence of all, but he came in later years to be accepted in every clubhouse in the kingdom. 'Nothing less would do that,' the sentence runs, '"than a nat'ral conwulsion", to quote Mr Samuel Weller.' Those opening words in *The Times* were inscribed on the silver salver given him by a host of golfing friends on his retirement as golf correspondent forty-six years later. They are balanced by the last words he wrote, on the Halford Hewitt tournament in 1953, it being rightly judged that such a bewildering tournament was hardly one for his successor to cut his teeth on. That dinner, attended by Cabinet Ministers, judges, Governor-Generals, and men distinguished in almost every walk of life, reflected better than words his achievement over half a century. There was a feeling that *The Times* should have given him more recognition than they did, but this was a gesture they could hardly have undertaken except in a spirit of self-advertisement. Its greatest servants had always departed unsung; the retirement of Delane, the paper's most powerful nineteenth-century editor, occupied two lines at the foot of the column. In those days of anonymity Darwin could expect no other treatment. Even a banquet given by his colleagues in Printing House Square, so few of whom had ever set eyes upon him, would have been a hollow compliment.

He never trained as a journalist. In *Pack Clouds Away* he admits that after writing for newspapers for thirty years he knew wonderfully little about them, such knowledge as he had of their offices being largely gleaned from Sir Philip Gibbs' *Street of Adventure*, which, he added typically, 'is a book that I read about once a year'. He once described writing about sport as a job 'into which men drift, since no properly constituted parent would agree to his son starting his career in that way. Having tried something else which bores them they take to this thing which is lightly esteemed by the outside world but which satisfies in them some possibly childish but certainly romantic feeling.' The same holds generally true today;

from Henry Longhurst, who started work selling advertising space in trade journals, down, the large majority had no firm intention of becoming golf writers before they first began to earn money that way.

If Darwin served no apprenticeship, he suffered no delusions that he was a professional in Fleet Street. On the rare occasions that he covered golf abroad he was vaguely alarmed at the prospect of sending off Press telegrams. In *The House that Fred Built* he describes how a French postmaster dotted the 'i's' and crossed the 't's' of a report Darwin wished to be dispatched, and having overcome the obstacle of the handwriting, remarked as he gathered up the sheets: ''Ole, what is zees 'ole?' Darwin's writing was crabbed and spidery, his dispatches were scrawled on small sheets of paper, and pinned to a telegraph form franked for wiring to London at the night rate of eighty words a shilling. Geoffrey Cousins, a doyen of golf writers, remembers delivering some late copy of his own to the Hoylake Post Office one night, and being told on inquiring how the other copy was flowing: 'It's nearly finished; at least we've got rid of Darwin. Terrible writing. Sometimes we just can't figure it out and have to put in what we think he meant.' It was only later, when the services of Charles Macfarlane had been secured as a kind of Telephonist Royal, his bell-like tones sailing undeterred through the most scholarly passages, that the nightmares of telegraphists were diminished. In fact, Darwin's writing was not impossible; it needed a practised eye and a steady nerve; like a traveller crossing a gorge by a narrow plank, the reader had to keep steadily on without pausing or looking to one side.

Darwin had no truck with punchy introductory paragraphs. He thought the way to convey a picture of the day's play, and it no doubt suited him to think so, was to start by taking account of the weather, make a few general comments on the scene before him and on the state of the turf, and then take things as they happened. Having discussed the morning's play over luncheon, he would settle down afterwards, armed with a glass of port, and start writing – always, it seems, fluently, apparently easily and without faltering until he had finished. When Jock Hutchison holed in one at the 8th at St Andrews and rimmed the hole for a second consecutive one at the 9th, that unusual occurrence must take its proper place in the sequence of events, and if in the process it got buried halfway down the second column, that was no concern of his. When Sarazen took eight in the hill bunker at the High hole in the Open of 1933 Darwin omitted to mention the fact. One sentence, attributed to his writing about the 1934 Open, has passed into the history of golf writing: 'Then it was time to go to tea,' he is said to have written after watching the first two holes of Cotton's famous round of 65. I have been unable to unearth the evidence required, but there are several examples of his ending his piece with the words, 'As for the rest the results must speak for themselves'. Thus spake the essayist, intent on the quality of his piece, and on saying what he had to say. No criticism of his methods is intended; he is in any case beyond it, and he wrote not for a different generation so much as for a different century. The fact that so much of what he wrote has stood the test of time is a tribute to his quality no less than to the enduring virtues of the game.

Any shortcomings he may have had as a journalist were more than made up for by his first-hand knowledge of the game. He started playing at Felixstone when he was eight, a slim figure in breeches and a white flannel shirt, insinuating himself between grown-up couples, endured by them only so long as he kept out of their way. In addition to his agonized victory with Joyce Wethered at Worplesdon (a more imposing event than it stands at the present) he won the President's Putter and the *Golf Illustrated* Gold Vase. Again both these events, in the absence of others at the time, ranked high on the list of achievements open to the amateur. He did not set himself up as a stylist. He complained in moments of bitterness that his style was too flamboyant and juvenile. A picture of him taken in his more active days shows a back-swing well past the horizontal, his left heel high off the ground to facilitate the full pivot, his whole position anticipating an explosive downswing.

He was probably too agitated a player ever to become a good putter and this may have prevented his reaching the top in the game. His opponent in that Worplesdon final remembers him muttering as he addressed the ball for a short chip from off the green made with an old cleek; 'Now then Darwin, come along Darwin, come along, keep it smooth,' and occasionally, 'Oh Darwin, you bloody fool.' The patter sounds like a remedy for an incipient twitch, especially as it was accompanied by a leapfrog movement of the clubhead behind and in front of the ball before the stroke was played. He had a peculiar horror, once he was in the lead, of the holes slipping away. Once, in writing about himself in the Worplesdon Foursomes, he described how, seized with the old terror of this happening, he went, 'weakly and weakly' into bunkers in front of his nose. The unique position he was in to write anonymously, usually disparagingly and always modestly about his own golf, was taken up in *The Times* by a correspondent, fully aware of the situation, who complained that the golf correspondent was unsympathetic and brutal in writing about a most worthy man and excellent golfer, Bernard Darwin. To read the paper, he never played a shot right in his life and was apparently suffering from every imaginable ailment in the second childhood of his life. *The Times*, the letter went on, made him sound decrepit, whereas the author of the letter had been pleasantly surprised to find him an upstanding man of early middle age wearing many clothes and a cheerful, if somewhat sheepish grin. But the years of his prime amateur golf were extremely strong, and he did reach the semi-final of the Amateur twice, managing at the same time, with the aid of trusty lieutenants, to send in lengthy despatches to *The Times*. His concentration was no doubt fierce when he was playing, so that even the voice of Dickens was stilled within him, but the writer-player is seriously handicapped by the thought of what he has to do. A strong intuitive sense combined with vast experience also enabled him to read a match correctly on the flimsiest evidence. In the 1952 Amateur at St Andrews he overcame his dislike of hysterical crowds enough to accompany Bing Crosby for a few holes in his second-round match. Crosby started 3, 3, 3, and was three up, whereupon Darwin turned to the companion with whom he was sharing an umbrella and said: 'Well, that's all we need to see; he will lose by 2 and 1 or 3 and 2'. And he did.

As for the Press interviews on which so much sports writing is now dependent, he left an example of his attitude towards them after Max Faulkner had won the British Open at Portrush in 1951. The winner had come down to talk to the Press; Darwin endured it for a bit, and was then heard to mutter as he rose to his feet and left the room, that what his readers were interested in, or ought to be, was what he thought of Faulkner's round and not what Faulkner thought of it himself. Hob-nobbing with professionals in order to make a report more colourful he viewed as odious familarity, because it suggested an intimacy with the personality which was a source of pride. 'I think it is the football writers who are the worst offenders, or rather those who write about them. Their wives and their twins, their houses and their jokes are all served up to us with a sense of penny-a-lining gossip. And worst of all, perhaps, their grievances and, but this applies perhaps rather to runners, their excuses. I have heard an amusing story about a baseball player who was called Alibi Ike. I wonder if the title might not be revived.'

He would have viewed the elaborate Press centres of today with abhorrence, glaring at the scoreboard covered with soulless figures, and stumping out of the marquee at the announcement of the next player coming in to be interviewed. Where others today would quote Nicklaus, Darwin, had he still been working, would have quoted Nickleby. But to pursue the comparison further would be to descend to fantasy. Darwin was moulded by the times in which he lived. In his day a writer of golf had to forage for himself. The bare figures were available to him when a round was finished, but there was nothing to tell him who was leading, who he should go and watch. There would have been nowhere except his knee on which to rest his typewriter, so why should he bother to learn how to use one? He did not drive a car, and would not have wanted to add to his luggage which probably already included his clubs and a present for the hostess of the private house where he was going to stay.

One journalistic quality he possessed to an enviable degree. He had the concentration to settle down and write his piece wherever he had to. He strongly approved of trains and of the opportunities they gave him to complete an article. The most likely place would be the corner of a lounge where, at the end of the day, the most information was to be found. Not that he would have needed to make much use of that. One pictures him slowly digesting what he had witnessed in the course of the day; making mental notes, for he never appeared to be writing anything down, reckoning perhaps that what he did not remember would not be worth reporting. He never tired of pointing out that he could not be everywhere at once, and his advice to young writers was to decide what was likely to be the most interesting round of the day, and to go out and watch it. Whatever happened they should write about the event, and if they could not make it sound the most readable event of the day, then they had no right to be doing what he was. What he practised he preached. He could make a 74 that he had watched sound more entertaining than a 67 which he had not. In the continuous freshness of his enthusiasm there is much to admire, especially in an age when television makes armchair critics of us all, and when over-exposure to sport numbs our sensitivity.

To mind about such things is not a bad philosophy of life, however trivial they may be. And he did mind. His zest for the game drove him at the double from vantage-point to vantage-point, as long as he was physically able, just as, in earlier days, he had once ridden a bicycle for three from Trinity to Hunstanton, a matter of seventy miles, in order to take part in a match. Yet in spite of this he kept a tight rein on his emotions when it came to writing. He deliberately made every superlative earn its place. That is why his most enduring work – if we are to believe him, none of it was meant to be enduring – was in the quieter moments. His description of Horace Hutchinson, a golfer and writer whom he much admired, might be taken as applying directly to himself. 'He had the enthusiasm, the light touch, the power of pleasant prattle, the occasional and skilful discursiveness that go to make the agreeable essayist.' He never lost sight of the fact that golf is only a game and that there was a world outside it.

PETER RYDE, *Mostly Golf*

Great musicians spend countless hours in
acquiring and perfecting their technique before
they pass on to interpretation, and the golfer
should take a lesson from them. ABE MITCHELL

Joe Kirkwood

'I'm sorry,' said Joe Kirkwood, the most imaginative shotmaker golf has known, 'I'd love to tell you some Hagen stories, but my publisher wants me to save them for my book.' His Australian accent was edged with regret. Kirkwood traveled with Walter Hagen for 25 years, taking golf to the world, and the two were fun-seeking confreres whose exploits defy embellishment.

We were sitting in the pro shop at Stowe Country Club in bucolic Vermont where he is head professional, surrounded by a vast melange of memorabilia – a rock collection, inspirational signs, some of his own verse – and incidentally, golf equipment.

Kirkwood apologized for not being able to relate any Hagen stories – and then told a string of them. There was the one about Hagen at Leo Diegel's funeral. Hagen and Diegel had been fierce but affectionate rivals in the 1920s. Remorseful over Diegel's death, Hagen imbibed at some length, and led Kirkwood into the wrong church. The pair sat through the longer part of a funeral service for someone else before realizing their error. Later they caught up with the Diegel ceremonies at the cemetery. Hagen told the minister he would like a word with Leo.

102

He approached the closed casket and knocked on it loudly. 'You in there, Leo?' he rasped, tears in his eyes. 'See you soon, old buddy. How in hell'd they get you in there anyway with your arms stuck out?' – a reference to Diegel's unorthodox putting style. Kirkwood says, 'It was one of the most touching things I've ever seen.

And there was the time irrepressible story-teller Kirkwood and Hagen, tiring of hitting golf balls out of their New York City hotel window at the bums in Central Park below, walked several blocks and launched a contest to see who could play his way the fastest back to the hotel, through the lobby, up the elevator, across the room, and into the toilet bowl! They played this game several times and Kirkwood defeated Hagen consistently. An infuriated Hagen always was first back to the room, but was inept at chipping his ball into the toilet, while Kirkwood never missed.

For Kirkwood, chipping into a toilet bowl was nothing. The first great trick-shot performer (a designation that he does not like but that he raised to the level of legitimacy), he could do more with a golf ball than anyone before or since. He could tee two balls and, with a 7-iron, hit them simultaneously and cause them to cross in mid-flight, one hooking and one slicing; he could pound a ball into the ground so that only the top was visible, and crack it over 200 yards with a 4-wood; he could play left-handed with right-handed clubs; he could demonstrate his unparalleled touch by taking identical full swings with a 2-wood to pantomime the development of a novice player, and barely topple the ball off the tee, then dribble it a few feet, then hit it 50 yards, and eventually 275 yards. Or he could flail at it and pop it harmlessly into the air so that he caught it without moving.

He could tee six balls in a row and, in quick succession and without looking, move down the line and cleanly strike one after another, making them alternately hook and slice.

'The most difficult shot was the one where I'd hit backward out of a bunker and the ball would finish close to the hole,' he says. 'I kept my hands low and didn't come up with my swing. The ball flew right over my shoulder. Grantland Rice made a Movietone short of that shot, and after I saw in slow motion how close I was to getting hit I didn't do it often.

'I used to swing a lead shaft that would wind around my neck, and one day I hit myself in the shoulder on my backswing and spit out all the teeth from one side of my mouth. People thought it was part of the act and I was spitting out corn. There was a time when I'd do anything for money.'

103

Money was something only other people had when Kirkwood was young in Australia. He left home at nine, encouraged, he says, by his parents, and dropped out of school. 'Three of the happiest years of my life were in the second grade,' he jokes. He became a boundary rider (cowboy) for a sheep ranch, in his free time playing golf on three makeshift holes with a gift club.

'There was nobody to copy, so I had to use my imagination,' he says. 'I never intended to be a showman, but I wanted to do something the other fella couldn't do.' In his early 20s he won the Australian Open Championship and, too young to fight in World War I, made a patriotic contribution by entertaining disabled troops. 'I tried to show them what could be done even though they were amputees,' he says. 'I would hit a ball with one hand, or standing on one leg. That's how I got started.'

Fifty years ago, Kirkwood came to America. A good player, he won several tour events and the Canadian Open, and finished high in the British and US Opens, but decided he could not live well enough on the skimpy purses of the day, and threw in with Hagen as a trick-shot pioneer. The two men were an immediate success around the world, the penurious, better organized Kirkwood complementing the carefree Hagen. They played exhibitions in places golf had never been, on islands without names. The story goes that they once stopped a war in China because no one wanted to miss their act.

They entertained loin-clothed natives, presidents or convention-goers, but they also entertained each other. In Scotland, Hagen wanted a lesson from an old teaching pro. So he concocted a scheme. He and Kirkwood passed themselves off as Canadian cattlemen just taking up golf, and for an hour the old Scot grappled with what he doubtless considered the two oddest swings he had ever come upon. As they left, he called after them, 'Haste ye back!'

Five years ago Kirkwood settled in Stowe. He says he was fishing in nearby Bethel, fell in fighting a big trout, and was washed downstream to Stowe. The club had no pro, Kirkwood was tired of a schedule that often called for three shows a day and a long overnight drive, and he figured he would never find a more attractive, relaxing environment. He stayed.

He kept his game in shape, occasionally going on the road to give exhibitions, and breaking par on his own championship course playing with members and using only a 5-iron. In 1960, at the age of 63, he fired a 62 at Deland (Fla.) Country Club to become the youngest man ever to receive a certificate from *Golf Digest* for shooting his age, the golfing feat of which he is proudest. Actually, there is some uncertainty about Kirkwood's age. He says he is presently 74, but his son Ron who helps him operate the Stowe pro shop, says Social Security records show 78 (another son, Joe Jr., was a competent tour player and played Joe Palooka in the movies).

The once husky Kirkwood has cancer of the liver and has lost 70 pounds since a year ago, and his doctor has told him bluntly that he will not live another year. The irony is that liver ailments are popularly associated with excessive drinking and Joe never drank. Medicines keep him out of pain, and, while he spends much of his time resting, he can still be lucid and entertaining, his sense of humor as lively as ever.

When a local doctor shot himself with a pistol, someone remarked that it had to be due to one of three reasons: love, money or illness. Said Joe, 'Or a very bad slice.' Always a bit of a dandy, he continues to dye his hair, and even now is attractive to women. On the summer weekend that I visited him, a pretty woman in her 40s was in town trying to ingratiate herself with Joe. 'She's gotta be crazy,' Joe growled later. 'A harem would do me no good.'

He is determined to finish his book, with a woman writer who belongs to the Stowe club.

'The only thing I regret is that I can't play golf,' he says. 'I love the game. But I've played 8,000 courses and been able to go everywhere I wanted to go. I've had a full life; plenty of money, good friends. I've bought a little plot of land to be buried on here, and I don't want any fanfare or crap when I go. I'd just like to think the boys will drive by and say, "Hi, Kirkie."'

NICK SEITZ, *Golf Digest, 1967*

It is the control of the tension of the grip in the fingers which counts. This is the golf secret if there is one. HENRY COTTON

Old Tom Morris

Tom, 'old Tom', is a character, an institution, a subject on which the most interesting monograph might be written. Wherever golf is played his name is a password; interviewers have interviewed him, journalists made copy out of him; photographers photographed him (including in this connection at least one very skilful lady amateur, who confesses to an absorbing admiration for him); artists have sketched him, with sometimes astonishingly happy results; and, truth to tell, he, as he is known to us now, lends himself somewhat readily to artistic effort – his characteristic attitudes, his hands always in his pockets, except when engaged in the congenial occupation of grasping a club or filling afresh a pipe (which, by the same token, is oddly enough always a brand-new clay of choice), his grey beard, all these and sundry other points go to form an individuality as striking as it is unique. The writer recently came across a remark which he noticed with some attention; it was that in writing, for any good results to be produced, the mind must be red-hot behind the pen. As to the results here produced, the readers of this chapter will of course be judges; but there is one particular as to which the writer's mind is as red-hot in its conviction as the most ardent scribe could desire: this point is, that never could there be met with a more perfect specimen of what is called 'Nature's gentleman' than old Tom. Nobility of character is writ on his handsome sunburnt face in letters as clear as day, and withal there is an admixture of naïve and unsophisticated simplicity which ·is charming to the last degree.

An illustration of what is intended to be conveyed may be given in the following anecdote: Many years ago, at the High hole at St Andrews, Tom was working away in difficulties to the extent of three more or thereabouts, and still a very·long way from the hole. Captain Broughton happening to pass by, remarked, 'Oh, pick up your ball, Tom, it's no use.'

'Na, na,' said he, 'I might hole it.'

'If you do, I'll give you £50.'

'Done,' said Tom, and had another whack, and by some million to one chance the ball did actually go into the hole.

'That will make a nice nest-egg for me to put in the bank,' he remarked, and, further to give the *ipsissima verba*, 'the Captain he pit on a gey sarous face, nae doot o' that, and passed on.'

Within a few days the Captain honorably appeared with the £50, of which, however, Tom resolutely refused to touch one farthing, remarking that the whole thing was a joke, and 'he wisna raly meaning it.'

From all parts of the country communications reach him on recondite legal questions connected with the game; as an arbiter his authority is acknowledged beyond dispute, in virtue of his vast stores of knowledge, of tradition, of golfing lore, of his years, and consequent wisdom. A veritable Nestor he: gifted, moreover, he is with the faculty of harmonizing the most hopelessly discordant elements. Is there a pull-devil, pull-baker sort of squabble on the teeing-ground as to who should start first, about fifty balls teed in a row, and their respective owners all swearing at one another, down comes Tom, oil-bag in hand, lets out a few drops, and the raging waves acknowledge the soothing influence and subside at once into the ripple of a summer sea. He is a man of whom it is impossible to conceive that he could ever have had an enemy in the world.

H. S. C. EVERARD, *A History of the Royal and Ancient Golf Club, St Andrews, 1896*

One point is common to all golfers – the legs are vital. DAI REES

Severiano Ballesteros

Sometimes the talent goes with the glamour. Severiano Ballesteros, the most handsome and exciting golfer in the Open, tore the entrails out of the opposition on the way home at Lytham.

When he put himself into history as a winner at 22 it was natural that his three brothers, all professionals who happily admit that he has set himself soaringly apart, should smother him in warmth.

'He is No. 1 helping me, my brother Manuel,' said the champion afterwards. 'I been caddy for him and all things I learn from his game.' He had praise, too, for Roberto de Vicenzo, the Argentinian who took the same title at Hoylake in 1967.

'He tell me, don't confuse,' said the young Spaniard, beginning to sound as if he had borrowed from that special tongue that Roberto called his PGA English. 'He say when you take the club from the bag just hit the ball. Don't think about bunkers or anything. Play with your heart.'

Neither brother Manuel nor de Vicenzo had to give him that advice. He knows no other way. Every shot is a declaration and the Americans who crowded in on him yesterday seeking to crush him with a frightening mixture of excellence and calculation were left trailing by his boldness.

He hit only one fairway with the driver in the last round, which gave him the same limited success rate as he had the day before, but waywardness stimulates rather than depresses him.

The narrowness of Lytham's playing areas worried him only because they were not narrow enough. He had said earlier that an Open without fairways might suit him. 'I don't know if I win but I go close,' he told us, 'I have plenty practice in the rough.'

There was much truth in the joke, even more when he said last night that he felt comfortable with his ball in the sand. 'Fifteen times this week I am in a bunker. Fourteen times I need only one putt after.'

Manuel, he insisted, had taught him soon after his start at the age of eight or nine, 'how to play tricky things.'

He was a good student. For a man who swings like a fiend on the tee, he has an unbelievable delicacy with the short game. Indeed, any stroke out of trouble is his meat.

The ball is lifted out of minor jungles and floated on a carpet of inspired technique over all the ambushes of hillocks and sand-traps to threaten the pin. Putts roll aggressively towards the hole along unlikely lines and distances.

And through it all is the impression of a young man flaunting pride in his animal power and his skill. The dark, strong face is the kind that stirs wives and worries husbands and the personality is no let-down for his looks. In action he has a flourish that is simply beautiful and when he talks there is intelligence and appealing humour.

108

As Jack Nicklaus, one of his victims yesterday, pointed out, the only credible barrier that stands between Ballesteros and a position of greatness in golf is physical. A bad back has troubled him for some time and he acknowledged that anxiety about it when it went with him through the four rounds of this Open.

'I don't have pain,' he said. 'I feel like in my shoulders I am heavy. I am stiff. The cold is bad for me. You notice I swing three or four times before I hit the ball I feel like I am carrying a weight.'

Throughout yesterday he was a weight on the spirit of every other golfer at Lytham. The sun shone but the wind blew so that the great course was, as it so often is, the smiler with the knife. Most of the Americans, notably Hale Irwin and Ben Crenshaw, were eventually disembowelled, but Ballesteros saved himself from the most damaging thrusts of the conditions.

At the 16th he went wildly to the right and into the car park. But afterwards he suggested, with a mischievously delayed grin, that the lie didn't bother him because the wind was favourable and the pin was in an encouraging place.

Around about that time he was seen to be running between shots, tugging at his blue windcheater, reaching for the clubs with a barely stifled impatience, looking up ahead as if he knew that every obstacle was there to yield to him.

The British crowd greeted him on the 18th as one of their own, and he was sincere when he said later that he felt his victory was for Europe as well as for Spain.

He knows that the American master of golf cannot help feeling a resentment of brilliant interlopers. Severiano Ballesteros is young and brave and gifted enough to irritate them for many years to come.

HUGH MCILVANNEY, *The Observer, 1979*

We are certain that in the whole range of sport or human exercise there is nothing that is quite so good as the sublime sensation, the exquisite feeling of physical delight, that is gained in the driving of a golf ball with a wooden club in the manner that it ought to be driven.
HENRY LEACH

Slow-Play Flo

Where I came from, a so-called lady golfer was always something to be hollered at, like an overheating '53 Buick blocking traffic, or a sullen waitress who couldn't remember to put cheese on the 'burger and leave off the onions, the dummy. Hey, you. You up there on the green with the legs like tree bark, and the schoolteacher skirt and the one-foot putt. It's *good*. I give you the putt, all right? So take your 135 shots back to the mixed grill and jump into your vodka martini with your nitwit husband who took your father's thieving money and built the country club and won't let you play here but once a week in front of *me*. Go shell some peas or crochet an afghan or do whatever women ought to be doing instead of cluttering up a golf course. Fore!

That's how it was growing up back in Texas. The most fun was to stand back there with your guys and then, after all the yelling and waiting, everybody would cut loose with a three-iron. And then when the shots would burn into the green and go between the putting stances of Slow-Play Fay and Play-Slow Flo, and when they would hop around like an assortment of Ruby Keelers' we'd sink to our knees in aching laughter.

We had it all worked out in our minds that we belonged on the course and they didn't. We were there to sharpen up for the Goat Hills Invitation and they – the women – were there to keep us from becoming the future Hogans. 'Women golfers are meece,' we said, referring to our plural of moose.

We never asked to play through. We just did it, often while they were studying their chip shots. And there would always be one of them, a slightly rotund, menacing, scowling soul who would

110

challenge us. 'Don't you boys know anything about manners?' she would say.

We would all very wittily ask each other if we knew anything about manners and, while we putted out, we would discuss it. One of us would say he thought he used to know something about manners, back when manners lived over the way. Manners was pretty good, we would say, but he had a tendency to snap-hook it when he got tense. We would be going on towards the next tee and the big lady would still be after us. 'I know who you are, and I'm going to tell your parents,' she would say.

One of us would say, 'That's gonna be a lot of phone calls because we all come from broken homes.'

The big lady would usually turn out to be somebody I'll call Mrs R. F. Zinger, 14 times city champion and president of the women's district golf association. She would be the first lady ever to pass the local bar exam, the first lady pilot, a former Curtis Cup girl, an ex-national spelling champion, the daughter of the city's first four-term mayor, the author of a textbook on the history of the Colorado River and the architect of the town's new motorway system.

With Mrs R. F. Zinger lecturing after us, we would bound off down the fairway, having successfully played through, but of course a couple of us would insist on calling something back at her from out of slung-wedge distance.

Such was my fondness for women's golf in those days. Not to suggest, however, that my attitude would be changed by a certain maturity or my advancement into newspaper work. Anyone who ever did time on a newspaper sports desk is familiar with the type of phone calls you get from lady golfers. Mine usually came when I was listening to the Kentucky Derby and the horses were at the post. I would get the call from Mrs Simcox reporting the net 77 that Mrs Slocum shot to win the local women's golf association's Tuesday Flag Tournament.

'I'm *sure* it was a net 77,' Mrs Simcox would say. 'Let's see. She bogeyed 1, double-bogeyed 2. . . .'

Yeah, yeah, yeah.

I guess my most favourite phone call of all time – true story – went something like this:

Me: Hi, sports fans. Pegler here. Runyon's out to lunch.

'Sports department, please.'

This here's it.

'Is this the sports department?'

111

Take it on one, Hildy.

'Hello? Sports department?'

Hi!

'This is Mrs J. D. Stephens calling for Mrs R. F. Zinger, the president of the women's district golf association. Mrs Zinger asked me to call you because she said you always wanted the results of our weekly tournaments.'

Oh, good.

'Mrs Zinger said you liked to print the results.'

Well, Mrs Zinger looks out for us pretty good.

'Mrs Zinger said to tell you that we played our weekly blind-flag bogey event today, and I have the results.'

You played a what?

'Our weekly blind-flag bogey tournament is what Mrs Zinger called it.'

What exactly is that?

'Well, it was sort of complicated, but we all played and I have the winners here.'

Fine. What was it again?

'It was our weekly blind-flag bogey tournament, a different type of event that Mrs Zinger thought up.'

O.K.

'I'm not sure I can explain it, but we all played 18 holes and then Mrs Zinger figured out who won.'

O.K. Just start with the winner.

'Well, first place in the championship flight was Mrs R. F. Zinger. . . .'

It was inevitably my experience that women didn't actually *play* golf. They casseroled it. They all stood there in front of my gangsome, poling at two-inch putts. They all had woefully slow, four-piece backswings with curious hip moves. They took the clubs back so far that the shafts whipped them on the shoulder blades, and then they lunged forward and the clubheads plundered into the earth and the balls went dribbling off into the weeds.

A lot of the time I figured it was the way they dressed that made them play so badly. And slowly. They all wore those goofy things on their feet that weren't socks and came up just above the shoe tops and reached down below the anklebones. Ugly. And they wore straight skirts that hit them below the knees, with white blouses that were too tight, and big-brimmed hats with red bows.

Then there was the cackling in the clubhouse. After their rounds,

112

I noticed that most women golfers could get into the booze better than most men. Several times I thought I saw two women having a bitter fight across a table, but they were just chatting over their Manhattans – or whatever women drink – about curtains and drapes.

I understand, of course, that there were supposed to be a lot of women golfers in the world who weren't like the ones I had always been exposed to. I knew about the lady pros. I knew they had a tour of their own, but I also knew what most guys felt about it: you would have bet that every one of 'em out there on the women's pro tour could overhaul a diesel truck if she put her mind and energy to it.

In recent years I have been presented with a number of chances to visit a women's pro tournament instead of hanging around the men's tour all the time. Each time I gingerly managed to escape, and the assignment most often fell to an associate in the golf department, a child star who writes too well for any of us to loaf much.

'You ought to go see 'em,' he would say. 'They're great.'

Wrong. Got to stay with the guys, I would insist. Tom Weiskopf is getting ready to issue his first quote of the year, and I don't want to miss it.

'It isn't like you remember it,' my colleague would argue. 'Most of them are cute and friendly, and they can play like hell.'

Well, one of these days, I would say. Can't now, though. Got a biggie coming up in Pensacola. Eichelberger's moving up on the points list. McGee's ready to bust out. Crampton smiled the other day. All very exciting with the men.

To be candid about it, one of the things that kept me away from the LPGA tour was the knowledge that the girls don't exactly travel the caviar circuit in terms of towns.

Also, the names of their tournaments were troubling. They all sounded like stockcar races. For example, there were things like the Shreveport Kiwanis Invitational, the Johnny Londoff Chevrolet, the Len Immke Buick, the Springfield Jaycee and the Lincoln-Mercury.

Then it happened. My young associate said early last spring he thought there might be a women's event coming up that I'd like. The $50,000 Sealy-LPGA Classic. Sealy makes mattresses.

That's *funny*, I said.

'No, seriously,' he said. The men's tour was quiet, after all. Terry Dill wouldn't be changing his grip for another week or so. Dick Lotz still had the same putter. Bert Yancy had postponed his annual interview till July.

'And it's in Las Vegas,' he said.

That was the magic word. Vegas. Now, I know that to some people Las Vegas is not all that fascinating. To some, it's Baghdad-in-the-desert, the mob's idea of chic, a neon-lit asylum, the blonde-wig, no-bra, no-brain capital of the Western world. To others, such as me, however, Vegas comes up as the only civilised city in the US, because it's the only one where there aren't a lot of lightweight lawmakers trying to tell you that you can't eat, drink, gamble or fall in love between two a.m. and noon. So I take Vegas whenever I can get it, even if I have to fool around with women's golf.

Judging from the number of blue Sealy blazers around The Desert Inn during one full week last May, there weren't many mattresses being sold anywhere. Sealy was venturing into golf for the first time, and the company had selected a women's tournament to sponsor for what it believed to be a tidy statistical reason. Women make or influence nine out of every ten mattress purchases, said a Sealy press release.

It didn't take long, in Vegas, for me to realise that one of the major differences between lady pros and men pros is that lady pros scream a whole lot more at a dice table. On the first night in town I was trying to have a quiet drink in the lobby bar at The Desert Inn with my old friend Bud Erickson, a former employee of the Detroit Lions and Atlanta Falcons who had been cast into the unlikely role of executive director of the LPGA when we heard these female noises ringing through the casino.

'I think those are my people,' Bud said.

We looked and there they were, nine of them, jammed around a dice table as if it were a washrag sale. One of them – Gerda Boykin, her name was – was shooting, and she had just rolled a seven. Almost everything in The Desert Inn stopped for the next few moments as Gerda Boykin, an attractive brunette who was once the only lady pro in Germany, made three more passes with the dice amid a chorus of some of the best shrieks since Arnie first hitched up his trousers.

What had happened was, a bunch of the girls, including Judy Rankin and Pam Higgins and this Gerda, had formed a syndicate on the tour a few weeks before Vegas. Every time one of them three-putted in a tournament, she put $1 into a pool, and they had this pact that they would take the money to Vegas for the Sealy. And on the first night there, one of them – it turned out to be

Gerda Boykin – would shoot the bundle at craps for three, maybe four rolls. They went in with $60 total, and the nine of them came out with an average of $40 after Gerda got through.

Bud Erickson said, 'Pretty good story, huh, right off the bat? Nothing like that on the men's tour, I guess.'

Right, I said. You can't find nine guys who'll speak to each other.

'Lot of good stories out here,' said Bud. 'There's a girl named Diane Patterson who used to be a trapeze artist. She took up golf after she quit The Flying Viennas.'

Really?

'Got a kid named Pam Burnett who throws her wig around when she gets mad, instead of breaking clubs.'

Good.

'How about the Watusi Kid? Donna Caponi. She'll dance all night and play great golf.'

Hmmmmm.

'Got a couple of Japanese girls on the tour now. Chako Higuchi and Marbo Sasaki.'

Ah, so.

'Hey,' said Bud. 'How about Sharron Moran? She's really attractive and she does these hat tricks. She's always wearing a different hat on the course. She must have twenty or more different hats.'

Z-z-z-z-z-z-z. Oh, excuse me, Bud. Almost dropped off there for a minute.

The Sealy-LPGA Classic had an odd format. It was a 72-hole tournament for the girls, of course, with a hefty $10,000 going to the winner. Well, that's big for the women. It's a shrug for the guys. Anyhow, John Montgomery, the tournament director, had it all worked out that to make it different – to give it something extra – it would be played sort of like the Crosby in reverse. The lady pros would have *men* partners every day in what constituted four separate Pro-Ams. In other words, each day the girls would play for some extra cash, and the amateur men would compete for what appeared to be just about all of the Steuben crystal that had ever been sculpted.

On Wednesday evening John Montgomery ran down the list of all the glittering male types from sports and show biz who had been invited to participate. There were Joe Namath, Glen Campbell, Mickey Mantle, Joe DiMaggio, Dale Robertson, Joe Louis, Vic Damone.

115

'And you,' he said.

I said uh-duh-*who*?

'You play at 8.42 a.m. with Donna Caponi and Glen Campbell,' John said.

Later that evening my lovely wife, whom I shall call June, and I were trying to decide where to go in Vegas – I was torn between *Vive Les Girls* at the Dunes and *Geisha'rella* at the Thunderbird – when she asked what I was going to wear tomorrow morning because there would be a gallery.

The usual, I said. My basic-blue button-down with the sleeves cut off and bush jeans. Maybe the grey sweater.

'You'll smother to death and look stupid,' she said. 'How's your game?'

Terrific, if I don't shank, I said.

'Then *don't* shank,' she said. 'What'll Glen and Donna think?'

Relax, I said. What do show-biz guys know about golf? And forget Donna. This is hardly the Masters, you know.

You could probably say that the crowd was fairly large around the first tee, most of them there to see Glay-yun. We stood around for a little bit, posed for pictures and waited for the PA to announce our pairing. Donna Caponi came over and said: 'You and Glen both have eight strokes. We've got a chance to win this today. We'll just play loose and see what happens.'

I told Donna that the tournament itself was the most important thing, where she was concerned. We'd try not to bother her, me and Glen, I said.

'Listen, we're going to have fun,' she smiled.

Donna teed off first and whipped it about 240 down the middle with a pretty solid swing, and it suddenly dawned on me that she was, after all, the US Women's Open champion of the past two years.

Glen Campbell stepped up next and flogged it about 260 down the middle with a very good swing, and I wondered where in the hell *that* came from.

I don't recall a great deal of applause when I was announced on the tee, but I do remember teeing up the ball, backing away for a practice swing and seeing my wife over behind the ropes. She was trying to tell me something in a whisper, hoping I could read her lips. Which I could. She was saying: 'Take . . . off . . . the . . . dumb . . . sweater. . . . Dummy.'

That didn't bother me, however. I opened up with the tee shot I always open up with – a howling slice which, when last charted, was

116

headed so far out of bounds that Glen Campbell said: 'Fore on The Strip.'

The provisional drive I hit was the same old second effort, a boring hook that hammered its way into the nearest fairway bunker.

'That completes our clinic, folks,' Campbell said. And we were off.

It wasn't the most comfortable triple-bogey eight I've ever made because, by notable contrast, Campbell put a spoon up near the green in two and had a couple of leisurely putts for a birdie. Donna raced over and kissed him.

Look, I'm just one, I said. Can I play through?

'If you're not going to *try*,' my lovely wife said, 'then I'll just go on back to the hotel and wait for you by the swimming pool.'

By the end of the third hole I had cost our team a net birdie by missing a two-foot putt – specifically, my wife said, because I refused to take a cigarette out of my mouth before I stroked the ball, and I had smashed another drive out of bounds and made a double bogey.

'You have a good swing,' Donna Caponi was kind enough to say, 'if you'll slow it down about four speeds.'

Yeah, I know what to *do*, I said. It's just that sometimes, if you drink a little. . . .

'You'll be O.K.,' Donna said. 'Just take it back low and slow.'

A little later my lovely wife came over and said, 'Can I go get anybody a Coke, or a *golf shirt*, perhaps?'

Billy Casper frequently plays in a sweater in warm weather, I pointed out, rather testily.

'You're soaked under that thing,' she said. 'Yuk.'

I'll tell you what else is making me hot, I said.

There were those in the gallery who, were they willing, could testify that for the next several holes everybody in our threesome, including the dummy, played pretty well. Donna Caponi certainly wasn't any Slow-Play Fay or Play-Slow Flo. She was hard at work on a 71. Glen Campbell, the celeb, was in the process of carving out a surprising 72. When I finally started helping, our team chewed its way down to serious under-par figures. My moment of real glory came at the 13th when I got into a good drive, and a decent eight-iron, and then casually dropped a 15-footer for a birdie. Smoking. Donna raced over and gave me a birdie kiss, the crowd clapped. Glen patted me on the damp sweater and I looked around for the wife. Wasn't there, naturally. Had gone to get another Coke. Figured.

You blew my birdie back there, I told her.

'Well, thank goodness for *something* good,' she said. 'I just wish you hadn't picked *today* to play so badly.'

Hold it, I said. It's not all that bad. I'll be about an 82 with a triple bogey and a double bogey. Take away those two holes and . . .

'Glen's played just great all the way,' she said.

. . . it's down to about a 77 or so, which isn't all that . . .

'He's really hit some wonderful shots.'

. . . bad, actually. And I've made a few pars. It isn't exactly like I never hit a single . . .

'I love his shirt and pants. Aren't they good-looking?'

. . . shot, all day long. I mean, it's not exactly my *profession*, playing golf. Considering that I only play . . .

'Did he say he'd get us a table for his opening tonight at the International?'

. . . a few times a year, living in Fun City, whereas certain show-biz guys don't have anything to do but play a guitar and hang around Riviera and Lakeside . . .

'Isn't he the cutest thing? And so nice and friendly.'

. . . and, anyhow, you sure missed seeing a good birdie back there.

Nobody I've ever known in my entire life has ever won a Pro-Am. I have played in maybe 7,895 of them over the past 25 years, with any number of fine partners – guys who could really play and guys who had a bundle of strokes to use – and I have very often been 'the leader in the clubhouse,' as the TV commentators say, but before nightfall every one of these Pro-Ams has been won by a bunch of guys from Sacramento or Tampa. The pro would be an unknown, and his amateur partners would consist of a real-estate developer, an electrical contractor and a priest. They would be 24 under par.

Obviously, then, it was quite silly for Donna Caponi, Glen Campbell or me to think that our measly little round of 14-under would win anything on that first day. And of course it didn't. Marilynn Smith had a team that featured Jerry Lucas, the basketball star, who went out with his 12 handicap and shot a two-under 70 – gross – just like most of the 12-handicappers I ever knew back in Texas. They won laughing.

At the daily cocktail party and prize-giving, where all the Sealy folks got to work on their autograph collections and wondered where Joe Namath was, Jerry Lucas apologised and Donna Caponi confided that she was taking a party of 12 to both Glen Campbell shows that night.

For Friday's round the dummy got himself a golf shirt, his wife stayed at poolside, he drew for a pro a nice young married lady from

118

Midland, Texas named Judy Rankin who had captured three LPGA tournaments last year, and, for his other partner, a guy from Tampa with a long drive and a lot of strokes. Guy named Bill. Land developer. I thought we were a lock.

For a long time we were. Bill from Tampa was a cheer-leader who called our pro 'Judy, baby', and liked to take out a nine-iron for a five-iron shot and announce, 'If it's only 170 yards, a nine's plenty for me, baby.'

We played the back nine first and didn't cause any particular commotion until the 18th (our ninth) when I did one of those things we all did every week when we were 15 years old. I holed out a chip shot for an eagle.

From up on the TV tower, where the Hughes Network people were rehearsing, Bob Toski was giggling. 'Where'd you learn that?' he called down. 'In a subway?'

Our gallery consisted primarily of one: Walter (Yippy) Rankin, Judy's husband, a golf widower, a big, good-natured guy.

Somewhere on the incoming nine, Yippy Rankin made the mistake of telling us, 'You know, you-all are 15-under and that's leading. I think you can win it today.'

The ninth hole at The Desert Inn course (which would be our last) is an unprintable annoyance as far as I'm concerned. You have two choices off the tee on this par-four. You can drive it into a pond on the left or out of bounds into some homes on the right.

Knowing we had it all wrapped up, then, Judy Rankin promptly hit her drive into the pond, and I promptly hit mine out of bounds. None of this seemed to bother Bill from Tampa, however. He just stepped up and split the fairway with a boomer. Nine-iron to the green.

'I'll handle it, baby,' he said.

When we reached Bill from Tampa's tee shot, we could see the scoreboard and absorb the fact that our team *was* leading. I reminded our partner that he had a stroke on the hole, on top of everything else, so there was no point in being brave. Just a little flip up there to the big, safe part of the green and two putts would give us 16-under, more than we needed. That'll be a sweet $500 for Judy Rankin and some Steuben for the good guys.

'Don't worry, I'll put her right up there, baby,' said Bill from Tampa.

Who cold-bladed it out of bounds, and we finished tied for second.

Saturday's round was fairly uneventful, except for the fact that I was paired with some of the best set decoration on the new ladies' tour.

119

She was Donna's sister, Janet Caponi, who wears hot pants and helps make the LPGA look a lot different from the way I remembered it. Donna had taken the lead in the Sealy Classic itself, and we spent a lot of time asking for reports on her round. It was hot and windy, and the round passed as slowly as you might guess it would for somebody who had now been in Las Vegas for five days, which is the equivalent of 17 years. I was sadly over-Bill Cosby-d, over-Juliet Prowse-d, over-dinner-and-late-show-d, over-black jack-d and soundly asleep on each and every backswing.

John Montgomery and Bud Erickson decided that I created something of a minor problem for Sunday's final round. They had quite an athletic event on their hands, what with Donna Caponi holding a one-stroke lead over Janie Blalock, who had a sweet personality and a fine, fine game, and Sandra Palmer, an old friend of mine, as it happened, from Texas, who had yet to win her first tournament. And bunched together right behind them were all of the other top lady pros: Sandra Haynie, who had just won three in a row, Marlene Hagge, Jo Ann Prentice, Kathy Whitworth, Peggy Wilson, Pam Barnett, Margie Masters, Judy Rankin and Carol Mann.

Not only were the girls going out there on Sunday and battling it out for what was a big pay day for them, they were going to have to play threesomes: two lady pros with one celeb of sorts. For example, Montgomery and Erickson (and Sealy) thought it would be nifty for national television if there was a Glen Campbell or Joe Namath in every group of girls. And no writers.

'Let's face it,' Bud Erickson told me. 'You're not much of a TV attraction.'

Just blurt it out, Bud I said. No need to doll it up.

'How about 7.37 a.m. with Mary Lou Daniel and Jan Ferraris?'

I said I thought I'd be off the tables by then. Fine.

Part of the Sunday offering to keep the men stimulated, was a competition for a huge chunk of Steuben shaped into the form of a trophy. The Heart of Variety Cup, they called it. A man took his handicap and used it, and took the best holes he could get from his two lady pros, and all of that counted as *his* score, best ball.

Inasmuch as I was a dew sweeper that Sunday, Mary Lou and Jan and I got around rather swiftly. In fact, we finished at 11 o'clock just as Donna Caponi, Janie Blalock and Glen Campbell were teeing off. Mary Lou and Jan had been excellent companions and pretty impressive shotmakers. I must admit.

120

Maybe I particularly liked the two of them because I beat them with a light-running 75 from memory. In any case, our combined scores gave me eight-under for the round, and I was the leader in the clubhouse.

When you finish early you get to be the leader in the clubhouse for quite a long time. At The Desert Inn, I suppose I was the leader in the clubhouse for, oh, three or four hours. As a matter of fact, I was the leader in the clubhouse for so long that I finally started worrying that I might win.

There is no rule, of course, which says the leader in the clubhouse can't leave the clubhouse. So I went out on the course to watch Donna, Janie and Sandra Palmer throw the lead in the Sealy back and forth in pure melodramatic fashion. Hell of a tournament. They were each making one immense pressure shot after another while the Namaths and Campbells tried to stay out of the way.

Presently, after glancing at a scoreboard, I realised that I was a *co*-leader in the clubhouse.

Then it fell apart. Namath, Mantle and Campbell went by me, and then here came Don Adams with 18 strokes and a couple of pretty fair partners in Sandra Haynie and Marlene Hagge. He would win by a stroke.

'You're tied for fifth in the clubhouse,' my wife said.

The Sealy-LPGA Classic came down to the very last hole where Sandra Palmer, who had never won a tournament, held a one-stroke lead over Donna Caponi, directly behind her. As Sandra hit her second shot into a front bunker by the 18th green, Donna smashed a big drive down the fairway. Everybody figured it would go into sudden death.

I curiously found myself standing out there half-way up the fairway watching both, pulling for both; for my old friend Sandra from the old home town, the ex-college cheerleader whom I had first seen play when she was 14; and for my new friend, Donna, the dancer, in many ways the solidest player of all the girls.

My wife said, 'You've got to admit this is pretty exciting.'

Big deal, I said. Ten thousand dollars. Nicklaus gets that much for marking his ball.

'You're phony,' she said.

Yeah, I know, I said. But keep it in the family. It's an image deal.

About then, Sandra Palmer hit a slightly stupendous bunker shot that took two hops and rolled straight into the cup for an eagle 3; for all of the whoops, all of the glory and the biggest chunk of the cash. For victory.

I saw her later. She was still in semi-shock from her first win.

'Did you have fun?' Sandra asked. 'I hope you got to see that we have lots and lots of really fine players out here and some awfully nice people.'

That's true, I said.

'It's great you could be here. I hope a lot of the girls have told you that,' Sandra said.

They had, and it was embarrassing.

'See you again somewhere?'

I grinned and said I'd have to check the towns first. See what the bus schedules were like.

Sandra laughed.

'We'll see you again,' she said.

DAN JENKINS, *Sports Illustrated, 1971*

Over the Spinney
and into the Pond

Golf, uniquely among games, has no defined pitch or court and much of its charm derives from the variety of countryside over which the golfer directs his erratic progress.

Turnberry, 6th Tee

The Links of Eiderdown

Given exactly the right conditions, there are few pleasanter things than a day in bed. We must not be rank imposters; we must just be ill enough to be sure that we shall be nearly well next day, or, indeed, quite well so long as we have not to come down to breakfast. We must feel equal not to gross roast beef but to a whiting sympathetically eating its own tail and to a rice pudding, not forgetting the brown sugar. Tobacco, though sparingly indulged in, must not take. on the flavour of hay, and though wholly incapable of answering a newly arrived letter, we must be well able to read an old book.

It is best, if possible, to feel some warning symptoms the night before, so that we may be assured that it would be very unwise to get up next morning. Thus we have the joys both of anticipation and of fruition. That such joys are selfish it cannot be denied. The telephone bell rings in the distance and we cannot answer it. The bell rings for luncheon, and there are sounds of scurrying feet as of those late in washing; we are taking a little holiday in that respect and our lunch comes up on a tray. With what heavenly malice do we hear a strange motor-car crunching the gravel under the window. Callers – ha, ha! The new neighbours – ho, ho!

We shall be told later that they proved to be very agreeable people and we are perfectly ready to take it on trust. With a last thought of them sitting ranged round the drawing-room, we drift away into a beautiful half-way house between sleep and waking without fearing any of the misery that ensues if we do the same thing in a chair. We shall come to ourselves as bright as a button and ready for another go of 'David Copperfield.'

This was my admirable choice last week, and I was so drowsily happy that I found even Agnes 'pointing upward' not unendurable. Only one thing disturbed my serenity. In my warped mind's eye I continually saw golf holes designed on the 'land of counterpane' before me. It is not an uninteresting one, this links of eiderdown, and is laid out on what an ingratiating prospectus would call fine, undulating country. Moreover, by undulating himself in bed the patient can in a moment change the contour of his course. In the ordinary way there is a broad hog's-back ridge extending down the middle of the course. It is doubtless possible to use it in several ways, but I always saw a long plain hole running nearly the whole length of it, slightly downhill with a fall to perdition on either side for the slicer of hooker. It seemed to me, if I remembered the number aright, rather like the thirteenth hole at Liphook. There were no bunkers on it of any kind; no 'lighthouses', as the more ferocious of architects scornfully term them, to guide the eye of the tiger and make superfluously wretched the rabbit's life; nothing but a wide expanse on which it would clearly be very difficult to judge distance.

When my eyes dropped to either side of this ridge I felt that I was in another country. Was I at Formby or Birkdale, or perhaps at the sixth hole at Prince's, Sandwich? Here, at any rate, was one of the holes that run along a narrow valley with slopes on either hand – on one side, to be precise, the patient's leg, and on the other the outside edge of the eiderdown. I have always had rather a romantic affection for such holes. I have heard with pain from those same 'highbrow' architects that they are not really good holes, because the mere fact of the banks (which will kick the ball back to the middle) give the player confidence, whereas the architect's duty is to make him hesitating and uncomfortable. I began to think that these irritating views were right; the valley might be narrow, but I felt as if I could drive straight down it, whereas when I looked at the ridge I did not feel nearly so happy.

There were other holes on the course but they were hardly so satisfactory. There was, to be sure, a big, blind tee-shot, to a one-shot hole as I imagined it, over a comparatively noble hill, made by my toes, but somehow it lacked subtlety; and when by a swift piece of engineering I moved the hill to see what the green was like on the far side, it proved flat and featureless. By separating and then adroitly manipulating my two sets of toes it was possible to make a crater green, with visions of the ball running round the side wall and back wall to lie dead at least for an unmerited three.

That brought back sentimental memories. I knew a beloved course once that had three such greens running, at the fifteenth, sixteenth and seventeenth, and many years ago I had three threes running there and won a medal thereby. Still, the sweetness of such threes has a cloying quality. No doubt it is all for the best in the most testing of all possible worlds that there should be no more greens like that nowadays.

To roll over on my side had a disappointing effect on the links. In fact it was obviously not a links any longer, but a mere course; one of those courses on downland which I have the misfortune to dislike, with long, steep slopes, equally tedious to play up or down, and too often adorned with 'gun-platform' greens. When tea came, however, the course took on a new aspect, for the tea-tray was on a bed table and the bed table had four legs. The course was now one cut out of a wood, on which the architect had wisely allowed a

126

solitary sentinel tree or two to remain standing in the middle of the fairway. The valley holes instantly became far more interesting, for each of them had one tree, acting in some sort as a Principal's Nose, for the tee shot, and another, like that capital tree at the first hole at Frilford, bang in front of the green. I spent some time trying to resolve on which side of those trees to go. At one hole it seemed best to try the right-hand line, because if I went to the left I might hook on to the floor, which was clearly out of bounds.

At the other hole an exactly converse policy was indicated, but even with the banks to help me the shot was far from easy.

Now I am, as Mr Littimer would say, 'tolerably well' again, and 'David Copperfield' is finished. I have no reasonable pretext for not getting up for breakfast, and indeed it is rumoured that there are to be sausages tomorrow morning. The links of eiderdown are fast becoming of the fabric of a dream. I have tried to fix the holes before they elude the frantic clutches of memory and fade away into one another.

BERNARD DARWIN, *Playing the Like*, 1934

Believe me, there is no easy way to better golf.
HARRY WEETMAN

Mullion

My ball is in a bunch of fern,
   A jolly place to be;
An angry man is close astern –
   He waves his hand at me.
Well, let him wave – the sky is blue;
Go on, old ball, we are but two –
   We *may* be down in three,
Or nine – or ten – or twenty-five –
It matters not; to be alive
   Is good enough for me.

127

How like the happy sheep we pass
    At random through the green,
For ever in the longest grass,
    But never in between!
There is a madness in the air;
There is a damsel over there,
    Her ball is in the brook.
Ah! what a shot – a dream, a dream!
You think it finished in the stream?
    Well, well, we'll go and look.

Who *is* this hot and hasty man
    That shouteth 'Fore!' and 'Fore!'?
We move as quickly as we can –
    Can any one do more?
Cheer up, sweet sir, enjoy the view;
I'd take a seat if I were you,
    And light your pipe again:
In quiet thought possess your soul,
For John is down a rabbit-hole,
    And I am down a drain.

The ocean is a lovely sight,
    A brig is in the bay.
Was that a slice? You might be right –
    But, goodness, what a day!
Young men and maidens dot the down,
And they are beautiful and brown,
    And just as mad as me.
Sing, men and maids, for I have done
The Tenth – the Tenth! – in twenty-one,
    And John was twenty-three.

Now I take my newest ball,
    And build a mighty tee,
And waggle once, or not at all,
    And bang it out to sea,
And hire a boat and bring it back,
And give it one terrific whack,
    And hole it out in three,
Or nine – or ten – or twenty-five –

It matters not; to be alive
At Mullion in the summer time,
At Mullion in the silly time,
    Is good enough for me.

A. P. HERBERT, *Mild and Bitter, 1936*

---

*If you have never golfed, I reckon you are missing
the best thing in life.* MAX FAULKNER

St Andrews

In writing of some celebrated golf links, there is one point which is
happily and incontestably settled for us – namely, with which we
should commence. The links of St Andrews – of the Royal and
Ancient Golf Club of the East Neuk of Fife – holds premier place as
indubitably as Lord's Ground in the kingdom of cricket. When two
stranger golfers meet upon some neutral ground, one of the first
questions that will pass from one to the other will most certainly be,
'Have you been to St Andrews?' – and should the answer be in the
negative, the questioner will immediately deem himself justified in
assuming a tone of patronage which the other will feel he has no right
to resent.

All the great mass of golfing history and tradition – principally,
perhaps, the latter – clusters lovingly within sight of the grey towers
of the old University town; and, to most, the very name St Andrews
calls to mind not a saint nor a city, nor a castle nor a University, but a
beautiful stretch of green links with a little burn, which traps golf
balls, and bunkers artfully planted to try the golfer's soul.

This is the great excellence of St Andrews links – the artful
planting of the bunkers. Not, of course, that they were planted by
any but Nature's hand; but planted by nature, one would say, with
an obvious artistic eye for the golfer's edification. Just around each
hole they lie in wait for the unwary and unskilful; and, along the
course, just in such ambushes as to catch the ball that is not driven
both far and sure. Kind Nature, too, has so laid out the ground that
the holes can be, and are, placed at such distances from each other

that every stroke tells – that is to say, that whereas at most links the majority of the holes are approachable with one or two full shots followed by an iron shot, at St Andrews the majority of holes are so disposed that they may be reached with two, or maybe three, real good drives. And the advantage of this, from the golfer's point of view, is that, whereas, in a hole at which an iron approach necessarily follows upon two good drives, the bungler who has foozled one of these drives may make up for it by taking a somewhat longer club for the approach shot than his opponent, and may be on the green in three, equally with the man who has played faultless golf; at St Andrews, on the other hand, a weak or foozly drive means, in very many instances, a full shot lost – the two faultless drives will send the ball up on to the green, while the player who has foozled a shot will suffer his salutory and inevitable punishment in not being on the green in less than three.

The great point in which we are inclined to quarrel with St Andrews as a golfing links is in the prevalence of banks and braes. Many of them one may avoid, but there are others so small, or so disposed, that it is the better wisdom to play to chance them, and it is very trying to the temper to see your adversary lying beautifully, a few yards back, while your own somewhat better drive has finished up hard under a brae, hopeless for any club other than an iron. Yet it probably comes all right in the long run. At the end of the round luck has probably equalised itself. It is true that the St Andrews links are much cut up by iron wounds. With the enormous amount of play which goes on during the autumn it is wonderful that they are not more so. Indeed a ground of more strictly golfing quality – *i.e.* of more sandy nature – would never stand the wear and tear to which St Andrews is subjected; but after all to a really first-class golfer a cuppy lie is of very little consequence.

Some of the putting-greens are not what they should be – notably the 'heathery hole' and the end hole – but others, again, are things of beauty. The green of the 'hole o' cross' is probably the best in all the world of golf. The eleventh hole – the 'short hole coming in' – and 'the road hole' – the seventeenth hole – are two very crucial tests – the two points in the course where more chances of medals have been ruined than at any others. The short hole coming in is, we may say, on a calm day, but a cleek shot; but such a nervous one! There is the shelly bunker ten yards to the left of the hole – the Eden river fifteen yards beyond it – and that little round trap of a Strath's bunker not three yards nearer you and to the right of it, with all the ground breaking in toward the bunker! Many a stout-hearted golfer, if his score is good, will take his light iron and play a half shot to the left, and short, giving himself a clear run up for his next – and many more would have done better had they done so; but never, in a scoring round, play it how you will, will the stoutest-hearted fail to draw a breath of relief when that slantwise-lying little catchy hole is over. Then we may go on, sailing and slogging, till, steering along beside the railway, we have accomplished the 'corner of the Dyke,' and are coming to that dreaded seventeenth – so near the end, and so dangerous! For after we have piloted our way through, or round, or over the corner of the wall enclosing the Station-master's garden, and the little bunker on the left, and have turned up towards the right, with our seconds, then we see that little Garden of Eden – very different from the river so called – where the hole, is, lying between Scylla and Charybdis (a dread vision such as may excuse any anachronism in our similes!), that horrid little round bunker to one side of it, and that hopeless hard road on the other. And the canny golfer we see approaching it in instalments, and the bold spirit, taking his fate in his hand, going for glory or the grave.

After that, the last hole is child's play. As long as we do not make an egregious top into the burn, or an equally egregious slice into a kitchen area of one of the houses on the links, we may go forward undeterred, and finish our medal round beneath the Club windows and the blessing of old Tom Morris, the guardian angel of the last hole.

And all the world is watching to see us do it! Yes, call it folly, vanity, what you will, it is this that lends to golf at St Andrews half its pleasure – the feeling that you are doing the right thing, the thing that has been the great absorbing interest of the whole atmosphere for years, the thing that is the great local interest of to-day. It makes a difference; and St Andrews is devoted to golf as no other place in the world is. The very houses and streets are called by names derived from the game. It is hard to believe but that the limbs of St Andrew's cross have sprouted into golf clubs.

HORACE HUTCHINSON, *The Badminton Library, 1890*

18 of the Best
St Andrews Old Course

At least one respected historian claims that golf was invented by students at St Andrews University and that the game started on the Old Course. Others have fuelled the legend of St Andrews as the birthplace of golf, but repeated assertions do not add up to an historical truth. It is all conjecture and speculation for there is not one item of evidence to support the claim. As for educated guesses, the best one looks to be the notion that golf was brought to Scotland from Holland, either by returning Scottish officers or by the Dutch merchants whose ships visited St Andrews regularly and who had to carry their wares over the linksland to the city from the harbour in the Eden estuary.

It does not matter. St Andrews enjoys a unique place in golf and has no need of claims, spurious or otherwise, to represent its origins. Five hundred years ago golf was a rudimentary and formless pastime and the distinction of developing the game, and continuing to regulate it, belongs to St Andrews and its Royal and Ancient golf club.

Visitors come to St Andrews with the reverential air of pilgrims and they tend to gaze in awe across the links and imagine that this is how it all began, unchanged since the days of King James II. Here stood the archery butts where the townsmen were obliged to practice once a week in order to maintain a citizen's army against the invading English. And here the locals preferred to play golf, neglecting their archery to the point that the game had to be banned by royal decree. Alas for fancy, the rolling duneland selected for such speculation was under the sea at that time.

A succession of sea walls has won most of the linksland within the last 150 years. The original common land along the foreshore was a narrow strip used by the community for a variety of purposes. Women hung their linen on the whins to bleach, men hunted rabbits or played football. The golfers had to negotiate these unusual hazards as they played out to the end of the links and then retraced their steps, playing the same holes in reverse direction. Only as the city fathers built embankments to reclaim the foreshore was it possible for golf to develop into the form we know it today, with separate fairways for each hole (although still communal greens in most cases on the Old Course).

One feature which puzzles visitors is the apparently haphazard siting of the myriad of bunkers, some of them only a few yards from the tee. That, say the knowing ones, is because they were originally made by sheep, shallow depressions scraped out to provide shelter from the North Sea winds. Such may indeed be the origin of bunkers – although wind erosion creates bunkers quite naturally in sandy country – but it does not explain their siting in the Old Course. Most are man made, or have had their original position ratified by man. The reason there are so many of them, many with individual names, and often in unlikely places, is that it used to be the regular practice to reverse the direction of play to save wear on the course. If you imagine yourself to be playing the course the wrong way round, from first tee to seventeenth green and so on, then those improbable bunkers take on a valid significance.

A number of technical advances (the gutta percha ball, hand forged iron clubs, rubber-core ball, steel shafts) changed the character of golf but none more so than the invention of mechanical grass mowers. These machines introduced putting as a fine art and it is from this era that the influence of the Old Course has been most marked.

Every golf course in the world owes something to the Old Course for, either by accident or design, it embodies every feature and architectural trick. Course builders have studied and analysed the Old Course and have been inspired to reproduce the elements to be found here, seeking not to create an exact replica (although that has been tried as well) but to copy the golfing challenges. In that sense the Old Course can be called the mother of golf and what a subtle, beguiling, exasperating and endearing old harridan she is, to be sure. Her mood changes with each shift of the wind. Men have devoted their lives to the Old Course, playing twice a day, rain or shine, until the day they died. Even then they have not exhausted her secrets, her whims and her tempers.

Augusta National

The best way to build a golf course is to start two hundred years ago. When Bobby Jones withdrew from serious competition he had just such an opportunity. He had recruited some friends to form a club and finance the creation of a course and he had a precise idea of the kind of site he wanted. It must be on undulating country, not so flat as to lack interest and not so hilly as to involve steep climbs. And it must be beautiful, for Jones insisted that golf was a game to be enjoyed and attractive scenery was an essential ingredient in the recipe for the pleasure of golf.

At Augusta he found just the place. On his first visit he stood on the spot which is now the practice putting green and looked out over the property. 'Perfect! And to think this ground has been lying here all these years waiting for someone to come along and lay a golf course on it.'

The ground in question had once been an indigo plantation. Then, in 1857, an emigre Belgian, Baron Louis Mathieu Edouard Berkmans, had turned it into a nursery for trees and shrubs. Each hole at Augusta is named for one of the original nursery stock: Tea Olive, Pink Dogwood, Flowering Peach, Flowering Crab Apple, Magnolia, Juniper, Pampas Grass, Yellow Jasmine, Carolina Cherry, Camellia, White Dogwood, Golden Bell, Azalea, Chinese Fir, Firethorn, Redbud, Nandina and Holly.

Jones invited the Scottish architect Dr Alister Mackenzie to help him with the work. It was a wise choice for both men shared similar ideas about the nature of golf. These may be expressed in two broad precepts: that the golf should be fitted to the land, leaving it as natural and untouched as possible; and that golf should be enjoyable for everyone, good and bad player alike.

Golfers do not want to have their games spoiled by searching for balls, or to be faced with gargantuan carries. By the same token, a bad shot often penalises itself; there is no need to build bunkers 100 yards in front of the tee. At the same time a course must present a severe challenge to the good player who seeks to beat par. The genius of Augusta lies in the compromise between these apparently contradictory concepts. Most of the fairways are 75 yards wide, more than three times the width which the United States Golf Association decrees for fairways in the United States Open championship. And if you should miss a fairway you can easily find your ball, often lying on a bed of needles fallen from the massive Georgia pines. Likewise, the greens are generous in size and so it is comparatively easy to reach your destination in the prescribed number of shots. However, if you are seeking a birdie, it is not good enough simply to be on the green, for these are putting areas of tantalising complexity. It is a feat of infinite skill and judgment to find that 4¼-inch hole from the edge. And for practical purposes (disregarding outrageous luck) the only way to create a birdie chance is to stop your ball close to the hole and below it. Thanks to the wise cunning of Jones and Mackenzie the only way to put your ball in this prime position is to play a shot of a certain type from a certain place on the fairway. Thus the golfer must know the position of the flag as he plans his tee shot and the challenge of each hole starts not with the drive but with the problem of where to drive. The target area may be no bigger than a tennis court and it may call for a controlled fade or draw, high or low, to find it.

No other golf course in the world so completely meets the true specifications of the game as an exercise first in thought, a severe mental challenge which is quite beyond some outstanding strikers of the golf ball, and secondly in execution.

When Augusta was being built they made two interesting discoveries. The site of the twelfth green, one of the most celebrated short holes in golf with its hump-backed green set hard against a bend in Rae's creek, was an old Indian burial ground. The wind funneling through the avenues of pines swirls capriciously over this green, leading the fanciful to believe that the spirits are angry at being disturbed by golfers. And in Rae's creek they struck gold, ore which in 1930 was not considered to be commercially viable. One day, no doubt, as the metal becomes scarcer, it may prove a worthwhile proposition to dig for it. Augusta National is one course where a true sense of values demands that the precious metal is left undisturbed under the even more precious real estate which covers it.

Gleneagles

Towns and countries do not always live up to their publicity. The world forms an impression of a place from songs and romanticised literature and often the visitor is disappointed by the reality. Catch it in a bad mood and Copenhagen can be anything but wonderful, wonderful. Switzerland is not all cuckoo clocks and edelweiss, nor Holland a vast carpet of waving tulips.

Scotland has been well served by its image makers. It is bonny, it is Landseer's Stag at Bay, it is hauntingly beautiful with morning mists o'er the glen, it is haggis and whisky, it is dour men in kilts, it is bagpipes, it is lassies doing the sword dance, it is gowff.

Wealthy visitors to Scotland who make Gleneagles their first stop are not disappointed. It is everything that mythology suggested about Scotland; Gleneagles makes sure of that. There is a distinct air of forced Scottishness about the luxury hotel and this even extends to the two 18-hole golf courses in the form of whimsical names for each hole, such as Whaup's Nest and De'il's Creel. Most visitors lap it up.

There is even some discord about the name, Gleneagles. The hotel's version is Glen of Eagles, and the official emblem is an eagle, but some people opt for a mediaeval French origin of the name, Glen d'Eglise, and point in corroboration to a small church in the distant valley.

None of this need affect the golf, of course, which on a fine day is nothing short of magnificent. The setting is the foothills of the Grampians and the terrain is steeply undulating, mountains in miniature with the fairways sweeping up hill and down dale and winding through valleys.

Of the two original 18-hole courses (a third was added in 1980) the King's is the sterner test but the whole point of golf at Gleneagles is to revel in the beauty of the surroundings and in this respect the Queens is in no way inferior. There is a feeling of spaciousness about the place, both in the uninterrupted views across the valley to the blue-tinted foothills and on the courses themselves, with each hole separated from its neighbour by acres of wild heather, whin, bracken, broom and wild flowers. At times, when the match is not too desperately important, it is a pleasure to tramp across that superb moorland in search of a wayward golf ball.

For those in pursuit of serious sport the courses are on the short side, especially as the turf gives a flattering roll to the ball, but the design is nothing if not sporty. James Braid overlaid his genius on land which might have been specially ordained by nature for the enjoyment of golfers and so this is the antithesis of target golf. Here you must read the slopes and use them to get your ball close to the hole. Neglect this preliminary, or allow your ball to stray from the correct line, even by a small margin, and you may see it swing the wrong way, to be gathered up by bunker cunningly sited to administer its reprimand.

At Gleneagles there is a high proportion of shots which carry a strong charge of special invitation. Every golfer will recognise what I mean by an inviting shot. You survey the scene ahead and enjoy a feeling of exhilaration. You itch to get your hands on a club; you feel strong and confident. Jack Nicklaus is one architect who well recognises the value of this feeling, and how to provide holes which inspire it. The easiest way is to play from a greatly elevated tee into a broad valley and thus create the subconscious notion that a well struck ball will fly vast distances.

A good architect uses this illusion as a trap. Having selected a site which induces this feeling of well-being, he then employs all his guile to thwart the unthinking player. Perhaps he will contrive that the second shot will be exceptionally difficult unless that carefree drive finds a precise area on the fairway, a trick which finds its finest expression at Augusta National.

On the whole, however, the visitor to Gleneagles will normally play above his usual standard and come away enchanted by his experience.

Oakmont

In the rules of golf a bunker is defined as a hazard and that is the only clue to the purpose of a bunker. It should, clearly, involve risk; the golfer who hits his ball into a bunker should be embarking on a hazardous enterprise as he reaches with thumping pulse for his niblick. In modern golf there is a tendency, much fostered by tournament professionals, to eliminate the hazardous essence of bunkers. Sand should be selected for its special properties of providing a lie from which recovery shots can be played with maximum facility; it should be allowed to compact for months before an important tournament and every irregularity in its surface must be raked smooth, under pain of dire penalties from the Professional Golfers' Association, so that players in the following matches shall have optimum conditions on which to wield their broad-soled sand irons. Specialist sand players, such as Gary Player, frequently direct their shots deliberately into bunkers because they are confident of playing a more precise stroke than, say, from short semi-rough. Oakmont scorns such permissive flouting of the true purpose of hazards.

Golfers who like to see courses in human terms would probably recognise in Oakmont an elder of the kirk, breathing hellfire and damnation from his pulpit and exhorting his trembling flock in a voice of thunder not to stray from the narrow and rocky path of Old

Testament virtue. Hard packed sand? Sacrilege! A good lie in a bunker? Profanity! At Oakmont the doctrine of the hazardous hazard has the force of holy writ.

Oakmont has no truck with such fripperies as beauty; golf is far too important for such distractions. It is irrelevant that a highway slices through the centre of this austere course near Pittsburgh. Golf is not for pleasure; it is an exercise in rectitude, unswerving devotion and virtue being its own reward. Wretched hedonists who approach Oakmont with a disregard for the solemn piety of the exercise, perhaps – ye Gods! – even remarking to each other: 'Let's go out and have fun', are soon chastised for their irreverence. They are accursed and, as often as not, depart cursing.

When Oakmont was built just after the turn of the century it had nearly 250 bunkers although a regrettable laxity among later trustees of this shrine to high moral purpose reduced the number by a handful.

And what bunkers they are, vast pits of sand which are daily ploughed with a specially designed mechanical rake which leaves furrows two inches deep. The iniquitous golfer who strays from the fairway gets his due deserts and, on the principle that suffering is good for the soul, emerges a better person. At the very least he emerges as a more careful golfer. Perhaps he may not emerge at all in the sense of retaining his competitive life because between the third and fourth fairways lies a hazard of diabolical severity. It is a vast expanse of sand, furrow-raked of course, with seven symmetrical ridges of turf about 18 inches high running from side to side at regular intervals, giving it the name of the Church Pews. If your ball plugs into the face of one of these ridges you may well be faced with the sole option of blasting with all your might at a ball and trying to direct it in exactly the opposite direction to your preferred line of play. Serves you right!

Oakmont is not content with having the most terrifying bunkers in the world. In the same spirit it goes in for par-fours which are only yards short of being par-fives, and par-threes which are at the limit of the average golfer's Sunday Special with the driver. Having reached the green the golfer's troubles are only just beginning. The greens are vast but this is not a measure of generosity. Quite the reverse. The purpose of their size is to provide maximum scope for taking three, four, five or six putts because they are notoriously the hardest, least receptive and fastest greens in the United States. They are shaven like a monk's tonsure and the areas round the cups are polished, or so it seems. Actually they are mown even closer, the aim being to produce that sickening illusion of a putt actually accelerating as it reaches the hole and rolling way, way past.

Naturally, the United States Golf Association reveres Oakmont and has selected it for the US Open on many occasions. Ben Hogan, the most accurate striker of modern golf, won in 1953 with a score one under par. Jack Nicklaus beat Arnold Palmer in a play-off for the 1962 Open with par golf. Then came the event which scandalised the high priests of Oakmont. In the 1973 Open a mighty thunderstorm was visited upon Oakmont, possibly as punishment for sinfully allowing the USGA to smooth the bunker sand. On a drenched and holding course, and playing well down the field with none of the pressures of contention, Johnny Miller went round in 63 to win. It was unprecedented, impossible even. But it happened.

Muirfield

It is impossible to state with certainty that the honourable Company of Edinburgh Golfers was Scotland's first golf club. The golf historian is thwarted in determing primacy by consideration of defining what constitutes a club and by the masonic nature of those early associations, with their practice of destroying minute books lest the secrets and ritual be revealed to outsiders.

However, the Honourable Company is the world's oldest club so far as surviving records are concerned, as opposed to vague references to earlier dates of institution, and it certainly led the way in shaping the structure of golf and golf clubs as we know them today. It pioneered open competition when it petitioned the city fathers of Edinburgh to provide a silver club for annual contest at Leith in 1744; its written rules remain the earliest surviving code for the proper playing of golf; and it promoted the first 72-hole Open championship.

That was in 1892 and by then the Honourable Company had outgrown two courses, moving first from Leith to Musselburgh and then to its present site on the Firth of Forth under the lee of Gullane Hill. Andra Kirkaldy, a prominent professional of the day, did not care for the new course at Muirfield. Kirkaldy was noted for his capacity to produce a breath-taking insult, which in Scotland passes for wit, and he castigated Muirfield as 'nothing but an auld watter meddie'. Thus began a tradition which endures to this day of professional golfers making pronouncements of stunning ignorance, misjudgment and vulgarity.

In fact Muirfield represents one area of common ground, perhaps the only one, where traditionalists and modernists can meet and agree that this is a superb golf course.

It is undeniably links golf, for the most part on undulating country rather than precipitous dunes, and it has all the virtues of links golf such as inviting fairway lies, remoteness, magnificent seascapes and keen greens. At the same time, the design is as fair as human ingenuity can devise, with only one blind shot on the course. The challenge is squarely presented to the golfer and what a challenge it is when the wind blows off the sea, as it mostly does.

Although Harold Hilton the Liverpool amateur won the first Muirfield Open, the course has always represented for me the decisive test for separating the good amateur from the good professional. To score well at Muirfield it is not enough to drive the ball straight and true. The pot bunkers, beautifully faced with terraced turf faces, are small by modern Sahara standards but their size is deceptive for they have subtle catchment areas which gather a shot which is not well shaped.

Muirfield's long history is rich in battle honours of the great players such as Vardon, Braid and Cotton but nothing surely can compare with the drama of the 1972 Open championship. Lee Trevino seemed marked for destiny that week because he had holed out with two bunker shots on his way to challenging for the title on the final day. However, after 16 holes Tony Jacklin had the initiative and was headed, as it seemed, for his second Open championship. At the seventeenth he safely found the green with his approach while Trevino faded his approach into a fearsome lie on a downslope wide of the green.

Trevino admitted afterwards that at this point he mentally conceded the championship to Jacklin. However, he had to play out the round and this required the formality of making a few more strokes.

Had he been concentrating fiercely on the shot under the burden of contention it would have been a terrifying stroke. As it was, relieved of all pressure under his assumed role as playing attendant to the conquering hero, he played a relaxed swing with the nonchalance of a practice swing. To his delight and astonishment the result was perfect and the ball ran into the cup. To Jacklin this outcome was a devastating blow. He was so shaken that he three-putted and he went one behind. He marched quickly to the tee, his face like granite in both colour and rigidity.

Trevino's fierce professionalism now returned. He took his time in sauntering to the last tee in order that the crowd could settle and he would be able to follow his favourite practice of pegging up his ball and hitting without delay. It helped, of course, to leave Jacklin fuming with frustration and disappointment for a few extra moments. Trevino played the last hole with copybook precision and Jacklin blundered from rough to bunker. He was never quite the same player again.

Pebble Beach

The ultimate accolade for an American golf course is that the United States Golf Association should confirm its status by taking the US Open championship back for a second time. That honour was conferred on Pebble Beach in 1982 and put the official seal of greatness on a course which had enjoyed international renown for many years.

Pebble Beach lies on Carmel Bay on the Monterey peninsula, just a mile along the coast from Cypress Point. With Spyglass Hill and the Monterey country club also a few miles further along the coast, this corner of California must boast the richest concentration of outstanding courses in the world, with just the possibility of a counter-claim from the sand belt of Melbourne.

Each course has a distinct character, and separate appeals, and Pebble Beach's special virtues are the strength of its closing holes and a string of highly demanding holes in the middle of the round. For many years this has been the magnificent setting for the climax of the Bing Crosby national pro-am in January, a time when the weather can almost be guaranteed to intervene with turbulent fury. The spectacle of America's finest professionals battling the elemental fates against a backdrop of a foaming Pacific ocean has become one of the nation's sporting rites.

The first few holes give no hint of the shocks ahead. You start in conventional American country club country, on sheltered fairways bordered by trees and the trim villas of millionaires. You may think the course difficult enough, because the undulating greens are small and viciously fast, calling for the combination of sureness and delicacy which marks the good putter. As you trudge up the steep rise to the sixth green perched on top of the cliffs you may well revise your opinion that the golf has been difficult so far. Gazing along the string of clifftop holes you realise that the real Inquisition of Pebble Beach is about to begin, with a fearsome array of thumb-screw, rack and white hot needles.

141

On preliminary scanning of the card you might have assumed that the seventh, at a mere 120 yards, was one of those fill-in holes which the architect had provided to make up the numbers because he did not have enough land to make a 'proper' hole. The reality is frightening. From the elevated tee you look down on an emerald set in a cluster of garnets, a minute green surrounded by bunkers, with the cliff falling away on two sides and the inland borders hardly less inviting. You have to find that target, that's all there is to it. So what is so difficult about hitting a wedge into a small green? The problem is that this is about the most exposed place on the course and as you struggle to keep your balance in the blasting wind you may conclude, like thousands of golfers before you, that you need a full wood to make the distance. Even in relative calm the canny player will probably decide on a punched 7-iron for precision.

Assuming that you have not shredded the card and decided to play out the course just for fun, the eighth bears down a little harder because now you have two challenging shots, a drive which must be kept short of a chasm which splits the fairway, followed by a booming second which must carry at least 180 yards if you are to have any chance of seeing your ball again. The demand for length and precision increases on the 9th and 10th until, with relief, you turn inland again. It may take some time to regain your equilibrium and you will need to have your wits about you as you come to the 17th, a long par-three to a green built on the rocky beach. The green is shallow and kidney-shaped, and you must hit the right sector or you face the unusual prospect of having to pitch from one end of the green over rocks to the flag. It was here in the 1972 US Open that Jack Nicklaus cracked a full 1-iron into the gale and his ball hit the flag with resounding clang and dropped to the side of the hole. That shot set him up for a unique American record, winning an Open as well as an Amateur championship on the same course. That is getting ahead of the story for there is nothing of a formality about the 18th, a par-five which follows the sweep of the bay, with watery disaster to the left, out-of-bounds to the right and two large pine trees slap in the middle of the fairway at driving length. This is a hole where you need a three-stroke cushion for comfort for treachery lurks on every inch of its 540 yards.

Turnberry

The problem with writing about links courses is that what may very well be true today is almost certainly poppycock tomorrow and questionable the next day. There are in fact two courses, the whin-lined Arran and the mighty Ailsa which is what everyone means when he speaks of Turnberry. On a fine, still day the golfer whose game is under reasonable control might well wonder what all the fuss was about as he played the first five holes. They are pleasant enough holes, and the views of distant Arran and the Mull of Kintyre, with the rock of Ailsa Craig in sharper focus in the foreground, are magnificent. But the golf, you may think, is not all that difficult.

The next day that opinion is likely to need drastic revision for when the wind whips in from the sea those opening five holes change character as if under the influence of Dr Jekyll's potion. And by some freak of geography the weather at Turnberry can achieve a ferocity quite outside the normal experience of the British Isles.

Rain or shine, calm or turbulent, Turnberry shows its mettle when you reach the short sixth, a long par-three across a valley to a green guarded by tumbling dunes and bunkers of such severity that a three looms like a triumph. Now Mackenzie Ross, the architect who restored Turnberry after its wartime duty as an airfield, really begins to show his hand. The drive at the seventh must be played across a wilderness of wild rough to a fairway cutting obliquely across the line of the shot, tempting the golfer to bite off more than he can chew. This is one of the oldest stratagems in the golf course architect's bag of trickery and nowhere is it employed with more subtlety. The eighth has more pitfalls for the unwary and then, just as the golfer has acquired a deep respect for the course and lost some of that false confidence in his own abilities, he is confronted by Bruce's Castle. It is an ordeal just to walk along the pathway which, to sensitive folk, narrows to the dimensions of a tightrope, and leads to the back tee, perched on a rock with the sea boiling below. One professional could only reach the tee by being blind-folded and lead by the hand. From a purely golfing point of view the prospect is no less daunting for the shot must be played across the corner of a rocky bay, spelling disaster for a hooked shot, to a hog's back fairway which will shrug off a misdirected shot into sundry horrors right and left.

There is more of the same to come, not quite so intimidating, perhaps, but with undiminished potential for drama. Then, with relief, the golfer turns inland and the pressure is reduced, finishing with the anti-climax of an undistinguished last hole.

An international professional tournament brought Turnberry to wide public attention because the only date which the sponsor could be given in a busy calendar was the week of the autumn equinox.

Those tournaments produced horrendous golf. Hurricanes, rain and hail storms brought tents crashing and the world's finest players battled to break 80.

The weather was fine in July of the long, hot summer of 1977 when Turnberry had its first Open championship. The rough was parched to impotence, eliminating the course's first line of defence. The intrinsic merit of the design was enough to cause severe problems for most of the field but two men, Jack Nicklaus and Tom Watson, undoubtedly the world's two best golfers of the day, led at the halfway stage. They were thus paired together and the Open became in effect a match. The match-play element turned the 1977 Open into the greatest championship of all time.

Battling head to head the two titans turned the championship into a gladiatorial contest, inspiring each other to produce golf of a lifetime. Both were round in 65 and so the duel continued on the last day. Again and again a Nicklaus thrust was countered by a Watson counter-thrust until Nicklaus made his first mistake in 36 holes. The birdie which was his by right of power and putter eluded him at the 71st hole and Watson was ahead by a single stroke for the first time.

At the last Nicklaus saw his drive run over the fairway among whins, with Watson safely on the fairway. Nicklaus fashioned a masterly recovery which put him just off the back of the green and Watson lofted a superb approach to within four feet of the flag. There has never been a golfer with Nicklaus's ability to will the ball into the hole in times of crisis and down it went for a birdie and a 66. Watson, who had proved himself to be no less doughty a scrapper, coolly holed his putt for a 65 and the championship.

Pine Valley

There is room on this earth for one Pine Valley just as there is a place in the entertainment industry for the horror film, the ghost train and the chamber of horrors. Here is the ultimate expression of sado-masochistic golf, the supreme example of the penal school of architecture.

A Philadelphia businessman, George Crump, conceived the idea, possibly during a nightmare, and he cast around for a suitable site to put his diabolical plan into action. Near the border of New Jersey and Pennsylvania he found the perfect spot, a wasteland of scrub and sand and pine. The modern developer's approach to such a place would be to demand a budget running into millions and then bring in an armoured corps of bulldozers and graders to mould the landscape before carpeting it wall to wall with emerald turf.

Crump's notions were quite the reverse. His fiendish scheme was to preserve this stricken wilderness as closely as possible, increasing the devastation where necessary to make it even less hospitable to golfers. He would build a tee but he would have no truck with wide ribbons of fairway. Instead he would prepare a small island of turf among the sandy wastes to which the golfer could direct his drive. Then he would select a particularly God-forsaken area of cratered sand and build a small green in the middle of it. He made no concessions to the weak and the wayward; they must suffer for their infirmities.

Wherever he saw the opportunity he introduced special difficulties which nature had overlooked. On the par fives he clipped the wings of the big hitters by restricting the length of his landing areas, making it impossible for anyone to get home in two strokes. He well understood the psychological effect on a golfer of water and used a pond and stream with telling effect.

Look at a plan of Pine Valley and measure the target areas and you will be forced to agree that they are theoretically within the scope of a reasonably accomplished striker. But on a plan, of course, you get no idea of the brain-washing effect of the horrendous penalties for missing a shot. Just as prisoners break down at the sight of the torturer oiling his thumb screws and testing his electrodes, so the golfer who runs the gauntlet at Pine Valley loses his nerve just waiting for the moment when he hits a loose shot and runs up a score of double figures. The normal condition of the first time visitor at the end of his ordeal is not unlike shell shock. One hot-shot amateur started birdie, eagle, hole-in-one, birdie and, since this opening loop brought him back to the club-house, popped in for a bracer before tackling the formidable fifth. The prospect of facing the fifth, one of the most demanding par-threes in America, followed by the mounting difficulties to follow, so preyed on his mind that he decided to stay safely in the bar.

Suffering is supposed to be good for the soul and certainly a round at Pine Valley is a salutory experience for anyone foolish enough to believe that he has conquered the game of golf. The only player who ever got the better of Pine Valley at the first attempt was Arnold Palmer. He had just turned professional and his parents had watched him fail to qualify in his first tournament. The reason was clear enough; Palmer's mind was not on the golf because he was in love. Deacon Palmer growled at his son: 'You had better marry the girl and get it over.' It was sound advice but there was one snag: Palmer was flat broke. Palmer's solution to this problem was typically Palmeresque; he struck bets with some friends that he would challenge the legend: 'Nobody breaks 80 at Pine Valley at the first try.'

The deal was that Palmer would get 100 dollars for every stroke he scored under par, and would pay 100 dollars for every stroke he was over par. Desperation sharpened his wits, for he was in no position to pay out a nickel, and his boldness was rewarded. He went round in 68, married on the profits and lived happily ever after.

Sunningdale

There is an unfortunate attitude among many club golfers that low scores are a reflection on the quality of their course. When professional tournaments are in the offing, committee members determine that 'the pros won't make a fool of our course' and to this fatuous end all manner of adjustments are made. To foil the experts, the rough is encouraged to encroach into the fairways, new tees are built to stretch holes beyond the scope designed by the architect and collars of thick grass are grown around the greens.

Anyone with a true appreciation of the game of golf realises that low scores are a compliment to the condition of the course. Indeed it might be held to be a basic truth of golf that one of the factors separating good courses from bad ones is that a good course will yield low scores to great golf. It would be all too easy to build a course on which scores in the mid-sixties were impossible, just as it is possible to prepare any course in such a way as to preclude any possibility of a low score.

Sunningdale Old is a good course, by this or any other standard. It was designed by Willie Park at the turn of the century on the Surrey heathland of birch, pine and heather, with a base of silver sand, and if it now seems slightly old fashioned because of a few blind shots we can forgive these blemishes because of the overall excellence of the golf. It is on the short side by championship standards and the words which most readily come to mind to describe the golf are subtlety and delicacy. Arthur Lees, the canny Yorkshireman who was the professional at Sunningdale for many years, epitomised Sunning-dale with his short but deadly game and educated hands which could fashion every shape of shot.

146

Sunningdale ranks as one of the premier clubs of England and it has never stooped to tricking up the course for major competition. It is difficult enough in all conscience and also hauntingly beautiful. There are few more exhilarating sights than the view from the high 10th tee across an inviting valley, with the fairway rising to the wooded horizon. Behind the green, discreetly camouflaged but never out of mind, even if out of sight, is the halfway house where the grateful golfer can refresh the inner man. If there is one hole in England which fantasists would like to take with them into banishment on a desert island it must be the tenth at Sunningdale.

Bobby Jones wished that he could take the entire course back with him to America. He did in fact take back cherished memories of Sunningdale and incorporated many of them in Augusta National. His enchantment was enhanced by his experience in the Open championship qualifying round of 1926. He played what has often been described (mistakenly) as the perfect round of golf, 33 shots and 33 putts for a highly satisfying 66. There have been many other notable rounds on the Old, a devastating 63 by Norman von Nida to clinch the Dunlop Masters and later a 64 by Gary Player to set the young South African off on his illustrious career. Sunningdale did not regard these scores as affronts but accepted them as confirmation of the rare skills of the golfers.

Within the club there is a faction which holds that the New course, designed by Harry Colt and added in the twenties, is the superior course. This is by no means an eccentric view, for the New, with its combination of richly wooded and open heathland holes, is also superb in its own way. It is different but hardly inferior to its famous companion and the Sunningdale club is indeed doubly blessed in the quality and variety of its golf.

Cypress Point

The language of golf is over generous. By common usage the word 'great' is applied indiscriminately to courses, players, shots, scores and club sandwiches which are noticeably above average, with the result that when we are confronted by genuine greatness we have no words left in the lexicon with enough impact to express ourselves. Great has been debased to the point where it may be promiscuously applied to a long par-four on a municipal course with a small green. We have to fall back on grunts and ejaculations. Wow! Fan-bloody-tastic! Such responses are inappropriate to Cypress Point for here we are in golf's Sistine Chapel and the masterpiece demands a reverential silence.

Besides, if you became too vocal they would probably run you off the property. It is that kind of club, the *sanctum sanctorum* for well-bred, well-connected, well-heeled, well-accomplished former Rhodes scholars. It is definitely not a club where you turn up in garish Bermuda shorts and demand a green fee ticket and an electric cart. Riff-raff below the social standing of, say, the ambassador of a major power are admitted only once a year, as paying spectators for the Bing Crosby pro-am. Seeing it even in that passive capacity, Cypress Point provides the golfing experience of a lifetime for it is, quite simply, the most beautiful and dramatic course to be found on earth. The coastline of 60-foot rocky cliffs winds acutely to form inlets and promontories and below the Pacific belies its name as it crashes belligerently against this boulder fortress, often throwing up spouts of spray and spume to sprinkle the toiling golfers.

Sea lions bask on sentinel rocks or glide through the heaving mats of kelp and their smaller cousins, the seals, pursue their amorous gambolling in the shallows. Inland the velvet fairways are bordered by shrubs and the gnarled, arthritic Cypress trees spreading their limbs in grotesque shapes and contortions. It would be a golfing Mecca even if the quality of the course itself were undistinguished, simply for the magnificence of the scene. In fact it is a gem to outshine Alister Mackenzie's other masterpieces of Royal Melbourne and the Augusta National. If ever a golf course could be said to have achieved perfection in combining scenery and golfing merit then this must be it.

The quintessence of Cypress is the 16th, the most photographed hole in the world. A finger of promontory extends some 250 yards into the ocean, just wide enough to accommodate a green and satellite bunkers at the tip. You do not play along this treacherous strip, that would have been altogether too obvious for the subtle mind of Mackenzie. He set the tee on the clifftop so that the shot must be played obliquely, every inch of its 233 yards to be carried across the raging ocean. Fail by a yard to make the carry and your ball strikes the massive cliff and rebounds down among the barking sea lions. In the unlikely event of being too strong then your ball disappears into the sea beyond the green. If you are bold enough, or foolhardy enough, to try this direct route then you must effectively pitch your ball onto a tennis court 240 yards away. Only two holes in one have been recorded here in the fifty-odd years since the course was built, one of them being by Bing Crosby.

Most mortals swallow their pride and flinch from the macho drive, par-three or no par-three. This is a case for a timorous mid-iron on the shortest route to the fairway and then a pitch to the green. Never mind if it adds up to four, that bogey is as satisfying as a birdie and it is a triumph to have escaped relatively unscathed, unlike the professional in the Crosby who doggedly persevered in his attempts to drive the green and ran up a score of 19. There are 17 other holes which are scarcely less demanding on the emotions, nerves, judgment and skill of the player so a round at Cypress is a unique experience.

Royal County Down

Ireland is a land of romance – at least that is how those of us who visit Ireland see it. As a matter of prosaic fact the members of Royal County Down are as hard-nosed and pragmatic as anyone else and their golf is no less cut-throat and down-to-earth than anywhere else. But we who arrive from abroad will have none of it. The romanticised view of Ireland is far too deeply ingrained in us to accept things as they are. We coo with sentimental delight at the sight of a donkey cart and sigh at the sound of a tenor's throbbing 'Danny Boy'.

Royal County Down exactly fits this tourist mood. Here the mountains of Mourne really do sweep down to the sea, and a constant delight they are as sun and shadow constantly change the patterns of purple and green on their heathery slopes. The view, with a magnificent seascape across Dundrum Bay and ranges of massive dunes on the golf course, is half the charm of the golf and it is best to approach the links in a poetic frame of mind. This is no place for fierce concentration on card and pencil and life-or-death struggles to beat your handicap. This is not an examination paper to measure the stature of a golfer; it is an experience to be savoured, to elevate the spirits and touch the soul.

There are too many blind shots for the modern concept of championship golf. The Amateur Championship was played here in 1970, and it made a memorable setting for a match-play event, but the rigours of stroke-play are not best served by the adventurous nature of the course, specially if large cash rewards are at stake.

Fortunately, it is all too easy to succumb to the notion that golf is just a game, a vehicle for enjoyment. Played in that spirit, golf at Royal County Down is exquisite. There is a sensual satisfaction in clipping the ball away off the crisp turf and watching it disappear over a sheer cliff, perhaps to find the fairway, perhaps to drift away into the rough. For once the outcome matters less than the execution of the stroke. Royal County Down is Ireland's answer to Old Prestwick, and much superior in my view. It was built in 1889 when the club was formed and the princely sum of £4 was allotted for Old Tom Morris to complete the work. Changes and refinements were made over the years in accordance with the evolutionary custom of those days until the present design was established in the early years of the century.

Naturally there have been subsequent proposals to modernise the course but these have been resisted. On such occasions the debate centres on whether a classic design should be preserved in the face of improving equipment and the argument rages most fiercely when a great architect's work is involved. Since golf courses are growing entities in a changing world I do not subscribe to the view that such courses are sacrosanct. The object, in my opinion, should be to preserve the stroke values and tactics which the architect conceived and it may well be that physical alterations are needed to achieve this end. In the case of Royal County Down I reserve the right to be inconsistent and add my vote to those of the conservationists who say that the course should not be changed by so much as an extra blade of grass.

This is a living museum of the game, a supreme example of period golf, and should be preserved, specially as it retains as strongly as ever all the challenge a golfer could desire, plus a unique aesthetic appeal.

Pinehurst No 2

The appeal of golf derives from many sources, not least the fact that the game defies simple logic. At every turn the golfer is confronted by paradox. In order to make the ball fly high he must strike it a descending blow; any attempt to scoop the ball into the air will result in its scuttling along the ground. By the same token, in order to hit the ball a long way he must hit it smoothly, with a lazy, languid action; if he seeks extra distance through extra power he is doomed to disappointment. The paradoxical nature of golf extends right back to its origins, to the truism that if you want to build the best golf course you start by acquiring the worst land. In this context that denigrating 'worst' is highly prejudiced, meaning that it has little value to agricultural and development interests. In short, it is cheap. The farmer and the builder may not have a good word to say about sand and because of their contempt sand has earned a bad name. Throughout the ages sand has been type-cast as the geological villain, shifty and impermanent, and its blackened character has been introduced into the language in such expressions as 'Getting sand in the works' or 'Building on a foundation of sand.' Sand's connotations of death (sands of time running out) and disaster (bleached bones in the desert) and starvation (shrivelled crops) mean nothing to the golf course architect. To the course designer earth has no finer prospect than a wilderness of sand dunes on which rudimentary plant life clings to life by a thread. Here is natural drainage; here is cleanliness, here the lack of nutrients is a positive advantage because impoverished turf on sandy soil provides a golfer with the perfect lie for his ball. And, of course, it is easily moved and sculpted by the landscape artist.

A Boston pharmacist named James W. Tufts had a good appreciation of the virtues of sand when he bought a parcel of sandhills in North Carolina for $1 an acre at the end of the last century. Tufts had the idea of building a golf course where his friends and their friends could escape the rigours of the New England winter. The course he built was rudimentary and that might have been the first and last anyone ever heard of Pinehurst but for two fortuitous events. Harry Vardon, the absolute king of golf at that time, played an exhibition match and fired the enthusiasm of the locals by his extraordinary prowess. Soon after, Donald J. Ross took up residence as professional to the new club.

Ross was a Dornoch man, from that original fountain of golfing truth and beauty on the north-east coast of Scotland. He had absorbed the wisdom of Old Tom Morris, who breathed his genius into the redesign of Dornoch. Ross knew how to coax life from arid sand and he was an accomplished player with a full appreciation of stroke-making and how to make the architectural punishment fit the golfing crime. Above all, he had vision, the ability to cast his eye over an unpromising sweep of scrub and transpose it in his mind to fairways and greens.

Pinehurst No. 2 was Ross's architectural baptism. When complete it measured only 5,860 yards but over the years following its completion in 1907 he lengthened and improved it into one of America's acknowledged masterpieces. The quality of Pinehurst No. 2 was quickly recognised and Ross was in great demand to build courses in America and Canada.

151

He stamped his philosophy of golf on his courses, putting the premium on accuracy and stroke-making above length. His greens were on the small side and heavily bunkered and he created courses which made golf a battle of wits no less than a trial of skill.

All those requirements are evident in Pinehurst No. 2 which today measures a majestic 7,028 yards. Sloppy thinking or sloppy striking is severely punished among the gigantic pine trees which border the fairways but the player who has the capacity to identify the optimum target areas, and the skill to hit them, can score well, as evidence the 62 of Hale Irwin.

The other great strength of Ross's approach to design was his belief that the beauty of the surroundings was an integral element in the enjoyment of golf. At Pinehurst No. 2 the golfer strolls through avenues of towering pines, remote from all other human life on the course.

With the creation of Pinehurst No. 2 the resort achieved a nationwide popularity and four generations of the Tufts family have been concerned in extending the golfing facilities, building five more courses for the enjoyment of visitors. Pinehurst is also the home of golf's Hall of Fame.

Royal Birkdale

The links of Royal Birkdale divide the world of golf. Those who adhere to the Pilgrims' Progress school of architecture, insisting that a round of golf should test a man's character as he battles against hidden perils, hold Birkdale in low esteem. It is unfaithful to the links tradition and not fit to be mentioned in the same breath as, say, Old Prestwick. The opposing view of modernists, much influenced by professional golf, claims that golf should be primarily a test of skill, and a fair test at that. For them Birkdale is the greatest of the English championship links. The argument can be encapsulated in the simple incident of a drive directed truly down the middle of a fairway and then being deflected by a hump into the rough. Is that golf? Yes, say the traditionalists in unison, for now the player must summon up those worthy qualities of stoicism, patience and fortitude and shrug off his misfortune with no more than a wry smile. No, say the modernists. If a player has the skill to hit a straight drive he is morally entitled to his due reward of finding the ball on the fairway.

It is specially irksome to traditionalists that Birkdale has the natural endowments of towering dunes to create a course which would try the patience of a saint. But Birkdale is uncompromisingly modern, with the fairways level enough to eliminate rub of the green bounces. Similarly, the greens are not perched on top of dunes, which is where the masochists would have them, but for the most part nestle in the hospitable cleavage between dunes. Above all, you can see what you are at when you play Birkdale. The challenge is squarely presented before you and in all conscience it is challenging enough without the lottery of blind shots.

It is a big, honest, he-man course which calls for accuracy rather than subtlety and also, when the wind blows, healthy power. Some of the carries off the back tee are formidable indeed into the wind and they mostly come at a time when you are least fit for them, at the end of a gruelling round. Like all links courses, the conditions change day by day, often hour by hour, and in its benign moods its length is not a paramount factor. But the need for accuracy never diminishes, for Birkdale is merciless on the wayward. The rough in its natural state is rough enough to satisfy the sadistic impulses of any championship committee but its capacity to wreck a card is compounded tenfold by willow scrub. This is a small and seemingly indestructible shrub, tough enough to resist all but the most violent attempts to extricate a golf ball.

J. H. Taylor and Fred Hawtree redesigned the original course in the early thirties but Birkdale really came into its own after the second world war as a championship course. It enjoys to a degree higher than any other of the championship courses the incidental amenities necessary for a major sporting occasion, such as space for parking and tented villages, easy road access and local hotel facilities. Birkdale has therefore attracted more than its share of great events, the Amateur Championship, English Amateur championship, Walker and Ryder Cup matches and regular Open championships. The history which accrues from these events adds noticeably to the enjoyment of playing Royal Birkdale. Who could suppress a feeling of awe at seeing a plaque in the rough celebrating a titanic recovery shot by Arnold Palmer in the 1961 Open, or fail to be moved by Jack Nicklaus's sporting gesture in conceding to Tony Jacklin a short but eminently missable putt on the last green to tie the result of the 1969 Ryder Cup match?

Then there is the indelible memory of Lee Trevino failing to thread his drive through the dunes at the 17th and nearly dishing his chances in the 1971 Open, with the grinning, hat-doffing Lu Liang Huan almost sneaking home on the post. It was also here that the teenaged Severiano Ballesteros of Spain first gave notice of his coming greatness when he disputed the climax of the 1976 Open shot for thrilling shot with Johnny Miller. The quality and stature of Royal Birkdale will undoubtedly be disputed for years to come but by one test of a golf course, the capacity to inspire exciting and dramatic golf, it has certainly earned its reputation for greatness.

National Golf Links

If anyone is to be nominated as the founding father of American golf then an obvious nominee must be Charles Blair Macdonald who, although not the first to introduce the game into the United States, was certainly the most influential of the pioneers. Macdonald, a mid-westerner with the build and personality of a Sherman tank, became a proficient and fanatical golfer while attending St Andrews University. He believed, not without some justification let it be said, that he was the best player in America and the only golfer who truly appreciated the style and spirit of the game. He managed to get the inaugural national championship declared void on the grounds that he had not won it, an outcome which was proof enough (to him) of the invalid nature of the competition. At the beginning of the century he conceived the ambition to create the world's greatest golf course and to this end he made five visits to Europe, analysing and measuring the most celebrated holes in Britain and taking copious notes. He was equally meticulous about choosing his site, finally settling on 250 acres on the Atlantic coast of Long Island, a hundred miles from New York.

The land, gently undulating and covered with trees and shrub, bore no similarity to the bleak duneland where he had found his inspiration, but Macdonald well appreciated that the essence of a golf hole is not the topography or the geology or the botany but the quality of the golfing challenge. Many visitors to the National who do not share his insight are disappointed when told, for example, that the third hole was inspired by the Alps at Prestwick. 'But it is nothing like it.' Visually it is not, but as the golfer stands on the tee he is beset by the identical problems, which route to select and how to shape the shots.

And so it goes on, the 3rd from Royal St George's, the Redan from North Berwick, the 11th and Road Hole from the Old Course of St Andrews. Homage rather than plagiarism motivated Macdonald in creating the National and he succeeded where many modern architects fail in creating a course which puts a heavy premium on

154

strategic thinking. Every shot presents the golfer with a variety of options and the best striker will not score well at the National unless he first solves the problem of picking out the optimum route, a solution which varies from day to day according to the strength and direction of the sea winds which are rarely less than frisky along this coast. The other virtue which Macdonald displayed in creating his monument was that he was faithful to the landscape, striving always to retain the natural appearance of the site.

The course was opened in 1909 and for once in his life Macdonald revealed a chink in the armour plating of his formidable ego. 'I am not confident that the course is perfect and beyond criticism today.' He continued to tinker with the design, altering bunkers and adjusting the lengths of the holes before he was finally satisfied. At that stage the course measured 6,100 yards and was subsequently extended to 6,745 yards.

Today it would not rank alongside a championship course and the reason, ironically, is because Macdonald sought to make it the ultimate championship course. He took as his inspiration holes which were old fashioned even at the time when he was first captivated by them. Macdonald's design was overtaken by a new golfing philosophy which demanded that the problem be fairly presented in plain view; the blind shot, which used to be regarded as an exciting venture into the unknown, is now an anathema.

For this reason the National has never had a major championship and the only event of stature to be played there was the Walker Cup match of 1922. That was the National's finest hour, at the height of the golden era when Scott Fitzgerald characters arrived in their private yachts to play the course. Something of the grace and flavour of those days lingers on Long Island, one of the last outposts, along with Boston, of that elusive quality of life called style. For this reason a visit to the National is doubly endowed with a time-warp quality of stepping back into a vanished age. That is not to say that there is anything quaint about the National, far from it. To play the course is to engage in a strenuous challenge to a golfer's character and skill in a rare atmosphere of solitude and enchantment. Charles Blair Macdonald may have failed in his objective but time has vindicated him. To refugees from the hustle and bustle of a world obsessed by commerce Macdonald built better than he knew.

Ballybunion

Mood and atmosphere are important to golf and the enchantment of Ireland strongly flavours Irish golf. Nowhere is this appeal more strongly felt than during the approach to Ballybunion, on the Atlantic coast near the mouth of the Shannon. Ballybunion is in a remote corner of Kerry, a county which is rich in remoteness, and so a visit perforce takes on the feeling of an expedition. That helps, of course, for the anticipation of pleasure magnifies the pleasure and with Ballybunion there is no possibility of anti-climax. No matter how high the visitor's expectations may be, titillated by such tributes as the judgment of Herbert Warren Wind, the American writer: 'Very simply, Ballybunion revealed itself to be nothing less than the finest seaside course I have ever seen', the reality comes as a delightful surprise. On very few courses is the golfer in such close involvement with the sea and the spanking winds which go with it. Dunes of majestic proportions, ranking almost as small hills, are cut abruptly by a high, sheer cliff with the Atlantic surf boiling below. On one tee the nervous tension arising from the challenge of holding up your drive in a blasting cross-wind may very well be increased by pangs of vertigo. The cliffs suffered severely from erosion, attacked as they were by wind and rain on the higher levels and by the sea at the base, and seaboard holes were in danger of collapse. Such is the hold of Ballybunion on the affections of the golfing world that an appeal brought donations from every corner of the globe and the cliffs have now been shored up by gabion walls, vast wire baskets filled with rock. The scale of the dunes indicates that the holes for the most part must follow the natural bends of the valleys and this arrangement introduces a premium on precision driving.

The golfer who has been conditioned to a driving philosophy of 'the longer the better' must readjust his ideas because here he is frequently driving to a fairway which runs obliquely to the lie of his shot. Your ball must carry a wilderness of wrist-breaking rough. Too short, and you will find yourself clambering and scrambling over the precipitous dunes and then having to swing like a contortionist in order to apply the club-face to your ball. Too long, and you suffer the chastening experience of watching your beautiful drive run through the fairway to finish in an extravagantly unpromising lie.

Here we have the essence of Ballybunion's appeal. Golf is a game of calculating risks and here the dangers are so horrendous that the satisfactions of success are greatly enriched. Ballybunion turns the screw gently, opening up with a run of five reasonably straightforward inland holes which may lull the visitor into a sense of false confidence. This is not too exacting, he may think, just as generations of golfers have been deceived by the early holes of courses such as Pine Valley and the Old Course at St Andrews. He is a lucky man, or an exceptional golfer, who gets round Ballybunion unscathed if the wind is at all fresh. The last shot of the round is perhaps the one disappointment, for you must pitch to an elevated green over a brow, a blind shot involving a strong element of hit-and-hope for the first time visitor. However the outcome is unlikely to be as expensive as the eight or nine strokes which you may well have expended on one of the holes among the dunes. Holing out on the 18th is not the end of it for golf in Ireland is essentially a 19-hole game. The crack and the jar are an integral part of the round, with a pint of smooth draught Guinness if only for the sake of local ritual.

If the weather is cold then the high priest behind the bar will create an ambrosia involving Irish whiskey, hot water and cloves which will magically restore circulation and morale and send you on your way vowing to return. Robert Trent Jones, the American architect noted for his lavish courses embellished with artificial lakes and ornate bunkering, has designed a second course at Ballybunion. He fell under the spell of the original course and sought to reproduce its unique mood and style.

Merion

If great golf is a reflection of the quality of the course on which it is played, the Merion must be ranked as the premier course in the United States. It was here at Merion, in a suburb of Philadelphia, that Bobby Jones completed the grand slam, that Ben Hogan limped painfully to his finest triumph in the U.S. Open, and where Jack Nicklaus and Lee Trevino disputed one of the classic duels of championship play-offs. Merion has been the stage for much of the modern history of American golf, including the only recorded instance of a championship competitor (Walter Hagen) putting out of bounds.

Merion sprang from curious and unlikely origins. The members of the Merion golf and cricket club wanted a second course which would stand comparison with anything in the country and they selected a young Scottish insurance salesman, Hugh Wilson, to undertake the design. Wilson was sent to Britain to study the great

157

courses and learn the secrets of the black art of design. He proved an apt pupil and returned with a sound grasp of strategy and a philosophical concept of golf as a game of skill rather than brute strength.

The course he built on undulating parkland was, and remains, short, at about 6,500 yards, with only two par-fives and a par of 70. More than any other American course, except perhaps Augusta National, Merion marries putting and striking into an indissoluble union. Every drive and every shot must be planned with the putting in mind and this is both the strength and weakness of the course.

When the small, slick greens are hard they will reject all but the most perfectly struck approaches and woe betide the golfer who leaves his ball above the hole in such conditions. In dry weather, when the course plays the way Wilson conceived it, Merion is the ultimate test in accuracy, placement, control and stroke making.

However, if rain intervenes to soften those greens and fairways, as it did for the 1981 U.S. Open championship, then Merion is prey to any target-golfer who can keep his ball in play. That was one occasion when, apart from the winner, David Graham, Merion failed to bring the cream to the top.

In its fiery mood, a round at Merion resembles a tip-toe through a minefield of cunningly sited bunkers, trees, out-of-bounds roads and creeks and the tension builds as you approach the most demanding finish you could wish for in championship golf. The topographical feature which dominates the finish is a worked out quarry with an almost vertical face. The 16th measures 430 yards and if you get a good drive away you now have to hit a precise, high-flying second and carry it every inch of the way to the green perched on the cliff top. For a handicap golfer it is a terrifying shot, because anything less than perfect contact with the ball results in the direst of penalties.

The 17th is a long par-three, 224 yards, to a green well defended by bunkers and offering only the narrowest of openings. Between them, these two holes have broken many strong men.

The 18th has been immortalised by Hogan. In the 1950 U.S. Open Hogan was still suffering from the effects of the road accident which nearly ended his life. His legs were swathed in bandages and the pain was so excruciating at times that he nearly had to withdraw because he could not walk. He forced himself to continue and came to the last needing a four to tie with Lloyd Mangrum and George Fazio. Hogan fired his drive over the quarry face to the centre of the fairway and was left with a one-iron shot to the moulded green.

158

Those who witnessed that stroke applauded it as one of the finest shots ever played in the championship's history. Hogan himself was not impressed as he watched the ball fly dead straight into the heart of the green. He had intended to impart a hint of fade into the flight of the ball and thereby swing it towards the flag for a possible birdie putt and outright victory. As it was, he had to wait another day for his moment of glory in winning the play-off. He could not have repeated that one-iron shot in the play-off. While he was signing his card a souvenir hunter stole the club from his bag.

Walton Heath

The most important part of a golf course is out of sight under the turf, the infrastructure of drainage and irrigation and the quality of the subsoil. The word 'heath' proclaims the geology, sour gravel and sand which support typical heathland flora of heather, bracken, gorse and silver birch. To the golfer these plants are friends for they represent the finest inland conditions to be found for golf, although that friendship can be sorely tried at times when a wayward shot carries the ball into the wiry heather. The heathlands of Surrey provide many fine courses, the greatest of them being Walton Heath on the fringe of suburbia south of London. The Old course claims many adherents to the view that it is quite simply the best inland course in the British Isles. Herbert Fowler laid out the Old course in 1904 on common land, only the first hole – a teasing par-four of some 300 yards – being on land owned by the club. Then the golfer must cross a public road, possibly the one valid criticism which can be made about Walton Heath. Over the years there have been adjustments, some of them at the suggestion of James Braid who served the club as its professional for 45 years until his death at the age of 80 in 1950. Some further changes were needed to accommodate the loss of the original eighth green to accommodate a motorway. One alteration which I rather regretted eliminated a hillocky band of heather set diagonally across the fairway about 250 yards from the second tee. This presented the golfer with a fine dilemma in his choice of tee shot. If he could summon enough nerve and confidence and skill he could take his driver and direct the ball into a hospitable flat glade at the furthest extreme of that treacherous heather, a prime site known as Braid's corner.

From Braid's corner the approach to the green was invitingly straightforward, with iron, but the fainthearted golfer who laid up short of the heather off the tee was left with a brute of a second, generally with wood off a steeply hanging lie. The triumph and the heartbreak of that magnificent second hole were thoroughly diluted by the building of a new tee and the removal of most of the heather. However there are plenty more opportunities to test the golfer's strategic acumen on the tee.

Many courses reduce the art of driving to routine. No thought is needed, simply a swing which will move the ball forward onto the fairway. At Walton Heath the decision is every bit as important as the execution, with a balanced scale of rewards for the player who can first determine the best target for his tee shot and can then shape the shot to find it. Nowhere is that initial conundrum more complex than on the tee of the 16th hole, surely one of the greatest holes in the world. It measures 499 yards off the medal markers and so in favourable conditions it presents the heady prospect of getting on or near the green with two spanking shots. Now the moment a golfer begins to think in terms of a bit of extra oomph with the driver he naturally goes for a running draw but the fairway ahead of him slopes from right to left, calling for a fade to keep the ball well up the slope and away from the thicket of heather down the left side of the fairway. Greed is now at war with prudence and the first objective of golf course architecture has been successfully achieved: a seed of doubt and mental turmoil has been planted. Let us assume that one way or another the drive goes a satisfactory distance and ends on the fairway. Now the battle of wits is rejoined and the question is whether to risk a shy at the plateau green with its formidable defences of vicious slopes, sand and undergrowth. Or does the balance of probability tilt towards a lay-up shot, leaving the desired birdie to the chance of a pitch or chip and single putt? There is, of course, no single correct answer to the riddles of golf. The right way for you may spell disaster for me but no matter how the birdie is achieved at this hole it represents one of the more satisfying rewards in golf.

The open heathland, often with frisky breezes, is an exhilarating place and this may contribute to the happy circumstance that many golfers respond to the challenge of Walton Heath by playing better than usual. It puts a golfer on his mettle and brings out the best in him, as has been demonstrated many times, specially during the years when the club was owned by the *News of the World* and the match-play championship was played there.

Seminole

Life frequently poses the moral dilemma of conflicting principles. Let us examine two propositions. Should a group of likeminded people be able to form themselves into an exclusive club for their mutual enjoyment? Most of us would surely say that, provided they do not break the law of the land, then the answer must be yes. Free association is a basic human right. Bearing that in mind, should the trustees of a national asset in the form of a unique golf course, the masterpiece of one of the greatest architects the world has known, deny public access to it? This question has concerned many golf clubs and a number of them have to a greater or lesser degree opened their doors to interested visitors.

Other clubs, such as Augusta National, jealously preserve their exclusivity and Seminole is among their number. That is a pity from the golfing public's point of view because here is a course which has greatly influenced modern course design and which offers an experience quite outside the normal. This is genuine links golf, probably the only course in America which captures the spirit and mood of its Scottish antecedents. How Donald Ross must have relished the opportunity to work with the natural ingredients of his native Dornoch when he was commissioned to design Seminole in southern Florida. He even had the element which adds the essential spice to links golf, constant and often frisky winds.

Of course Ross did not make the mistake of trying to reproduce a Scottish links in every detail; he respected the integrity of the local landscape and flora, so Florida palm trees add to the zest of Seminole. The first impression is that this course is all bunker and no fairway. More than 200 bunkers of dazzling white sand call for precision which few golfers can hope to command. Ben Hogan, probably the most accurate striker in the history of golf, felt that Seminole came closest to his ideal in a golf course and he liked to pit his wits and skill against the course as preparation for tournament play.

The intrinsic excellence of Seminole, with its premium on strategic thinking to avoid the gauntlet of bunkers and the large central lake which casts a powerful spell on the nervous, is matched by the immaculate condition of the course. This is millionaire country and when the members from the icy mid-west fly south for the winter they want the best golf that money can buy. The large Seminole greens are lovingly manicured and are as true as any putting surfaces in the southern states. So here we have everything

161

that golf should be and this may be as good a place as any to define the idea.

A large element in the appeal of golf must be the sheer aesthetic pleasure of enjoying the surroundings, of walking on soft turf and breathing clean air. The next, and most neglected requirement, is that a game of golf should be in large measure an intellectual pursuit, not unlike chess. You should have to balance risks against rewards and think two or three moves ahead and you should be punished if you do not plan your moves well. This is where the design of the course plays such a vital role. Then the course should be well conditioned because golf can only be played to its true potential if the golfer has closely mown turf from which to play his shots and true putting surfaces. The weather, of course, can enhance all these ingredients and at Seminole in winter time the climate could hardly be more agreeable. People often ask what merit there is in making golf courses so difficult; would not there be more enjoyment in the game if fairways were wider and hazards fewer? The answer is that scoring would be easier, and those for whom the score is the be all and end all of golf might prefer it. But the satisfaction of golf is directly proportional to the strength of the challenge. Just as the mountaineer scorns the easy climb, so the real golfer is drawn to the great championship courses. Seminole is definitely one for the connoisseur.

Take a Fertile Imagination and a Golfing Theme

Few games have inspired writers as much as golf. The items which follow comprise the merest trial tasting of an extensive cellar of vintage golf fiction.

Sotogrande, Spain

The Strange Case of the Ambitious Caddy

Once upon a time there was a boy named Robin Bideawee.

He had chronic hiccups.

He had hay fever, too.

Also, he was learning to whistle through his teeth.

Oh yes, and his shoes squeaked.

The scoutmaster told him he had better be a caddy.

He said, Robin, you aren't cut out for a scout, you're cut out for a caddy.

At the end of Robin's first day as a caddy the caddymaster asked him how he got along.

Robin said, I got along fine but my man lost six balls, am I ready yet?

The caddymaster said No, he wasn't ready yet.

At the end of the second day the caddymaster asked him again how he got along.

Robin said, My man left me behind to look for a ball on the fourth hole and I didn't catch up to him till the eighteenth, am I ready yet?

The caddymaster said No, he wasn't ready yet.

Next day Robin said, I only remembered twice to take the flag on the greens and when I did take it I wiggled it, am I ready yet?

The caddymaster said No, he wasn't ready yet.

Next day Robin said, My man asked me whether he had a seven or an eight on the water hole and I said an eight, am I ready yet?

The caddymaster said No, he wasn't ready yet.

Next day Robin said, Every time my man's ball stopped on the edge of a bunker I kicked it in, am I ready yet?

The caddymaster said No, he wasn't ready yet.

Next day Robin said, I never once handed my man the club he asked for, am I ready yet?

The caddymaster said No, he wasn't ready yet.

Next day Robin said, I bet a quarter my man would lose and told him so, am I ready yet?

The caddymaster said, Not quite.

Next day Robin said, I laughed at my man all the way round, am I ready yet?

The caddymaster said, Have you still got hiccups and have you still got hay fever, and are you still learning how to whistle through your teeth, and do your shoes still squeak?

Robin said, Yes, yes, a thousand times yes.

Then you are ready, said the caddymaster.
Tomorrow you shall caddy for Ogden Nash.

OGDEN NASH, *The Face is Familiar, 1954*

Temper never got anyone anywhere in golf.
BOBBY LOCKE

Naval Occasion

The seventeenth hole at Chumpton is in many respects typical of life in general. You can see only a very little way ahead of you. A tall hill confronts you as you stand on the tee, and you have to get over the middle of that hill. The way is not long, but ah! it is strait and narrow. If you slice, there are bunkers deep; if you pull, there is tiger country. It is almost exactly like a thing out of the *Pilgrim's Progress*.

Admiral Juddy's opponent was a Mr Twine, a good Christian but, like so many of the better Christians, an indifferent golfer. A fair, average, heathen eight-handicap man could reach the green from the tee with a mashie iron. Mr Twine, by means of a full blow with a Dreadnought driver, had managed to hit his ball as far as the right-hand bunkers, whither he had now proceeded. Admiral Juddy's caddie, who in the course of the afternoon had heard a lot of new and startling information concerning himself, was looking for the lost ball with but little enthusiasm and an implied cynicism regarding the length of the admiral's tee-shot. The admiral himself delved and cursed in the tiger country. And at this point Miss Kyte, most strapping and masculine of all the up-to-date strapping and masculine daughters of St Andrew, teed her ball on the seventeenth tee, tossed her cigarette to the ground, addressed, swung, and smote.

She carried her own clubs, preferring to dispense with a caddie. So did her opponent, young Harry Chinney, an assistant preparatory schoolmaster, who couldn't afford one. But there was no need

166

to explore. The admiral and Mr Twine must either have played the hole by this time or have lost a ball. Miss Kyte accordingly smote.

Her ball curled over the tall hill and away to the left. With it we take flight from the strait and narrow line of reason into an adventure of the wildest improbability.

Admiral Juddy waded out of the worst of the tiger country and stood on a bank of smooth, short grass, breathing great snorts of rage from his nostrils like a very old and very angry dog. His caddie had now, perhaps in self-defence, entirely disappeared. Twine was one down and would take at least six to get out of the bunker, and would have lost the match for a certainty. Now he would have to be presented with the hole. It wasn't that the admiral minded losing a ball or a hole or a match, or anything else. It was simply blast and curse life in general, and golf in particular. Why the multi-coloured eternity of woe was one such a fool as to play golf, or, if it came to that, to live this blasted life? Oh, completely, finally, and eternally, blast and damn everything!

Miss Kyte's ball fell with a thud behind him and came bouncing gaily along the grass. A great spasm of rage shook every nerve in Admiral Juddy's frame. That one should live and golf was bad enough. That one should be smitten into without warning in this off-hand manner, and at this moment accursed, was literally *pswee-bo*. Blind with fury, the admiral slashed wildly at Miss Kyte's perky little bouncer with his murderous niblick. He hit it.

It sailed, spinning merrily, into the air again. It fell on the green, bounced, ran, settled into a staid trickle, trickled to the edge of the hole, hesitated coquettishly, and flopped home.

Next moment Twine, a short, agreeable gentleman, who should never have worn plus-fours with those legs, and should have forsworn a drooping moustache, but who was very well-meaning and affable, came trotting eagerly towards the tiger country.

'Oh, good shot indeed!' he cried. 'Beautiful! My word! In the hole – absolutely in! I was just coming over to help you find the ball. I suppose that's only your second? I'm on the green, but I've played five. Well done, I say. A magnificent shot!'

To each of us comes the devil at his chosen moment. Oh, don't dispute it – you sin; I sin; we all of us know that insidious whisper, and yield to it; and who are we to judge others? At that moment, quelling the fire and tempest of wrath and sorrow, whispered the subtle voice of the tempter into the rather reddened ears of Admiral Juddy.

He pulled his beard, frowned at the gushing Twine. For a fatal second he wavered. The fatal second gave birth to another, during

167

which he shot a quick glance towards the spot where he had last seen his caddie. The caddie had reappeared, but his back was turned, and he was still searching listlessly. Admiral Juddy toyed with Satan.

'It certainly was a pretty good shot,' he muttered.

'Marvellous!' agreed Twine. 'Well, well, that's the match; but I don't mind losing to a shot like that. Hallo, here's somebody playing behind us!'

As he spoke, Mr Chinney gained the top of the high hill guarding the green, where he proceeded calmly to play several shots without further notice; while round the foot of the hill came the striding and swinging figure of Miss Kyte.

'I suppose they think we've lost a ball,' said Twine, with a nervous smile at Admiral Juddy. The latter, overcome perhaps by his supreme effort with the niblick, exhibited an unusual hestitation to move on.

'It – er – it *was* your shot, wasn't it?' asked Twine.

'Hell d' yer mean?'

'What? I mean – it *was* you that hit that ball, that ball that went into the hole, that *was* you?'

'Of *course* I flaming well hit it! What the——?'

'Exactly. Quite. Well done. Only, I mean – shan't we go on?'

Admiral Juddy decided mentally upon a compromise. At a more convenient moment he would reveal the truth to Twine. But as for this swaggering hoyden with her confounded presumption, bursting in upon him with a cigarette in her mouth and practically knickerbockers on her legs, he would teach her a lesson. She could dashed well stay and find his ball, and he'd carry on with hers. Serve her right, the dragon's whelp! With an oath of summons to his caddie, he turned towards the green.

'Seen my pill?' inquired Miss Kyte.

'No,' replied Twine pleasantly.

'Found your own, then?'

'Ye-es,' said Twine. 'Admiral Juddy has just found his and played it. Magnificent shot, too. Holed it from here.'

'Oh, come on!' commanded Admiral Juddy. 'Don't stand gossiping there. And another time,' he added, addressing Miss Kyte, 'you kindly wait till I'm off the green.'

'Well, look nippier,' said Miss Kyte. 'Besides, if you were standing here, I must have almost hit you. Are you sure you didn't play my ball by mistake?'

'I can positively swear to that,' replied the admiral. 'Twine, will you come on? Caddie, come on, will you? Come on; run, you son of a duck!'

168

'What ball were you playing with – a Dunlop?' asked Miss Kyte.
'Yes. Why?'
'Yes? So was I. What number?'
'What number was yours?'
'Four,' said Miss Kyte.
'So was mine,' said Admiral Juddy. 'So *pung-ti* to *that*.'
He stumped away. 'Hell!' said Miss Kyte, and, throwing her golf-bag aside, plunged into the tiger country.

BEN TRAVERS, *The Temptation of Admiral Juddy*

Action before thought is the ruin of most of your shots. TOMMY ARMOUR

How to Become a Scratch Golfer

The first tee on this chilly Sunday morning is in its usual state of tension.

The constituents of half a dozen four-balls stand about, swishing their drivers, waiting to get off.

They are all handicap players, and look like it. That is, they wear clothing specifically designed for the game. Zippered jackets with gussets let into the back to provide an easy movement of the shoulders. Rubberized, waterproof shoes, felt caps and hairy jerseys. Some of them, looking like post-operative lobotomys, wear white woollen hats with bobbles. Others have gone so far as to tuck the ends of their trousers into their socks. Nearly all of them have trolleys.

They are joined by a common emotion. Acute anxiety.

This is caused by the fact that they don't know from Adam what's going to happen when their turn comes to strike off – when they have to step up on to the tee and balance the ball on a peg and, in death-like silence, have a rigid waggle or two and then, rather suddenly, a bash at it, with everyone watching.

The north-east wind is making their eyes water. They may not be

169

able to see the ball at all, so that it will shoot off the tee of the club into the car-park where they'll have to rootle about for it under a lot of Mini Minors with the match behind them growing more and more restive on the tee.

Alternatively, they may hook it, as usual, into the long and tangled grass behind the third green and lose a brand-new ball first crack out of the box while the next two matches play through, getting the day off to a jagged start from which it will certainly not recover.

Some of the fourballs have not yet been fully organised. They toss for partners and get the very chap they didn't want so that an argument develops about tossing again, on the grounds that one of the coins came down sideways.

No sooner is this matter settled than two of the players refuse to play for ten bob a corner, because they thought it was only going to be a dollar, so they have to toss all over again to decide this, too.

Someone, feeling his muscles stiffening in the chill wind, tries a practice swing and cracks someone else on the head with his driver. The apologies fatally interrupt a player driving off at that very moment.

Just as his partner is about to strike someone else finds his caddy is missing and starts roaring across to the caddy master, causing the man to top his drive.

In the midst of this nervous chaos the man who looks like a Scratchman appears on the steps of the clubhouse, and one sees at once how it ought to be done.

He is dressed, for a start, in a way which gives the onlooker no clue that he is going to play golf at all.

He is, in fact, in so little hurry that he pauses on the steps of the clubhouse to exchange the time of day with two pretty women whose husbands are already waiting for him on the tee. Laughter rings out. He leaves them, with the gloved left hand raised in formal farewell.

The husbands urge him to hurry. They're off next. He gives them a reassuring wave – and walks thoughtfully across to examine the surface of the eighteenth green. It takes a little time. He presses his spikes in the turf, making – one would hazard a guess – a test for moisture content. As he is about to walk away he stops and looks across the green, head slightly on one side. Facts – we imagine – are probably being correlated about the length and texture of the grass which may be useful for one of those awkward 15-footers later on. He concludes his examination with a slight shrug of the shoulders, indicating – we can only presume – that conditions are not nearly as good as they are, say, at a real course like the Berkshire, but will have to be endured. He joins the other players on the tee, to be greeted with a barrage of complaint that it'll be dark, if he doesn't hurry up and get on with it.

The Scratchman is entirely unperturbed. 'There's ample time, gentlemen,' he tells them calmly, 'for all of us to notch our usual ninety-three.' He looks round. 'Where's my lad?' he enquires. 'Or perhaps he's still in bed.'

His caddy steps forward. The Scratchman's caddy is always there before him. No shouting at the caddy master is ever required. 'Morning, Jigger,' says the Scratchman. 'I hope you spent a quiet night. Sir's just this side of the grave.'

Sir, of course, always knows his caddy's name – or, rather, the nickname by which the caddy is known from Troon to Sandwich by other caddies on the tournament circuit.

Jigger nods, without saying anything. He knows better than to try to get in on the act. He isn't, in fact, too stimulated by it, having seen it too often before. He only hopes that the news about Sir being just this side of the grave isn't true, or they'll be spending even more of the day than usual in the long grass.

The Scratchman ties the arms of his cardigan round Jigger's neck. 'We'll keep that in reserve,' he says. 'The blood's liable to thin out just before lunch.' Fastidiously, Jigger removes the cardigan and puts it in the bag.

'Well, now,' says the Scratchman, 'who's playing with what, and for how many?'

The other players, in an effort to get *something* moving, have already tossed for partners, so that Willy, the odd man out, gets the Scratchman.

Willy, in fact, owing to a habit of twitching his chip shots clean over every green, is absolutely useless off a handicap of fourteen. The Scratchman, however, appears over-joyed to have him as a partner. 'The result,' he announces, 'is unclouded by doubt. We can only hope they save themselves a couple of shillings on the bye-bye. All right,' he tells their opponents, 'why don't you two top it first.'

The opponents point out that it isn't their honour.

The Scratchman is surprised. He doesn't understand the complexities of handicaps, as he doesn't use one himself.

'Our honour?' he says. 'Well, it's only the first of eighteen. Have a slash at it, Willy, while I have an attack of the shakes.'

171

While Willy goes through the contortions that propel his tee-shot 125 yards into the rough on the right the Scratchman puts on a comedy expression of delirium tremens so acute that not even the experienced watchers can make an estimate of what he was doing the night before. The Scratchman fills it in for them.

'Pernod,' he explains, 'with tiny actresses. Never again, till tomorrow night.'

Willy steps down off the tee. It's the Scratchman's turn to play, and all at once a remarkable change comes over him.

He becomes extremely serious. All trace of the earlier comic element is switched off.

He throws his cigarette away – half-smoked – and mounts the tee, his gaze fixed on a point 300 yards away, down the middle of the first fairway. Slowly, he peels the paper off a new ball, handing the paper to Jigger, who resignedly drops it into the tee-box immediately beside them.

Still looking at the distant target, he goes over to Jigger and rests a hand on top of his woods, in their leather jackets.

'What d'you think, Jig,' he says.

This is the part that Jigger can't stand. The first hole is wide open, and mainly downhill. It's more than 400 yards in length and no human being on the face of the earth could conceivably take anything else except a driver. Jigger starts to take it out.

The Scratchman stops him. 'I'm not sure – ' he begins. He comes to the big decision. 'Okay,' he says, 'you're probably right.'

He occupies the whole of the next half minute with a clinical survey of the ground, looking for the exact position on which to tee his ball, eventually choosing a site far over on the left. He tees the ball and puts the clubhead behind it. Delicately, like Menuhin at work on a Stradivarius, he eases his fingers round the shaft of the club, into the Vardon Grip. At the moment when it might be presumed – and many of the handicap men are deceived – that he might be about to settle himself to hit the ball, the Scratchman suddenly loses all interest in it. He steps away, holding the club out almost horizontally, his eyes once again fixed on the target 300 yards away. 'Keep her leftish, Jig?' he enquires, very seriously.

Jigger nods. He wishes to God he was carrying for one of the other cripples who, if they can't hit it out of their way, at least do it quicker.

'Right,' says the Scratchman. And at last he steps up to the ball. He looks really menacing. The jaw sets. He beds his ferocious spikes deep into the ground. He turns his head a fraction, to pin-point the

172

target 300 yards away. Then he cocks his chin, so that it points an inch behind the ball.

It's the long-awaited signal – a gesture matched only in suspense by the officer in charge of a firing-squad raising his right arm. HE'S GOING TO DO IT NOW!

The Scratchman starts slowly back, club-head low to the ground, left arm and left side all in one piece. He hasn't the faintest idea what the result of the shot will be. Probably the usual whistling hook into the nettles behind the third where Jigger, as usual, will hardly make any effort to find it, so that it's the end of a new ball. About half-way up the Scratchman takes a muscle-wrenching grip with his left hand, letting the right go slack. If he can only cut it, or push it, it'll finish up on the thirteenth fairway, where at least they'll be able to find it. . . .

He starts down too quick. His head comes up. With a single split-second to spare the club-head just catches the upper half of the ball, launching it straight down the middle, very low, but all of 240 yards.

'Great shot,' murmurs the audience, who genuinely believe, in view of the ceremonial preceding it, that it was.

The Scratchman steps to pick up his tee; using the opportunity to take a quick sideways look down the course. He's no idea where the ball went to. He lost sight of it the moment he started his down swing, and never caught a glimpse of it again. If anything, it felt hooky, and is almost certainly in the nettles. The Scratchman suddenly sees it, a white dot on the verdant fairway, a surprising distance away.

'Well,' he allows, to the profoundly envious handicap men, 'it's adequate.' With apparent sincerity he commends the revolting strokes played by both his opponents, and then strides off, relaxed and easy, and already launched upon a conversational theme which has nothing whatever to do with golf.

The reputation he leaves behind is secure. It is, the handicap men agree among themselves, the concentration that does it. They could see, from the moment he stepped up on to the tee, that he knew what he was doing, that he had a clear mental picture of the shot he was going to play. And he played it. He *looked* as though he was on top of the game.

It is, perhaps, fortunate for the Scratchman that they don't see his second shot, a rather snatchy little jerk, so that he plays his third from under a tree and subsequently just manages to shovel in a curly 4-footer for a half in five, but by this time they're too busy with troubles of their own. And in any case the Scratchman, if he's up to his work, greets the snatchy little jerk with a cry of such genuine amusement and surprise that even his partner Willy, who was confidently anticipating a three, is moved to look upon it in the same light – i.e., a laughable aberration, solely due to Pernod and tiny actresses, and one which will certainly not occur again. When it does occur, again and again, the Scratchman's pantomime of bewildered astonishment is so amusingly played that Willy almost comes to the conclusion that he was doing it on purpose, even after they've been beaten four and three – despite some extraordinarily gallant putting, with a lot of green-sweeping and line assessing, by the Scratchman, none of which actually finished in the hole. Even their opponents feel they were pretty lucky to win and can't make out, indeed, exactly how they did, specially by such a large margin.

They have been dazzled by Scratchman's Aura.

Let us – before we, too, are blinded – set down the principles of this vital factor game.

Principles of Scratchman's Aura

(1) An absolute ban on all clothing specifically designed for golf, with particular reference to zippered jackets, rubberized shoes, felt caps and hairy jerseys. All these suggest an earnest, painstaking approach, the antithesis of Scratchman's Aura, which is alive with a swashbuckling quality, making it plain that he could play equally well in white tie and tails.

(2) Be deadly serious, however, about the shoes, which should outspike everything in the pro's shop. The shoes are the player's sole contact with the ground, and the source, therefore, of all power. Truly ferocious spikes indicate power unlimited.

(3) An absolutely leisured approach to the first tee, even at the risk of losing your place and generating a sense of grievance among the other members of the fourball which may poison the rest of the day. A real stinker played in an agitated hurry looks like a real stinker. A real stinker, played after long deliberation with the caddy and a serious assessment of wind force, driver, or brassie, line to the hole, etc. looks incomprehensible.

(4) No trolleys, please, over the age of twenty-one. You can't discuss the next shot with a trolley. A slashing 3-iron into the teeth of the wind, finishing a yard from the stick, looks as if you've done it on purpose, if it follows a low-voiced confer-

174

ence with a caddy. Without the conference and the caddy it looks like the fluke which it is.

(5) Never call the caddy 'Caddy', but use the nickname by which he is known only to other caddies who work with professionals on the tournament circuit. Drop it, without explanation, to handicap players who've never heard of him. Over-tip him sickeningly and in private at the end of the round, so that his eagerness for your patronage will be ascribed to the brilliance of your game.

(6) Never complain about the partner you get stuck with. It suggests anxiety about the result, which will probably be exactly the same anyway.

(7) Always confess, using a broad comedy routine, to a crippling hangover, in case you get an opening blow which finishes behind the ladies' tee-box. Indicate, clearly, that the hang-over comes not from beer swilling in the golf-club bar, in which handicap men might engage, and probably have, but from an evening out with Ava Gardner at the very least, so that even your partner will think it reasonable for you to start with three sixes and a seven

(8) Get a crippling hangover, if you've never had one, and make a careful note of the tottering, pole-axed symptoms so that you'll be able to play them up to the hilt on return performances.

(9) Never, ever, have a practice swing. You've got to be very good indeed before a practice swing looks like the harbinger of 270 yards straight down the middle. A practice swing often hits the ground or someone else's trolley. Even if it doesn't it will only represent a panic-stricken attempt – obvious to everyone – to try to assess what's likely to happen when and if a golf-ball intrudes itself into the carpet-beating flog which this morning appears to represent your normal method of striking.

(10) Instantly drop all larking about, jokes and hangover mimes when your turn comes to play. It suggests a Palmer-like concentration which may not be borne out by the results, but at least gives you the opportunity to look genuinely astonished when your tee-shot trickles along the ground.

(11) When your tee-shot trickles along the ground reveal first of all astonishment and then honest amusement, in which all pres-ent should be freely invited to join in. When you top the next one, leaving it still in the rough, return to the hangover mime.

(12) If you do get a good one, instantly start to talk about something else, or, preferably, elaborate the theme you were on when the

175

others were playing theirs. This shows that 250 yards down the middle is routine, and not a profound surprise.

It should be noted here that the creation of Scratchman's Aura has nothing whatever to do with Gamesmanship.

Gamemanship is an introverted defence mechanism fundamentally concerned with winning, an ambition which is actually despised by the true Scratchman who hasn't won a match in years because his handicap really ought to be eleven.

The Gamesman who, in action, often resembles an elderly charlady beating a carpet in a gale of wind, seeks to depress his opponents below his own level of incompetence by playing upon their neuroses, because only victory can provide an assuagement for his own.

The Scratchman, on the other hand, cares nothing for victory. He accepts it cheerfully, if it comes without a struggle. It would never occur to him, however, to try to bring victory about by putting his opponents off. Their game is of absolutely no concern to him. All that he asks, while paying out yet more folding money in the bar, is that they should believe him to be infinitely better than they are and that he would certainly have been round in 69 gross with a little better luck.

The Scratchman often does, in fact, win matches by the sheer bravura of his performance.

Inexperienced players, dazzled by the radiance, often find it difficult to spot him, and go down without a struggle five-and-four. It is only afterwards, in the bar, when the Scratchman is talking modestly about being 'a couple over fours', that if they take the trouble to add it up they find he was actually round in 83, though it looked as if it was a great deal less.

There are two methods of piercing this shining armour. (1) Ask the Scratchman to hole short putts on the first four greens. If he's a genuine Scratchman he'll hit the back of the hole with all four of them, taking extreme pains with each. If he's one of the flash boys he'll miss at least two and, despite his merry incredulous laughter, you'll know him for what he is.

(2) Have a little chat with his caddy, heaping excessive praise on the fluency of Sir's swing. The caddy, who carried Joe Carr's bag in the Amateur of '52 and therefore has his own reputation to consider, will quickly put you straight.

Quite a number of handicap players, wearing zippered jackets and green berets, with their trousers tucked into the ends of their socks, go out of their way, even to the extent of incurring a special

176

rebuff, to invite the flash Scratchman to demean himself by joining in their rough fourball.

They know it will pay for their lunch.

Patrick Campbell, *How to Become a Scratch Golfer*

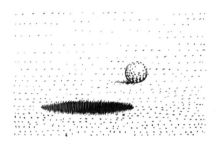

Oddments Retrieved from behind the Locker

Golf is often described as life in microcosm. Some people would have it the other way round. Either way, the game provides rich scope for literary diversions of one kind or another.

Sunningdale Old Course

Swearing

Expletives more or less vigorous directed against himself, the ball, the club, the wind, the bunker, and the game, are the most usual safety-valve for the fury of the disappointed golfer. But bad language is fortunately much gone out of use; and in any case, the resources of profanity are not inexhaustible. Deeds, not words, are required in extreme cases to meet the exigencies of the situation; and, as justice, prudence, and politeness all conspire to shield his opponent from physical violence, it is on the clubs that under these circumstances vengeance most commonly descends. Most players content themselves with simply breaking the offending weapon against the ground.

But some persons there are whose thirst for revenge cannot be satisfied by any such rapid or simple process. I have been told of one gentleman who threw the offending club on the ground, and then with his niblick proceeded to punish it with piecemeal destruction, breaking its shaft into small pieces very much as criminals used to be broken on the wheel. Even this procedure seemed inadequate to one infuriated golfer of whom I have heard. A shaft, be it broken into ever so many fragments, can be replaced and the implement be as good as new. Nothing less than destroying both head and shaft can insure its final disappeance from the world of Golf. The club must not merely be broken, but must be destroyed, and from its hated remains no new race must be permitted to arise for the torment and discomfiture of succeeding generations of golfers. This perfect consummation can, it is said, be attained by holding the club upright, the head resting on the ground, then placing one foot upon it and kicking it with the other, just at the point where the head and shaft are bound together. By this simple expedient (which I respectfully commend to the attention of all short tempered golfers) a 'root-and-branch' policy may be effectually carried out by destroying at one stroke both the essential parts of the club. It is better to smash your clubs than to lose your temper.

A. J. BALFOUR, *The Badminton Library, 1890*

The Charm of Golf

When he reads of the notable doings of famous golfers, the eighteen-handicap man has no envy in his heart. For by this time he has discovered the great secret of golf. Before he began to play he wondered wherein lay the fascination of it; now he knows. Golf is so popular simply because it is the best game in the world at which to be bad.

Consider what it is to be bad at cricket. You have bought a new bat, perfect in balance; a new pair of pads, white as driven snow; gloves of the very latest design. Do they let you use them? No. After one ball, in the negotiation of which neither your bat, nor your pads, nor your gloves came into play, they send you back into the pavilion to spend the rest of the afternoon listening to fatuous old stories of some old gentleman who knew Fuller Pilch. And when your side takes the field, where are you? Probably at long leg both ends, exposed to the public gaze as the worst fieldsman in London. How devastating are your emotions. Remorse, anger, mortification, fill your heart; above all, envy – envy of the lucky immortals who disport themselves on the green level of Lord's.

Consider what it is to be bad at lawn tennis. True, you are allowed to hold on to your new racket all through the game, but how often are you allowed to employ it usefully? How often does your partner cry 'Mine!' and bundle you out of the way? You may spend the full eighty minutes in your new boots, but your relations with the ball will be distant. They do not give you a ball to yourself at football.

But how different a game is golf. At golf it is the bad player who gets the most strokes. However good his opponent, the bad player has the right to play out each hole to the end; he will get more than his share of the game. He need have no fears that his new driver will not be employed. He will have as many swings with it as the scratch man; more, if he misses the ball altogether upon one or two tees. If he buys a new niblick he is certain to get fun out of it on the very first day.

182

And, above all, there is this to be said for golfing mediocrity – the bad player can make the strokes of the good player. The poor cricketer has perhaps never made fifty in his life; as soon as he stands at the wickets he knows that he is not going to make fifty today. But the eighteen-handicap man has some time or other played every hole on the course to perfection. He has driven a ball 250 yards; he has made superb approaches; he has run down the long putt. Any of these things may suddenly happen to him again. And therefore it is not his fate to have to sit in the club smoking-room after his second round and listen to the wonderful deeds of others. He can join in too. He can say with perfect truth, 'I once carried the ditch at the fourth with my second', or 'I remember when I drove into the bunker guarding the eighth green', or even 'I did a three at the eleventh this afternoon' – bogey being five. But if the bad cricketer says, 'I remember when I took a century in forty minutes off Lockwood and Richardson', he is nothing but a liar.

For these and other reasons golf is the best game in the world for the bad player. And sometimes I am tempted to go further and say that it is a better game for the bad player than for the good player. The joy of driving a ball straight after a week of slicing, the joy of putting a mashie shot dead, the joy of even a moderate stroke with a brassie; best of all, the joy of the perfect cleek shot – these things the good player will never know. Every stroke we bad players make we make in hope. It is never so bad but it might have been worse; it is never so bad but we are confident of doing better next time. And if the next stroke is good, what happiness fills our soul. How eagerly we tell ourselves that in a little while all our strokes will be as good.

What does Vardon know of this? If he does a five hole in four he blames himself that he did not do it in three; if he does it in five he is miserable. He will never experience that happy surprise with which we hail our best strokes. Only his bad strokes surprise him, and then we may suppose that he is not happy. His length and accuracy are mechanical; they are not the result, as so often in our case, of some suddenly applied maxim or some suddenly discovered innovation. The only thing which can vary in his game is his putting, and putting is not golf but croquet.

But of course we, too, are going to be as good as Vardon one day. We are only postponing the day because meanwhile it is too pleasant to be bad. And it is part of the charm of being bad at golf that in a moment, in a single night, we may become good. If the bad cricketer said to a good cricketer, 'What am I doing wrong?' the only possible answer would be, 'Nothing particular, except that you can't play

183

cricket.' But if you or I were to say to our scratch friend, 'What am I doing wrong,' he would reply at once, 'Moving the head' or 'Dropping the right knee' or 'Not getting the wrists in soon enough', and by tomorrow we should be different players. Upon such a little depends, or seems to the eighteen-handicapper to depend, excellence in golf.

And so, perfectly happy in our present badness and perfectly confident of our future goodness, we long-handicap men remain. Perhaps it would be pleasanter to be a little more certain of getting the ball safely off the first tee; perhaps at the fourteenth hole, where there is a right of way and the public encroach, we should like to feel that we have done with topping; perhaps –

Well, perhaps we might get our handicap down to fifteen this summer. But no lower; certainly no lower.

A. A. MILNE, *Not That it Matters*, 1919

Mostly it is a composed golfer who wins.
BRUCE DEVLIN

Once You've Had 'em, You've Got 'em

There can be no more ludicrous sight than that of a grown man, a captain of industry perhaps and a pillar of his local community, convulsively jerking a piece of ironmongery to and fro in his efforts to hole a three-foot putt. Sometimes it is even a great golfer in the twilight of his career, in which case the sight is worthy not of ridicule but of compassion. He will battle on for a year or two, but twilight it is, for 'once you've had 'em, you've got 'em.' I refer, of course, to what Tommy Armour was the first to christen the 'Yips.'

When he wrote a book called *The ABC's of Golf*, Armour had no difficulty with the letter Y. The Yips drove him out of tournament golf. On a somewhat humbler level they drove me out of golf, too, and a long and agonizing process it was, ending on D-Day, 1968, the anniversary of the invasion of Europe. On that occasion I put my

25-year-old clubs up into the loft with the water tanks, where they remain to this day because I am too mean to give them away.

Armour wrote graphically of 'that ghastly time when, with the first movement of the putter, the golfer blacks out, loses sight of the ball and hasn't the remotest idea of what to do with the putter or, occasionally, that he is holding a putter at all.' This confirms the description of that most distinguished of all sufferers, Bob Jones, who recorded that just before the moment of impact the ball 'seemed to disappear from sight.' Jones also recorded how he once was partnered with that sterling character of the late 1920s and early '30s, Wild Bill Mehlhorn. Poor Mehlhorn! He was only three feet from the hole, said Jones, but gave such a convulsive twitch at the ball that it shot across the green into a bunker. He then had the humiliation of exchanging his putter for his niblick, and, we may assume without being unkind, that was the last seriously competitive round he ever played.

Contemporary with Jones and Mehlhorn was Leo Diegel, whose extraordinary spread-elbowed putting style put a new phase into the golfing vocabulary – 'to diegel.' I watched him on the 18th green at St Andrews in 1933 when, from some yards above the hole, he had two to tie for the British Open title. While his partner holed out, Diegel paced up and down, much as an animal in its cage, repeatedly taking off his felt hat and mopping his brow. When his turn came, he charged the ball down the slope, several feet too far, chased after it, and, almost before it had come to rest, yipped it a foot wide of the hole. Everyone knew, as I am sure he did, too, that Diegel would never win an Open now.

Armour wrote, 'Yips don't seize the victim during a practice round. It is a tournament disease.' Here the great man was certainly wrong. My mind goes back to a conversation at Augusta with Craig Wood, who was robbed of the 1935 Masters by Gene Sarazen's historic double-eagle. Craig told me that he even got the Yips on the practice green, all by himself and with nothing at stake. Again, Armour says, 'I have a hunch that the Yips is a result of years of competitive strain, a sort of punch-nuttiness with the putter.' Wrong again, surely, for you will see any number of compulsive yippers, though many may not admit it, in Sunday foursomes whose members never play serious competitive golf at all.

In winning the 1931 British Open, Armour, having perpetrated a most frightful Yip to miss from two feet on the 71st hole, found himself faced with a three-footer to win. 'I took a new grip, holding the club as tightly as I could and with stiff wrists, and took a different

185

stance. . . . From the instant the club left the ball on the backswing I was blind and unconscious.' Next day that greatest of golf writers, Bernard Darwin, recorded in the London *Times* that he had never before seen a man so nonchalantly hole a three-foot putt to gain a championship!

Who, would you guess, wrote the following, and in what book?

'As I stood addressing the ball I would watch for my right hand to jump. At the end of two seconds I would not be looking at the ball at all. My gaze would have become rivited on my right hand. I simply could not resist the desire to see what it was going to do. Directly, as I felt that it was about to jump, I would snatch at the ball in a desperate effort to play the shot before the involuntary movement could take effect. Up would go my head and body with a start and off would go the ball, anywhere but on the proper line.'

That was written by Harry Vardon, winner of six British Opens and one U.S. Open, indisputably the greatest golfer that the world has yet seen. And the book was entitled *How to Play Golf*!

Americans sometimes refer to the Yips rather unkindly as 'whisky fingers,' and sometimes no doubt they are. Perhaps the last word on 'whisky fingers' – and almost my favorite quotation – was uttered by Harry Vardon to a lady who was trying to persuade him to sign the pledge. 'Moderation is essential in all things, madam,' said Vardon gravely, 'but never in my life have I been beaten by a teetotaler.'

Sam Snead, whose fluent style has lasted longer than any other man's in the history of the game, was reduced to putting between his legs, croquet-fashion – and he was a total abstainer for years. The croquet putter gave many a golfer, myself included, an extended lease on life and the banning of it was an act of cruelty to many hundreds of miserable wretches for whom the very sight of a normal putter set their fingers twitching. The ease with which you could line up one of these croquet putters to the hole was quite remarkable. By holding the club at the top with the left hand, thumb on top of the shaft, and loosely lower down with the right arm stiffly extended, the most inveterate yipper could make some sort of stroke at a four-foot putt which would not expose him to public ridicule. We did not ask to hole it; all we wanted was to be able to make a stroke at it, and this we could do. The United States Golf Ass'n not only decided to ban a method which had brought peace to so many tortured souls but the group let its decision become public before the Royal and Ancient Golf Club of St Andrews had time to consider it, thus putting the latter in the impossible position of either banning the club or falling out with the USGA. So they banned the club.

Further proof that the dread disease is not traceable to a dissolute way of life was furnished by the 'Iron Man' of golf himself, Ben Hogan, who of all men who have played golf since the game began would have seemed most likely to be immune. The rot set in, so eye-witnesses have assured me, on the 71st green at Rochester in 1956, when he was well placed to win a record fifth U.S. Open. Not only did he miss the three-footer, which anyone could do, but he yipped it, and that was the beginning of the end. At any rate, my last memory of Hogan in competitive golf is at the Masters some years ago. Every green, as usual, is surrounded with spectators and, as the familiar white-capped figure steps through the ropes, everyone spontaneously rises to give him a standing ovation. And a moment later he is stuck motionless over the ball, as though hypnotized, unable to move the ironmongery to and fro.

Is there any cure for this grotesque ailment? Few people can have made a more penetrating research than myself. The first led me to a psychiatrist-cum-hypnotist, who solemnly tried through my inner self to talk the ball into the hole. This, of course, was ridiculous since all that I was seeking was that, on surveying a four-foot putt, a massive calm should automatically come over me instead of the impression that I was about to try to hit the ball with a live eel. Better hope came from an Austrian doctor, who wrote to say that he knew the solution and would be willing to reveal it to me. Within a matter of hours I was visiting him in his rooms in London. 'It all comms,' he said, 'from ze angle of ze right ell-bow.' Something in that, I thought, recalling how, with the right arm stiffly extended, one could at least make some sort of stroke with the croquet putter. The theory seemed to be supported by the fact that, if you have difficulty in raising a glass to the lips, it is when the arm bends to approximately the putting angle that your drink is most likely to make its bid for freedom.

Innumerable 'cures' for the Yips have been tried and passed on from one sufferer to another. Looking at the hole instead of the ball; putting left-handed; putting cross-handed with the left hand below the right, and putting with the hands wide apart (probably the best bet of the lot). A friend of mine has had his hands about a foot apart, with the left elbow below the right, and then pulls down as hard as he can with the right – and he a one-time runner up in the British Amateur.

As an ancient and finally defeated warrior – three putts from a yard on the 18th at St Andrews, and only as few as three because the third hit the back of the hole, jumped up, and fell in – I listen politely

187

to all their tales. But the bitter, inescapable truth remains. Once you've had 'em, you've got 'em.

Henry Longhurst, *Golf Digest*

---

*To me, the performance of the perfect golf stroke
is as much a thing of beauty as can be found in any
of the performing arts.* Bobby Jones

Gamesmanship

The first impact of Hagen struck us before I was fully alert to the possibilities of golf. A visiting American golfer, I read, on the way over, had practised by 'driving golf-balls into the sea from the deck of the Mauretania'. Later, he 'loosened up with iron shots into the Thames from the roof of the Savoy Hotel'. It all happened a decade or so ago before the principles of gamesmanship were properly settled in my mind. 'Typical,' I said. I was prone to find things 'typical'. Hagen was 'showy'. We liked our professionals to be quiet and quietly clothed, salt-of-the-earth and with a way of calling you 'sir' which meant that we were all free men but shared a sense of degree, priority and place. We did not mind, we rather liked it if the dark flannel trousers of our professionals were a little muddied round the turn-ups. We were quite prepared to allow them into our changing-rooms, and indeed into the front door porches of their own clubs. And here was Hagen, perfectly polite, but without a touch of deference. Immediately after '14–'18, the British were still feeling that they were as pleased with Quimet's victory as the Americans had been. But now was the time to get things back to normal. A young generation of British stars was represented by Duncan the Scot and Abe Mitchell the strong and silent Englishman. Even Duncan had remodelled his swing under the spell of Vardon, so that when he won the first post-war British Open of 1920, it was regarded as a particularly British return to normal. Hagen, a young over-dressed American, paying his first visit to this country, aroused some head-shaking sympathy in that championship by taking over 80 for every single round. Although he himself had two championships already to his credit, they were both American. So that was American golf.

Next year, 1921, it is true that for the first time the Cup went to the States: but it was to Jock Hutchinson, till so recently a Scot of Scots, and still basically a St Andrews man, who, moreover, finished level with an English amateur, R. H. Wethered. He was lucky to beat him in the play-off since Wethered manipulated a remarkably advanced gamesmanship ploy – he 'didn't want to stay up because he had promised to play in a cricket match in England that Saturday morning'. In 1922 things had settled down again for good, surely, Havers calmly refusing to crack under foreign pressure. It was this Havers who did so well later at Moor Park by acquiring the silver hair and presence of a Benedictine abbott. Abe Mitchell, country squire to the last, never accepted stroke play. He would have agreed that medal play 'was little better than rifle practice'.

But the year of the gamesman was at hand, and for Britain it was Hagen, in 1922. He was to win our Open four times. I do not say that he ever won entirely by gamesmanship. To be winner of the U.S. P.G.A. in four successive years showed that he had a thread of skill as well. But I do say that had our small manuals of the gamesman's art existed at that date, his success could have been partly countered. And what were his chief gambits? There was of course the majestic use of clothesmanship, which is in essence the art of looking the opposite of the Opposition – the shoes, and the plus fours which were almost plus sixes – the butterfly among the drones. Let me mention also his famous last-minuting, his strolling onto the first tee with 30 seconds to spare, and, on occassions when this would not bring disqualification, using his ability to keep his opponent waiting 40 minutes on the first tee at the beginning of a 72-hole match.

There were counterploys, even then. The great Englishman, Archie Compston, was perfectly capable of a gamesmanship counter. He was no mean clothesman himself, though he concentrated on the rough tweeds and the loosely knotted scarf approach. He was large and leonine. He could keep waiting the man who kept everybody waiting: and in one famous 72-hole match, he beat Hagen 18 up and 17 to play.

The very size of this disaster suggests that a gamesman is involved. If the defeat is big enough one is inclined to dismiss it. The victim is 'off colour', or is suffering from some excess. (In ordinary Club play it is possible, by suggesting that 'Somebody has a very generous handicap', to have the winner pretty well sent to

189

Coventry.) Be this as it may, just before the coup de grace in the Compston/Hagen match, Hagen paused by the pond to the left of the 15th green on the High Course at Moor Park, sat on his haunches and stared at the water. 'Marvellous, isn't it?' he said. He was looking at the tadpoles.

It was when he was fighting against odds in a close match that Hagen was at his best. Bernard Darwin describes the occasion when, having driven his ball deep into a wood, he had the crowd moved back as if he intended to come out sideways and then 'as if suddenly spying a loophole of escape, played a magnificent iron shot through a gap in the trees right onto the green. His opponent was finished.'

Hagen is my first choice among living gamesmen. By such touches, finely conceived in themselves, he built up a character in which gamesmanship grew naturally, and to which gamesmanship was naturally credited. I remember as if it were yesterday – it must have been 40 years ago – reading a report in *The Times*, by Bernard Darwin, of Hagen in play and finding his ball lodged against a boundary post on the left of the course. 'Without pausing for a moment' (I am quoting from memory) 'he took out of his bag, like a conjuror producing a rabbit out of his hat, a left-handed club, with which he knocked the ball 150 yards down the fairway . . .' In the days when a golfer could carry round thirty clubs if he wanted to, I guess that a left-handed club was a fairly normal addition. But such was the power of Hagen that he was able, I have no doubt, to suggest that this notion was invented by himself. Impossible stories were told, most of them mythical. It was said that, not having been to bed the night before, he once arrived for an important match, and played it, in a dinner jacket. Untrue; but when it was said that as Captain of his Ryder Cup team he somehow outdiddled or flummoxed the opposition – well, the truth of that is that Hagen was Hagen, a mixture, it has been said, of the man who was blessed with strength and shrewdness, and who could at the same time enjoy the appearance of being the most carefree and happy-go-lucky character in the world.

Bob Jonesism

Perhaps we are too close to the later history of this subject to see its developments clearly. At the end of the twenties Hagen was of course eclipsed by Mr Robert Jones, who, for all his brilliance in golf has always been a disappointment in the world of gamesmanship. Many heads are shaken when his name comes up. Pure play and unquestioned excellence is the death of technique. Against the bravest opposition, merit and sportsmanship emasculates the gambit and nullifies the ploy.

Gambit of Henry Cotton

Through the twenties and thirties, England and America exchanged gamesmanship techniques. For a time – and on almost all team occasions – England faded. We bred excellent golf gamesmen within our own walls, including charmers of the old school, hard luck men, regular guys, and infant prodigies. All played their parts. One restored our prestige. Few will immediately agree with me that the most successful as a golfer, Henry Cotton, was also the most successful as a gamesman. But the Cotton gambit was a powerful one, as useful in life as it is in golf. No Unnecessary Smiling, as we might name it, is as effective as it is simple. Suddenly there was a man on our golf courses who looked serious, who looked as if he meant it, who was going to take the nonsense out of 'only a game'. One can dance mad boleros as soon as one is in the changing room; but Not Smiling within the boundaries of the actual course is a powerful weapon. Not smiling on the green or on the tee. Not smiling when held up. Not even smiling when watching another match.

Not smiling is something totally different from looking displeased. It suggests single mindedness and concentration. It was interesting to watch Cotton *v*. Alf Padgham. It was only at his peak that Padgham was able to counter-establish his more immediately attractive approach of easy chat which sometimes included a remark to the crowd. Or there was Cotton *v*. Dai Rees, who, equally determined, had to live up to the gambit of Volatile Welshman invented for him by the headline writers.

How was Cotton so successful? Remember that besides the discipline of his expression there were no untidy ends about his appearance, his personality, or his game. His trousers were no less well cut than his head and his hair. For clothes and general appearance he did for English professionalism what Hagen did for American. He not only accepted Hagen's black and white outfit, he improved on it.

When at last Cotton broke through, and won his first Open at Sandwich in 1936, I followed him on his last round. It was a tricky one. In the end, in spite of Cotton's big lead, the man who came second was only two strokes behind. At last Cotton drove straight down the 72nd fairway and the crowd started to clap as they all speeded to the last green. At this point a development took place, which has since been the subject of endless argument between historians. Cotton, realizing he had won, smiled *although still in play*.

STEPHEN POTTER, *The Complete Golf Gamesmanship*, 1968

The aim is to deliver a swift blow, not a heavy one.
ERNEST JONES

Golftopia

My comments on the virtues of the small canvas drainpipe golf bag as against the trolley brought a volume of support as gratifying as it was surprising, together with numerous suggestions for a tie for the society to be formed among those of us who carry this antiquated form of equipment.

On the other hand it has to be confessed that views were that I (*a*) was trying to do honest men out of a living, and (*b*) must have had a liver when I wrote it – one of which could have been true but wasn't; the other, never. Others suggested that it was time I stopped living in the past.

Well, sometimes the past has something to contribute to the present. Some things are better than they were and others were better than they are. It all set me wondering. Given the general conception of golf, which is now played by more grown-ups than any other game in the world, what would be the ideal conditions under which we should play if we could begin all over again?

We each have our own ideas of Golftopia and these are mine. I see a course ranging, according to the tees, from 6,000 to 6,200 yards (the present championship courses average about 7,000, plus 1,200 yards of walking between green and tee). This will include four short holes, two very long ones, one or two drive-and-a-pitch, and several where the second shot calls for a wooden club or 2-iron.

The short holes will face the four points of the compass and one of them will be very short indeed.

Like every other hole, however, it will conform to the principle that the size of the target varies in ratio to the size of the shot, and the green will therefore be microscopic. This will apply also to the long holes since, at about 480 yards, they will be out of range of two shots and the third will be only a pitch – provided you have hit the first two. If not, you will be hard put to it to get a five.

For the long handicap player, the beginner and the elderly, there will be no bunkers into which they can drive. These will be reserved for the longer and more skilful, and will be placed diagonally and with devilish ingenuity, tempting them to bite off as much as they think they can chew.

We shall have three tees in permanent use at each hole, the middle one within a few yards of the previous green; there will be several alternative starting points, and the eighteenth green will be under the club-house windows. As a consolation to those who are temporarily off their game, the course will enjoy magnificent views and an abundance of wild life.

Since it is easier (though this has not dawned in the last twenty years) to fit one ball to 1,500 courses than to alter 1,500 courses to fit one ball, we shall have a ball which the local scratch player can hit about 220 yards from the tee on a fine spring day. Perhaps Dr Barnes Wallis, of 'Dam Buster' fame, who I see has invented a new cricket ball, can help us on this before frustration causes him to emigrate.

The club-house will be unpretentious, rural in aspect, and something between the original tin shed and the converted mansion – an old farmhouse maybe. No other dwelling-place will be visible from it, and from the verandah we shall be able to venture a modest wager on our friends performing on a practice putting course of superlative excellence, enclosed by rambler roses.

Within, there will be a small and somewhat austere men's bar, but elsewhere and on the course women will have equal rights, except when it is inconvenient for the men for them to do so. In the main rooms, at any rate at week-ends, the drinks will be laid out on a side table, and everyone will help themselves, putting the money in a pudding basin provided for the purpose with the same punctilious exactitude that they accord to an absent news-vendor when buying their evening paper.

Lunch will consist of one hot dish – after all, we don't get a choice at home – and a number of cold things on the side, including blue Cheshire cheese and a host of salads and vegetables grown in the steward's garden without the aid of chemical fertilizers.

It will be a tradition of the club that you can come up without a game and always be sure of getting one; that foursomes will be

193

played on Sunday afternoons; and that the members not only patronize the professional's shop, but frequently invite him to play. Innumerable small boys will, of course, be on hand to carry our clubs.

There will be no annual subscription. At the end of the year the hon. secretary will inform each of our 100-odd members how much he owes. I hope that it will not, as happened in an American club of my acquaintance, come to $5,000 a head, but what if it does? With income tax at ninepence in the pound we shall be able to afford our Golftopia.

HENRY LONGHURST, *Only on Sundays, 1956*

To try to play golf really well is far from being a joke, and lightheartedness of endeavour is a sure sign of eventual failure. J. H. TAYLOR

The People in Front

Hazlitt thought it one of the best things in life to be known only as 'the gentleman in the parlour,' and certainly it is a pleasant title. There is something so respectable about its anonymity, and yet it suggests all the romance of wayfaring. Other titles formed on somewhat similar lines suggest nothing but feelings of hatred and contempt. Such is that of the large class of golfers whom we call simply 'the people in front.' When the clocks have been put back and darkness falls prematurely on the links, they are more than ever detestable.

It is true that they are not, as a rule, in the least to blame for the delay; so much we grudgingly admit, but it does not make their little ways the less irritating. They waggle for hours; they stroll rather than walk; they dive into their monstrous bags in search of the right club and then it is the wrong number, but they are not sorry that we have been troubled; their putting is a kind of funereal ping-pong. We could forgive them all these tricks, from which we ourselves are conspicuously free, if it were not for the absurd punctilio with which they observe the rules. They will insist on waiting for the people in front of them when it must be palpable even to their intellects that

194

the best shot they ever hit in their lives would be fifty yards short.

The one thing to be said for them is that when they are in front of somebody else they can give us a little malicious gaiety. Some while ago I was playing on the same course as was an eminent person. My partner and I started in front of him, but others of our party were less fortunate. For some time we could not quite understand why there were several empty fairways behind us. Then we noticed that on the tees couples were rapidly silting up. It was if a river had flowed placidly on until there was thrown a mighty dam right across it. As in our old friend, 'Horatius,'

> 'The furious river struggled hard
> And tossed his tawny mane,'

but the dam held; in front, steadily, methodically on went the eminent person, studying both ends of his putts with all that intense power of forgetting for the moment the affairs of State which is the hall-mark of his class. And I am bound to confess that we laughed, like Mr Mantalini, 'demnably.'

Generally, as was said before, the people in front are not the real culprits. 'I know it's not their fault,' we say in the tone of the man who, as he broke his putter across his knee, exclaimed, 'I know it's only a d——d game.' That being so, it ought to make no difference to us who are the people for whom we have to wait. We should go no faster and no slower if Bobby Jones and Harry Vardon were playing in front of us instead of that old lady who scoops up the ball along with a club that goes up so obviously faster than it can ever come down. I suppose we must be golfing snobs, because it does make a great difference. To be kept waiting by the eminent (I mean the eminent in golf) is to be reconciled to the inevitability of things, whereas we always believe that the scooping lady could get along faster if she tried. Moreover, there is the disquieting hope that she may lose her ball. It would be of no real help to us if she did, but instinct is too strong for us. Every time her ball is seen heading for a gorse bush our heartfelt prayers go with it, and though attainment will swiftly prove disenchanting, it is a great moment when at last she waves us on and we stampede courteously past.

It is at that precise moment that we are most likely to hit our own ball into a gorse bush, for it is a law of nature that everybody plays a hole badly when going through. To be there and then repassed is one of the bitterest humiliations that golf can bring; it must be akin to that of being rebumped by the boat so gloriously bumped the night before. But, of course, no rational being will endure it; far rather would we surrender the hole and make a rapid though undignified rush towards the next teeing ground. By this time, it is true, we are hot, flustered, and angry, and wish that the woman had kept her ball on the course. Nevertheless, we shall soon be wishing that the new people in front will lose theirs. What fools we are! and in nothing more foolish than in this matter of passing.

My original list by no means exhausted the crimes that can be committed by the people in front. They can call us on and then, finding their ball in the nick of time, go on themselves, but that is an offence so black and repulsive that I cannot write about it. They can try over again the putt they have just missed, and this crime has become more fashionable since we have been taught to admire American assiduity in the practising of putts. They can take out a horrid little card and pencil, and, immobile in the middle of the green, write down their horrid little score. In that case, however, there is compensation, for there is no law of God or man that can prevent us from letting out a blaring yell of 'Fore!' To see them duck and cower beneath the imaginary assault may not be much, but it is something. They may think us ill-mannered, but what does that matter? The worst they can do is to write an article about the people behind.

BERNARD DARWIN, *Playing the Like, 1934*

You must play boldly to win. My whole philosophy is based on winning tournaments, not on finishing a careful fifth, or seventh or tenth.
ARNOLD PALMER

Swing Time

'Simpson disappeared after breakfast with his golf clubs. He is in high dudgeon – which is the surname of a small fish – because no one wanted to see his swing.'

'Oh, but I do!' said Dahlia eagerly. 'Where is he?'

'We will track him down,' announced Archie. 'I will go to the stables, unchain the truffle-hounds, and show them one of his reversible cuffs.'

We found Simpson in the pigsty. The third hole, as he was planning it out for Archie, necessitated the carrying of the farm buildings, which he described as a natural hazard. Unfortunately his ball had fallen into a casual pigsty. It had not yet been decided whether the ball could be picked out without penalty – the more immediate need being to find the blessed thing. So Simpson was in the pigsty, searching.

'If you're looking for the old sow,' I said, 'there she is, just behind you.'

'What's the local rule about loose pigs blown on to the course?' asked Archie.

'Oh, you fellows, there you are!' said Simpson rapidly. 'I'm getting on first-rate. This is the third hole, Archie. It will be rather good, I think; the green is just the other side of the pond. I can make a very sporting little course.'

'We've come to see you swing, Samuel,' said Myra. 'Can you do it in there, or is it too crowded?'

'I'll come out. This ball's lost, I'm afraid.'

'One of the little pigs will eat it,' complained Archie, 'and we shall have india-rubber crackling.'

Simpson came out and proceeded to give his display. Fortunately the weather kept fine, the conditions indeed being all that could be desired. The sun shone brightly, and there was a slight breeze from the south which tempered the heat and in no way militated against the general enjoyment. The performance was divided into two parts. The first part consisted of Mr Simpson's swing *without* the ball, the second part being devoted to Mr Simpson's swing *with* the ball.

'This is my swing,' said Simpson.

He settled himself ostentatiously into his stance and placed his club-head stiffly on the ground three feet away from him.

'Middle,' said Archie.

Simpson frowned and began to waggle his club. He waggled it carefully a dozen times.

'It's a very nice swing,' said Myra at the end of the ninth movement, 'but isn't it rather short?'

Simpson said nothing, but drew his club slowly and jerkily back, twisting his body and keeping his eye fixed on an imaginary ball until the back of his neck hid it from sight.

'You can see it better round this side now,' suggested Archie.

197

'He'll split if he goes on,' said Thomas anxiously.

'Watch this,' I warned Myra. 'He's going to pick a pin out of the back of his calf with his teeth.'

Then Simpson let himself go, finishing up in a very creditable knot indeed.

'That's quite good,' said Dahlia. 'Does it do as well when there's a ball?'

'Well, I miss it sometimes, of course.'

'We all do that,' said Thomas.

Thus encouraged, Simpson put down a ball and began to address it. It was apparent at once that the last address had been only his telegraphic one; this was the genuine affair. After what seemed to be four or five minutes there was a general feeling that some apology was necessary. Simpson recognized this himself.

'I'm a little nervous,' he said.

'Not so nervous as the pigs are,' said Archie.

Simpson finished his address and got on to his swing. He swung. The ball, which seemed to have too much left-hand side on it, whizzed off and disappeared into the pond. It sank . . .

Luckily the weather had held up till the last.

'Well, well,' said Archie, 'it's time for lunch. We have had a riotous morning. Let's take it easy this afternoon.'

A. A. MILNE, *The Holiday Round, 1912*

Anytime a golfer hits a ball perfectly straight with a big club it is, in my view, a fluke.
JACK NICKLAUS

Par for POW at the Stalag

Nobody knew where that ancient hickory-shafted ladies' mashie came from. It turned up one day in 1943 at Stalag Luft 3, Hitler's main prisoner-of-war camp for RAF officers in the forest of Sagan, and worked a remarkable change in the lives of hundreds of men.

Stalag Luft was one of the better camps. The Luftwaffe, which ran it, believed in a velvet glove policy towards POWs, on the principle that, if they were left alone and made reasonably content, their will to escape would be lessened. There was little of the bullying arrogance and stupidity common to other camps and, within severe limits, the prisoners could pursue their own activities. In their half-life of noise, dirt, insufficient food, discomfort and lack of privacy, what made life bearable for the prisoners of Stalag Luft was sport.

Soccer and Rugby – seven a side on a half-size pitch – soft-ball, introduced by the Canadians and swiftly popular, and even cricket were played with an intensity and passion the like of which I have never seen since. Years of frustration were subliminated in games that could become tough and even brutal. The Germans soon banned Rugby because the sick quarters were filled with broken collarbones, torn ligaments and the rest.

One sport the camp failed to provide – at least before I got there – was golf. Then, shortly after I arrived, that little mashie turned up! I seized on it like a starved dog would seize a bone. Eager to put it to proper use, I and another man, a journalist named Sydney Smith, made ourselves a ball by wrapping yards of string around a lump of wood and covering it with cloth. It was not much of a ball, but it served, and we chipped it 50 yards back and forth for hours and hours. Others wanted to play, but Smith was firm. 'Go make your own balls,' he said, 'and we'll let you use the club.' And so they did.

Within days several new balls appeared, some even better than ours. As more people began to swing that overworked mashie, we designed a course, using doors, tree stumps and telephone poles for holes. Soon there were 12 of us, enduring the tolerance and good-humoured scorn of the rest of the camp. The game was revolutionized when Danny O'Brien, a scratch golfer in Scotland, used some strands of rubber in his ball and outhit us by miles. Like the golfers of old, who mistrusted the Haskell rubber-cored ball and bemoaned the passing of the gutty, so we resented the usurping of string as the essential ingredient, but progress would not be stayed. By now balls were covered with elastoplast, the innovation of Ronnie Morgan, another scratch golfer, and tremendous pressure was put on the officer in charge of the medical stores for supplies, but this phase passed. The revolution in ballmaking was really under way, and the first one made entirely of rubber appeared.

The ingenuity of prisoners was considerable, and the collective skills of 800 men within a confined space were almost limitless. Within months ballmaking had become an art, rubber more priceless than food or tobacco, and its value soared on the camp market exchange. It came from soles of shoes, tobacco pouches and air cushions, and people wrote home for these things to be sent in quarterly clothing parcels. Brand-new rubber-soled shoes would be torn to shreds on arrival, the precious rubber cut into thin strands with a razor blade, wound round a core of metal and covered with leather, usually from the shoes.

Trial and error soon achieved the right tension in the winding and the right weight. The method of covering was similar to that of a baseball: two figures of eight. Thread and twine became commodities precious beyond reckoning. Eventually we were making balls exactly to the British specifications of 1.62 ounces and 1.62 inches in diameter. These homemade affairs would fly true and could be hit to within 10 to 20 yards of a proper ball with a medium iron. From dawn to dusk every day, balls of every kind flew like tracer bullets around the camp; the miracle of it was that no one was seriously injured. Our finest ballmaker was an Australian named Samson, and a sample of his work is now enthroned in the Royal and Ancient Museum at St Andrews.

Within a few months real balls began to arrive in answer to our fervent appeals to friends in Switzerland, Turkey, Britain and even some occupied countries. Better even than the new balls, some of our friends sent us real clubs and the precious mashie could at last be rested. I calculated that it had hit more than 300,000 shots, been tossed from one player to another thousands of times and yet its sturdy little shaft never yielded. It must have been fifteen years old.

Among the new clubs was a limbershafted driver. Its use was banned because of the potential lethal effect within so small a space, but temptation was too strong for me. One frozen day when everyone was inside I teed a real golf ball at one end of the camp and let fly. The ecstasy of that impact, the first full shot in four years, was unforgettable; so was the apprehension as it soared away in a great booming slice over the kitchen building. The inevitable plunk followed and, as I soon discovered, the occupants of the room had flung themselves down as the ball crashed through the window, thinking a bored guard had opened up with a gun.

The Germans protested against the breaking of windows, which was not as amusing as it seemed for they had to be boarded up with wood.

The highlight of such episodes happened when a friend of mine shanked his tee shot into the window of a German lavatory in the kitchen building. An *Unteroffizier* was showered with glass, but the only repercussion was a request to move the tee. The original course included all kinds of spectacular holes, with blind shots over huts, but these had to be abandoned as more and more people played. Anyone standing by a window was in the target area.

Out of bounds was a far greater hazard than it ever is on a normal course. Inside the double barbed-wire fence surrounding the camp was a low rail, leaving a no-man's land of some 10 yards width. If you stepped into this you could be shot. The Germans grew tired of fetching balls, so they gave us white coats to wear while retrieving them. This, in effect, was a parole that one would not attempt to escape. If a ball went over the outside wire, there was nothing for it but to wait for a passerby, sometimes guided by a guard from the watchtower, to throw it back.

As ball manufacture evolved, so did course architecture. Within months, greens – or rather browns – had been fashioned, roughly eight to 10 yards in diameter, with shallow banks around them. The sand surfaces, carefully smoothed, were true and fast for putting, especially when watered, and a nine-hole par-3 course of 900 yards emerged, with the longest hole about 150 yards.

Even with a seven-iron, hitting these greens was not easy, but we became pretty accurate. I always recall my first game on a proper course after the war – the greens looked enormous, impossible to miss, but that illusion soon vanished.

Before the supply of clubs became plentiful, several artists made their own. Some were incredible contraptions. One, weighing about 20 ounces, became known as 'Abort Annie'. The patience, ingenuity and craftsmanship necessary to construct a playable club defies imagination when it is realised that the shafts were hand-carved from ice-hockey sticks, the heads moulded from melted-down water jugs and stovepipes and the whole job done without any proper tools except a knife. The moulds for casting the heads were made of soap or sand. At first it seemed impossible to make the heads strong enough without their being too heavy, but an American named Lee Usher and others succeeded, until the Germans unsportingly objected to their stovepipes being sacrificed to the cause of golf.

Stalag golf was wonderful for your game. At first, when we played with only the one club, real versatility of shot-making was needed; pitch, pitch and run, cut shots, explosions, putts – all of them with the mashie. Competitions and exhibitions given by the best players always drew crowds, and few of us had any experience at being watched before, especially by highly critical people who knew you well. You learned to concentrate, just as in a tournament at home.

201

There was quite an atmosphere to it – the practising before breakfast; the crowds, intent and silent, wearing only the scantiest of clothes; the players, working on every shot; and the sun shone so hot that you could scarcely walk on the sand barefoot. Reputations in a prison camp were jealously preserved; no one wanted to make a fool of himself on the golf course any more than a professional does in public, and our public was always with us – a few feet away.

By the end of that first golfing summer, the disease had fairly taken root. More than 300 had played the course, causing problems of congestion and control far beyond those of any public links. Wherever one looked, someone was swinging a club or a piece of wood, having a lesson from one of the comparative aces, practising shots or talking golf. We saturated ourselves in it, and people, who a few months earlier had never touched a club, talked glibly of draw, fade, shoulder turn, backspin and so on. Beginners had a great advantage over those at home; daily practice and constant tuition: one I knew shot in the 80's when he first played a proper course.

The Germans watched with the bored tolerance of attendants at a funny farm, little knowing that one of the most ingenious and daring escapes of the war was taking place right under their noses.

All through the summer a wooden vaulting horse, with enclosed sides, was carried out each day to a point some 20 yards from the wire, behind the sixth green. It carried a man who for hours on end lay almost naked in a terribly confined space, always with the possibility of being buried alive, digging the tunnel, foot by foot, which took three men to escape and freedom. The venture became world famous as The Wooden Horse. Eric Williams, the leader, and his two companions were the only successful escapers from that compound. They completed the tunnel after months of labour, while a guard in the watch-tower, not 30 yards away, looked down on the stupid British as they fooled around on the wooden horse, with the golfers passing by and the footballers and softballers on their nearby pitches.

When the tunnel was discovered after the three men had gone, the Germans threatened to close the golf course for good because they thought it had been used as a blind for the tunnel. In fact, it had not. That would have been too obvious, as the Germans later realised. So, a few weeks later the browns were smoothed, the banks and bunkers rebuilt and the Sagan Golf Club was back in business once more. It remained active, a precious part of our lives, until the camp was captured by the Russians early in 1945.

P. A. WARD-THOMAS, *Yesterday*

If I had my way, no man guilty of golf would be eligible for any office of trust or profit under the United States. H. L. MENCKEN

Match Days

Match days, for me, began the evening before. I went back to my rooms usually directly from Mildenhall. I was always too excited to read. I played my gramophone. Oh desperate solitary drinking! I gave myself a glass of sherry – sometimes, even two. Sometimes I gave myself the finale of Beethoven No. 7 with the second glass, but generally I preferred Ellington's slow gloomy Blues-tunes. My landlady brought me a boiled egg and bread and butter. About seven I went to bed. I wonder, now, if there was any stirring of the black cauldron of The Feras. I lay and thought of tomorrow ('cras amet'). I wondered what the course would be like: all were strange to me. Who would I play against. Then, how would I play? There was no set pattern, but at some moment I was overcome with nerves. I lay physically trembling all over for lifetimes of blank minutes. I was powerless to combat this. Sometimes I was sick. These attacks lasted anything up to an hour. Then I slept, like the living, deep and lost until my landlady's daughter woke me with a jug of shaving water and a cup of tea at five-thirty. I was confidently nervous when I came to play. The day was in an envelope, like a love-letter. There were pre-ordained generalities but would there be, in it, some positive message. You put it away into a pocket of delicious trepidation.

Walking through Cambridge in the dawn twilight of autumn was like the chilling promises of a mermaid. In the dim watery air moved the shapeless forms of 'bedders' more antediluvian and undiscoverable than the undiscovered coelacanth. Else a vast silence reigned. The silence that emanates from stone is wholly different from brick-silence. We drove west into opening day. We ate an enormous breakfast at a pub in St Albans. By half-past nine we were changing to play at Sunningdale, say, or Woking. A serious innocence in golf in those beautiful birch and heather and emerald green gardens kept me straight. Caddies told me to aim left, or right, of the pitfalls of knowledge. I did. Worplesdon shone in the autumn dew and dewy filaments and patterns of dew on fallen leaves and tiny wakes of dew behind your ball on the long putts though the greens had been 'swept'. I went round in seventy-one. By some kind of divination Hugh (Hugh Neilson, Captain of Cambridge University) had paired Laddie* and me as foursome partners. I had complete faith in his powers to get me out of trouble, consequently I seldom put him crooked. Never once were we at odds with each other – not even at the eighteenth at West Hill where my drive was a couple of feet in, on the fairway, to the right, just by a holly tree. Being left-handed he had to stand mostly in the tree. Like two actors do, who are en rapport, we produced and improved each other. I never had any doubt which was the star-player. I know that whatever gifts I have as a producer of poetry-readers has a deep root here.

Laddie and I were always likely to win. This gave me great confidence for the afternoon 'singles' matches. After tea, and possibly a drink, there was a tedious drive back to Cambridge, eastward into darkening night, sometimes against time, for cars had to be in by 8.30. It never seemed a long day.

Laddie, early and duly, got his Blue. Then came a home match at Mildenhall, in which for the first and only time our partnership was beaten. I went on for the second act in a curious and cussed frame of mind, both resilient and resentful. I thought, damn Laddie for letting me down, damn me for letting him down, if I don't win this afternoon its no use. I was playing against Henry Longhurst. Already amongst golfing journalists who were doubtable, he was known to be re-doubtable, like Bernard Darwin. I had no reason to doubt or re-doubt Henry's golf. In the gathering gloom we walked up to the last tee. We were all square. I needed a four for a seventy-two. As I walked towards my drive which I had prudently, or fearfully, placed up left, I saw Hugh and Tony slip from the clubhouse. I would have seen an ant. The hours, days, months, concentrated upon this. I knew exactly how to play this shot. I had no qualms at all. I took my mashie-niblick and put my ball a yard from the hole. Henry's second was at the back of the green. His putt

* Laddie Lucas

204

was inside where my ball lay. He too had seen Hugh and Tony. He too had captained Cambridge. I conceived he might give me my putt. For the first time for two-and-a-half hours, Henry stopped talking. The silence lay heavy between my ball and the hole. I think I held my putter about an inch from the head, shut my eyes, and shovelled. I can hear the ball drop. I shall never see it. Then I heard Hugh ask in his soft diffident voice: 'Would you care to play against Oxford?' as if, really, I might have something better to do. I said I would. I read Yeats almost all night for sheer joy and relief and to convince myself that this had really happened. I understood why Henry did not give me the putt, and blessed him.

Patric Dickinson, *The Good Minute, 1965*